Topicality and Representation

Topicality and Representation: Islam and Muslims in Two Renaissance Plays

By

Hammood Khalid Obaid

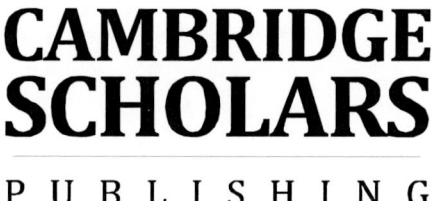

CAMBRIDGE SCHOLARS PUBLISHING

Topicality and Representation: Islam and Muslims in Two Renaissance Plays
By Hammood Khalid Obaid

This book first published 2013

Cambridge Scholars Publishing

12 Back Chapman Street, Newcastle upon Tyne, NE6 2XX, UK

British Library Cataloguing in Publication Data
A catalogue record for this book is available from the British Library

ISBN (10): 1-4438-5060-8, ISBN (13): 978-1-4438-5060-5

To Mike, Heba, Dad and Mum

TABLE OF CONTENTS

LIST OF ILLUSTRATIONS

PREFACE

The primary objective of this work is to examine the role played by topical concerns in the "representation" of Muslims and Islam in two important Elizabethan plays. The two plays are George Peele's *The Battle of Alcazar* (1589) and William Percy's *Mahomet and his Heaven* (1601). The former play was the first to introduce a Moor in a major role, while the latter was the first play to be purportedly based on Quranic material and the first play to present the Prophet of Islam as a dramatic character. My study views topical interests as the major factor informing the depiction of Muslims in both plays and questions the term "representation" of Islam after taking these interests in consideration.

My methodology is akin to the New Historicist approach in that it tries to posit a close relationship between the two selected plays and their political and religious milieu. The presence of an ideological commitment in both authors, albeit to different currents of thought, is seen as an important factor that challenges the very idea of a representation of Islam. Briefly, I argue that what we see in these two plays is less a representation of existing knowledge of the Muslim Other, and more a topical construction reflecting contemporary issues and events.

Chapter One focuses on Peele's *Battle of Alcazar* as an ideologically-based pro-government work. The play was written shortly after the Spanish Armada in 1588, a time when England was undergoing serious political turmoil. Of special interest is the visit of the first Moroccan ambassador to London in 1589, which probably coincided with the play's performance. Special attention is paid to the dramatic side and characterization in the play with the aim of showing how, in his play, Peele was interested in promoting Queen Elizabeth's new allies, the Moors, more than presenting a good or an evil Moor.

Chapter Two studies Percy's *Mahomet and his Heaven* as the product of a tense and complex set of circumstances relating to both the playwright and late Elizabethan England. Contemporary views on magic, women, and the Catholic-Protestant schism all play a role in forming the final outcome which constructs a topical allegory of England rather than a representation of Islamic Arabia.

Together, my analyses of these important plays show that the Muslim figure was, more often than not, constructed from topical and local material that was hardly based on original existing knowledge about Islam. In my conclusion, I suggest that the same may be true of other plays and texts of the period.

ACKNOWLEDGEMENTS

The production of this work benefited from the help and support of many people and some words of acknowledgement are due to all of them.

I owe a deep debt of gratitude to my supervisor, Professor Michael Pincombe, who has been extremely patient with my work and helped me pass through many a difficult time. His notes and guidance were invaluable and his support unlimited. Thanks Mike.

I am also immensely thankful to my examiners, Professor Lisa Hopkins and Dr. Ruth Connolly, for their thoughtful and thought-provoking comments on my work.

I must also thank the staff at the Robinson Library for their help. The Alnwick Castle archives staff were generous enough to allow to me use their collection. I am especially thankful to Christopher Hunwick, Archivist.

My family was the emotional rock against which I could always lean. My wife Heba's never-ending love and support has been indispensable for my work. My children Anas and Areej have been my bundles of joy and sources of endless light.

The prayers and love of my mother, Souad, have been the spiritual guidance I always needed. She has been patient beyond belief in waiting for my return after finishing this work.

I have to make a special mention of the soul that always supported and guided me. I shall never forget that, at the age of thirteen, upon achieving top scores in school, my father Khalid assured me that in my path seeking knowledge and education he would always be there for me. And he has always been. I regret that his sad departure, before my completion of the degree, deprived me of sharing with him the pleasure of having achieved my life-long dream, which was also his. Thanks dad and may God bless your beautiful soul.

ولله الحَمدُ مِن قَبلُ ومِن بَعد

BIBLIOGRAPHICAL NOTE

1. For all works printed before 1800, I use the Early English Books Online (EEBO) version. Reference is made in parentheses to image numbers unless otherwise stated.
2. For the works of George Peele I use the three-volume edition, *The Life and Works of George Peele* (1952), edited by Charles Tyler Prouty. The only exception is Peele's *The Battle of Alcazar* where I use Charles Edelman's 2005 critical edition in his *The Stukeley Plays*.
3. For William Percy's *Mahomet and his Heaven*, I use Matthew Dimmock's 2006 critical edition. For his *Aphrodysiall*, I refer to the unedited manuscript in the Alnwick archives MS509. For his *Faery Pastorall*, I use Robert Denzel Fenn critical edition in his unpublished PhD Thesis (1997).
4. For the works of Shakespeare, I use *The Norton Shakespeare* edition edited by Stephen Greenblatt et al. (1997).
5. English citations from *The Quran* are from Abdullah Yusuf Ali's Translation in *The Holy Qur'an: Text, Translation and Commentary*.
6. For all Biblical references, the edition used is *The Bible: Authorized King James Version* edited by Robert Carroll and Stephen Prickett (1998).
7. These are the editions used with their respective works: the New Mermaids Edition of *Dr Faustus* edited by Roma Gill; Revels Student Edition of *The Spanish Tragedy* edited by David M. Bevington; "The Wanton Wife of Bath" in Thomas Percy's *Reliques of Ancient English Poetry* (1877); King James's works, *The Selected Writings of James I* edited by Neil Rhodes et. al.

GENERAL INTRODUCTION

Do not ask what the Jews are, but what we have made of the Jews
Jean-Paul Sartre

Islamic characters and motifs appeared frequently on the Elizabethan stage and the study of this issue has been a very active area of research in recent years. This work proposes analysing two landmark Elizabethan plays in the light of their cultural milieu, especially the interplay between the play's image of Islam and contemporary ideology. The two plays are George Peele's *The Battle of Alcazar* (1589) and William Percy's *Mahomet and his Heaven* (1601). Topical references in the two plays are key points in this approach. The two plays were composed at important historical points for Elizabethan England and their composition was duly influenced by the events that surrounded them. This work adopts the view that this influence was so immense that it can hardly be possible to use the term *representation* in relation to the image of Islam in the two plays, and the term *construction* is proposed as an alternative. The words of Jean-Paul Sartre above succinctly say what this book wants to argue (qtd. in Pieterse 9).

This work is a study of Islam and Muslims in two landmark Renaissance plays. This book chooses two works that were both "firsts" in the history of Islam and Muslims on the English stage. Peele's *Alcazar* is generally acknowledged as the first play to present a Moor in a major role. Percy's *Mahomet* is the first play to present the Prophet of Islam as a dramatic character and the first play to be based on Quranic material. The general view of Islam in Elizabethan culture was a negative one. The two plays need to be seen against this background and their cultural work in portraying some Islamic motifs positively and others negatively runs along the lines of their background ideological concerns.

Studies of early modern England are showing more and more awareness of the Muslim Other in Elizabethan England. The area received little interest in historical and literary studies until the turn of the twentieth century. Since then, however, many works have tried to explore this field of research, with some interesting results. One silver lining of the events of September 2001 was an increased attention towards everything Islamic. Historians tried to trace the earliest instances of Muslim-Western encounters in an attempt to contextualize current tensions. Setting the crusades aside, diplomatic and commercial relations between England and Muslim states can be seen as the earliest forms of cultural interaction with which the modern English-speaking world could reckon: an Anglo-Saxon nation involved in peaceful and diplomatic relations with Muslim nations. This model is seen as quite distinct from later imperialist relations starting in the late seventeenth and early eighteenth centuries, which were duly theorized in Edward Said's seminal work *Orientalism* (1978). So what was the nature of this relationship?

Writing in the late sixteenth century, Fynes Moryson gave the following views of the Grand Turk:

> Touching forrayne Princes, England was so farr remoued from Turkye as from the forces thereof the Turkes could expect neither good nor ill, and when the Emperor beheld England in a Mapp, he wondred that the king of Spaine did not digg it with mattocks, and cast it into the Sea. But the heroick vertues of Queene Elizabeth, her great actions in Christendome, and especially her preuailing against the Pope and king of Spaine, her professed enemyes, made her much admired of the Emperor, of his mother, and of all the great men of that Court, which did appeare by the letters and guiftes sent to her Maiestie from thence, and by the consent of all strangers that liued in that tyme at Constantinople. (Moryson 31)

For the Turks, England was an insignificant and small island that only came to attention because of its opposition to the major Catholic European forces and its success in keeping them at bay, thus distracting them from war against the Turks. Quite the contrary was England's view of the two major Muslim entities: Turkey and the Barbary States. While Turkey had been, since the mid-fifteenth century, the terror of Europe, the North African states were worthy allies and, strategically, enemies of the Spanish king.

But what did Elizabethan England know of and imagine about Islam? Near the end of the sixteenth century a great deal of information was coming into England about the Muslim Other. Many translations were made from European authors who gave details of the world to the East and South of Christendom. London was also receiving exotic goods from the East like spices and carpets. English men and women who encountered Muslims (diplomats, merchants, travellers, pilgrims or captives) spoke and wrote of their experiences with varying degrees of verisimilitude (Schmuck "England's Experiences of Islam" 543). The English stage joined in through presenting Muslim characters and themes. Thus, this availability of information meant that Islam "could be written about, debated, denounced, admired, and scrutinized without bringing the Briton into contact with a single Muslim man or woman" (Matar *Turks, Moors* ix); hence comes the importance of studying the theatrical representation of Islamic figures. Theatre was one of the most popular forms of literature and its representations reached a wide and varied audience. This is a key point for understanding this study and it needs to be kept in mind throughout.

This study has as its focal point the circumstances that surrounded the production of the two plays under scrutiny. It is my belief that the depiction of Muslims and Islam in these two plays is heavily influenced by several political, religious and ideological contemporary factors that render the term "representation" extremely elusive. In the two plays, we see how the topical is masquerading as the historical and how history and source material are tampered with through ideological factors.

One key fact in the two plays, and one that is essential to this work, is that the two playwrights use Islamic motifs as a *medium* through which agendas are passed and messages conveyed. In order to highlight this fact, I use an approach akin to both New Historicism and Cultural Materialism in that the two plays are studied in terms of the historical moment of production and reception. The study shows how, while both plays seem to present the "Other," they actually tend to present extremely English themes and motivations. Especially in the case of *Mahomet and his Heaven*, it would not be too daring to say that what we get from the playwright is an England in Islamic clothing. Thus, in line with Sartre's words quoted at the beginning of this work, Muslims were made to be the object of an extremely local discourse. What the New Historicists might see as "representation" in these plays is closer to topical construction than anything else. Thus, we should not ask who the Muslims were in Elizabethan eyes and art but what Elizabethans made of Muslims. Before going further into the discussion, we need to define some terms that recur in this study and are vital to its proposals. These are *representation*, *topicality* and *construction*.

1.1. Definitions

This study uses a number of terms that need to be clarified before the discussion is taken any further. I shall outline a short explanation of each of these terms starting with a linguistic definition then move on to an overview of the term's history in literary criticism, and end with how this study uses this term. As already mentioned, this study proposes scrutinizing the effects of contemporary events on the representation of Muslims in two Elizabethan plays through studying topical allusions in the plays. The conclusion reached is that the image of Muslims was mostly the result of interplay between existing material and topical issues; thus it was a construction more than anything else. Topicality made representation a construction by moving it away from a mere conjuring of an image to a construction that accommodated temporal and local elements. Therefore, the terms *Representation*, *Topicality* and *Construction* are discussed below.

1.1.1. Representation

The concept of representation is an old question in the history of human thought especially when it comes to literature. In the book *Critical Terms for Literary Study*, the editors choose "Representation" to be the first entry in their book. The book section, by W. J. T Mitchell, stresses that representation is both historically and conceptually fundamental for our thinking about literature especially in its role in "aesthetics (the general theory of the arts) and semiotics (the general theory of signs)" (11).

Lexically speaking, the word "represent" means *inter alia* to "bring into presence," "symbolize ... serve as a visible or concrete embodiment" and "stand for or in place of" (*OED*). Semantically speaking, the word "representation" has a complex history. However, it is possible to distinguish between two main meanings, taking into consideration the possibility of overlap. The first meaning comes from "re-present" or make present again. Thus, something that is absent is made present again. The second and more widely used meaning relates to "standing for something." In this case, a present term stands for an absent term, with linguistic representation being the most familiar example of this meaning. An abstract or a physical object is "represented" by a linguistic sign. In this sense of the word, the sign or the copy substitutes the original, which is not present.

Anne Freadman distinguishes three areas of meaning for the word "representation": the symbolic, political and cognitive (Freadman 306). In the symbolic sense, a "sign" stands for a referent (like sleep being a "representation" of death). In the political sense, the house of representatives is a case in point where a person or a party stands for and defends the political interests of their voters and constituents. In the third sense, a cognitive representation "arises upon the mental formation of a cognition" (Freadman 306), i.e. the mental image of something.

In the literary world, and especially in New Historicist criticism, *representation* is a widely used term and the chosen title for New Historicism's flagship journal is nothing other than *Representations*. The idea of overlap mentioned above comes into play here as the use of *representation* in literary criticism mixes elements from various meanings of the word. Far from the political sense, this meaning of representation is a mixture of the symbolic and the cognitive meanings of the word. Indeed, a literary representation can be seen as both a sign standing for an original and a cognitive representation of an abstract idea. However, New Historicists give *representation* wider applications and meanings. For example, one can talk about the representation of royal power in a masque for example and discuss how the work of art presents the figure of the king to its viewers. However, and this is how New Historicists prefer to put it, the masque's representation does not 'show' that the "kingly character in a masque is all powerful [but] it enacts and produces this power" so much so that it becomes part of this power (Colebrook 98). Thus, the masque "re-presents" the power of the king or makes it present again.

The idea of representation becomes more problematic when talking about the Other. Unlike the example of royal power cited above, a representation of the Other tends to be more of an unopposed substitution due to the Other's disadvantage in being mostly absent from the world outside the literary work. Seldom did Elizabethan Londoners meet Muslims in real life and thus the theatrical representation they saw on their theatres almost had the final word on what these Others were like. The problem I see in the concept of "representation" is its claim to stand for an original object or idea, which in my view cannot be true in the presence of political and topical forces influencing the writer's output. In my two plays, topical factors played the role of both the catalyst for writing and the filter or prism through which ideas were seen. The result is a complex hybrid construction that incorporates many sources of input, many of which are topical rather than historical. The following section tries to define what is meant by topicality in this view.

1.1.2. Topicality

The relevant entry for the word *topical* in the *OED* defines it as "of or pertaining to the topics of the day; containing local or temporary allusions." The word comes from the Greek topos (τόπος) meaning a *place*.[1] In this study, I use the term "topicality" to refer to the sensitivity and responsiveness, conscious or subconscious, displayed in a text towards certain contemporary "motifs" which could be events, currents of thought or personalities.[2] My approach is to find these topical motifs in the life and works of the author in question, as well as landmark historical events, and then study the reflection or manifestation of these events in the work under study in relation to Islamic themes and characters. Such motifs remain historical only until they feature or play a role in a work of art, and only then can they be called topical.

---

[1] Hence the other expression used to refer to "topical reading" as "local reading" which in turn comes from the Latin *locus* meaning a place also.
[2] Examples of these in this study are: the Spanish Armada, anti-gynaecocracy and Queen Elizabeth respectively.

My views here meet to a certain extent with Leah Marcus's proposals in her book *Puzzling Shakespeare*. Aware of the criticism directed at topical reading, or local reading as she would have it, Marcus proposes a more sophisticated approach that escapes the pitfalls of mere allusion-spotting by being aware of its own "ruling methodologies" (*Puzzling Shakespeare* 36). She further explains this approach as follows:

> We can explore connections between particular "local" details which would have been immediately available to contemporary audiences and broader ways in which the text can be seen to function if those details are taken as central to meaning instead of marginal (*Puzzling Shakespeare* 36–7).

This study takes two plays that include Muslim themes and characters and examines their rich "local" and topical background. The aim is to gain a better understanding of the reasons these Muslim elements in the plays are portrayed the way they are through bringing apparently marginal issues to the centre of discussion.

Marcus is right in asking about the susceptibility of some works to topical reading and it is my theory here that the presence of Muslim themes and characters plays a key role in this regard. Europe was painfully aware of the Muslim presence in the east and Elizabeth's England was commencing normal relations with both the Ottoman and the Moroccans. Thus, the Muslim presence in a play from this era has to take into consideration such historical facts and their interplay with concerns. This is especially the case with Peele's *Alcazar*. Moreover, the far-fetched and exotic nature of Muslim land presented a versatile setting for passing dangerous messages and criticism, which is the case of Percy's *Mahomet*.

An important concept applied in this work and that goes hand-in-hand with topical reading is that of authorial agency, which Marcus calls "putative intentionality" (41). Marcus admits this to be a construct and has always been. However, if we "[demote it] from its traditionally privileged position as the overriding determinant of meaning," it becomes a useful tool (42). Similarly, my use of this idea focuses not on the unattainable intention of the author but rather on the general modes of thinking in which the author was usually involved. For example, George Peele's intention in writing *Alcazar* is beyond our reach, but it is imperative to know along which lines he generally wrote his works and whether or not his depiction of the Muslim Other can be separated from these lines. By the same token, Percy's responsiveness to issues affecting his family and sect certainly need to be taken into consideration when discussing his conception of Muslims in the play.

What remains to be introduced is the concept of *construction*. Why is it used here and how does it replace representation as a more proper term for approaching the image of Muslims and Islam?

1.1.3. Construction

The word *construction* in the context of this discussion will be defined then discussed in relation to the previous two concepts. In this study, *construction* can be understood to be a synonym of "putting together" as well as "making up." The relevant *OED* entry defines it as "a formation of the mind or genius." The meaning thus relates to something that is dissociated from reality. Another, more widely used, meaning of the word *construction* relates to building and creating, from which this study also takes the idea of forming something new from existing materials. Thus, the combination of these two meanings leads to the concept of making something new in the mind that does not have to be a neutral reproduction but at the same time is made up of readily available material.

The construction I study here is what my two playwrights did by way of presenting the Muslim Other to their audience. The outcome cannot be described as a straightforward representation because it is influenced by topical factors as well as by readily-available source material.

Thus, based on the above discussion, the three concepts relate to each other as follows. At the disposal of the playwright, there are various images and ideas which are already available before the work of art is produced. What the author does is *re-present* this material. The meaning of re-present here is to make present again, not only physically but time-wise as well. The material becomes present through formative topical factors that revive it from the archive of available knowledge, then help re-shape it.

This work puts forward the proposition that despite the existence of raw material on Islam and Muslims, the re-presentation of this material in dramatic form is always filtered through topical interests and ideological relations. What these topical writers do is take this material and combine it in different ways to suit a particular situation. Thus, their topical writing, or re-presentation, was *present* in a limited temporal frame of reference, or immediate reference in other words. The construction I describe here means "putting together," with a particular intention, material or building blocks which were already in existence. Writers did not reflect notions simply like a mirror nor did they represent them directly but they *constructed* new forms out of what they had. Mediation, or authorial agency, is always present and must be taken into consideration.

It becomes imperative at this point, then, to make a short survey of existing material on Islam and Muslims in the period under study. In the section below, I select significant examples from the sources of knowledge that were available to intellectuals in this period. The time frame starts from as early as possible and extends to the date of composition of the second play (1603). However, some works do fall beyond this frame but are used due to their relevance to ideas already present in the plays or other works discussed here.

1.2. Existing knowledge about Islam and Muslims

During the Middle Ages, and up to the late Renaissance, England knew little and cared less about the Muslims and their culture (Schmuck "England's Experiences of Islam" 544). However, several factors combined to bring Muslim-related issues to the forefront of public, political and commercial attention during the period under discussion. Before going into the details of the way our two plays handle the issue of representing Islam and Muslims, it is necessary to give an outline of the factors that could have played a role in forming a late-1500s-early-1600s conception about the Muslim Other.[3] The aim is to gain an understanding of the cultural work that the two plays were doing. In other words, what was available on the cultural arena before these two plays and how they dealt with it.

The period under discussion in this work falls between a dark and unaware past and an imperial and "Orientalist" future. As far as the history of East-West relations is concerned, the Renaissance is strategically located between the long years of medieval seclusion and the period of European colonization marked by Napoleon's invasion of Egypt in 1798 (Said's chosen landmark start of Orientalism.[4]) Renaissance knowledge of Islam was influenced by medieval sources and in turn, it had its influence on the imperial future of England.

To start with, the terms used to refer to Muslims were not crystal clear. Due to misinformation, stereotype and fantasy, the terms were of obscure

---

[3] The primary sources mentioned in this overview were mostly referred to by critical studies. I did, however, return to the original sources and select relevant material for my discussion.

[4] According to Said, "Quite literally, the [French] occupation gave birth to the entire modern experience of the Orient as interpreted from within the universe of discourse founded by Napoleon in Egypt, whose agencies of domination and dissemination included the Institut and the *Description*" (Said 87, italics in original).

origins and their uses overlapped. According to Anthony Gerard Barthelemy, the words Turk, Saracen, Oriental, Indian and Moor were "difficult to define precisely." He further explains:

> In the fifteenth, sixteenth, and seventeenth centuries, the words meant different things to different people. All these words, however, shared a common connotation: alien, or foreigner. Because these words were used so imprecisely—frequently they were used simply to identify any non-Christian—they came to denote a rather general category of alien (Barthelemy 6).

However, critics have tried to draw fine distinctions between these terms in an attempt to fathom their deeper meanings and connotations.

1.2.1. Terms used in reference to Islam and Muslims

The terms "Moor" and "blackamoor" had multiple meanings. Ania Loomba notes that term "Moor" could mean both "Muslim and black" (45), and Daniel Vitkus sees in the Renaissance use of the word a "generalized Islamic identity" (*Turning Turk* 91). The word was also indicative of black African origin, though perhaps less than "blackamoor," but Barthelemy notes that it was "synonymous with black African" (1). The two words were often conflated and "blackamoor" was used to refer to "dark-skinned non-Muslims" as well as "all Muslims" (Loomba and Burton 16). In 1555, English physician Andrew Boorde in his *Fyrst boke of the introduction of knowledge* distinguished between two types of Moors: "Barbary is a great country and plentiful of fruit, wine, and corn. The inhabitants be called the Mores, there be white Mores and black Moors,[5] they be infidels and unchristened" (Boorde 48).

The term "Saracen" was more of a Crusader's relic. European invaders used the term indiscriminately to refer to the inhabitants of the Levant. The origin and etymology of the word seem untraceable. Many theories exist but none gives an ultimate answer. Most medieval and Renaissance writers linked the term to Sarah, Abraham's wife, claiming that Muslims who in fact descended from Hagar, Abraham's bondwoman, tried to link themselves to Sarah in attempt to raise themselves above base ancestry. In 1599, shortly before Percy's *Mahomet*, George Abbot touched upon the origin of the term in his *Briefe Description of the Whole World*:

---

[5] See Chapter One, Section 4.3.2.2. "Muly Mahamet" for more on the distinction between two types of Moors.

> The Booke of his [Muhammad's] Religion is called the *Alcaron*. The people which are Sectaries (whereas indeed they came of *Hagar*, the Handmaid of *Sarah*, *Abrahams* wife, and therefore should of her be called *Ishmaelites* or *Hagarens*) because they would not seeme to come of a bond-woman, and from him whom they suppose a bastard; they terme themselves *Saracens*, as comming from Sarah (Abbot 145).

Another source for the term was proposed in 1615 by William Bedwell in his "The Arabian Trudgman," which was a concise dictionary of Arabic words inserted as an appendix to his *Mohammedis Imposturae*. Bedwell found the term to come from an Arabic word not from Abraham's wife: "Neither were they so named of *Sara*, Abrahams wife, as some men do thinke, but of *Saraka*, which signifieth *Furari*, to rob or steale. And indeed the Arabians haue bene and are to this day accounted great sharkers and robbers" (Bedwell 51).

Apart from the pejorative terms derived from the name of the Prophet of Islam,[6] the terms "Muslim" and "Islam" were hardly if ever used to refer to followers of Islam. The *OED* documents the first usage of the word "Muslim" to Bedwell. Under the entry "MVSLIM, or *Mussliman*," Bedwell notes the meaning to be is "one that is instructed in the beleefe of the Mohammetanes" (50). Explaining the meaning of the term in Latin, he writes that it means "sanae fidei" or "sound in faith" (50). The word "islami" was mentioned in Richard Knolles's 1603 book *The Generall Historie of the Turkes* where he defined it as "they call themselues *Islami*, that is to say, men of one mind, or at peace among themselues" (Knolles 5).

The word "Turk" gained special significance with the rise of the Ottoman Empire and became a *pars pro toto* for all Muslim nations. The special importance of the term came from the fact that faraway peoples, like the English, had little actual contact with Muslims and used the Turkish threat as a trope for Islam. As a result, myths and legends about the Turk were conflated with Islam and Muslims in general. Negative images of the Ottomans were rife in the fifteenth and sixteenth centuries. Thus, the term "turke" acquired "stereotypical features" which included "aggression, lust, ... murderous conspiracy, ... cruelty, merciless violence rather than 'Christian charity,' wrathful vengeance instead of turning the other cheek" (Vitkus *Three Turk Plays* 2). Islam as a result was associated with these values due to Europe's negative experience of Ottoman invasion. Furthermore, the term "turke" was often used in religious

---

[6] e.g. Mahometan, Mohametan, Machometan. ("Mahometan, *a.* and *n.*" *OED*).

polemic to refer to any perceived heretical approach to religion, most
notably between Protestants and Catholics accusing each other of heresy.[7]

1.2.2. History of contact

Chronologically speaking, the earliest point of contact between
Muslim and European cultures came through the "Moorish" invasion of
Spain. The Muslims ruled Spain for more than seven hundred years (711–
1492). The *Reconquista* of Spain by Isabella I of Castile and her husband
Ferdinand II of Aragon was seen as a victory for all Christendom. Thus,
centuries of real-life and first-hand encounters between Europe and Islam
ended with a note of hostility and expulsion instead of shared history and
culture. The Crusades were another chapter of hostility. Between 1095 and
1291, pope-led Europe launched nine consecutive crusades against the
Levant with the aim of reclaiming the holy land from the rule of
"Saracens." Again, hostility was the major feeling spread on both sides
during these years of war. Nor did the crusades end with the above date;
rather fighting against Muslim was more often than not called a crusade
well into the late sixteenth century.[8]

In the later middle ages, European-Muslim relations became mainly
dominated by the Ottoman incursions on the eastern front of the continent.
The fall of Constantinople in 1453 was a landmark in modern history.
Muslims saw it as a great victory and conquest while Europeans in their
shock saw in it a result of their distance from God as well as punishment
for their disunity. England was at the far end of the continent, which was
relatively safe from Ottoman threat. But Islamic danger was still felt in
England, or at least it was used to address sentiments of unity and
nationalism. In 1575, the bishop of Chichester gave a sermon in which the
queen was present and he speculated on a possible way for the Ottomans
to reach England by invading Spain first (Schmuck "England's
Experiences of Islam" 546). The Turkish threat was felt so deep that
English men actually travelled "to fight against the Ottomans, whether in
Crete (1522) or Algiers (1541)" (Matar "Britons and Muslims" 215). In
the same year 1575, in his introduction to his book *A Notable Historie of
the Saracens*, Thomas Newton warned against the approaching Turkish
threat because the Turks "were (in deede) at the first very far of from our

---

[7] Dimmock's *New Turkes* studies this phenomenon in depth.
[8] See Chapter one, section 4.2, where the battle of Alcazar is discussed as the last
crusade.

Clyme & Region, and therefore the lesse to be feared, but now they are euen at our doores and ready to come into our Houses" (Newton 3).

Scholars studying medieval and Renaissance relations between Islam and the West have often tried to find exceptions and permeations of the general negative vicious circle of misrepresentation and demonization. In a collection of essays, entitled *Western Views of Islam in Medieval and Early Modern Europe: Perception of Other*, Blanks and Frassetto try to argue against a "uniform" enmity between Islam and the West (4).[9] The very task undertaken by this book testifies for the prevalence of negative attitudes towards Islam and the need for finding instances of positivity in order to gain richer knowledge of the medieval and Early Modern views on Islam.

The period under study comes against this long history of distrust and hostility, and the two plays' views and representations of Islam need to be seen against a dark backdrop where relatively positive impressions need to be sought and looked for due to their scarcity. Taking into consideration these attitudes, what were the sources that an Elizabethan playwright could use or have access to about Islam and Muslims? The following section tries to answer this question.

1.2.3. Sources of knowledge

Writers who wanted to write about Islam had a store of sources to which they could refer. From the point of view of this work, these sources constitute the "non-topical" repertoire of ideas and images which could then be mobilised and made topical by poets in response to contemporary events. The sources informing Renaissance intellectuals and laity about Islam can be divided into four roughly defined categories. These include tales and narratives by travellers to the Muslim lands (including pilgrims and merchants); religious texts discussing Islam; chronicles and books of general history dedicated to the subject of Islam and Islamic countries; and finally and most pertinently literary works which included Islamic themes and characters.

1.2.3.1. Travel and trade

When the crusaders returned home, they brought with them stories of the far Levant where they met and fought the infidel Saracen. Crusader accounts were possibly the earliest form of travel writing concerning Muslim regions. Schmuck correctly observes that the accounts were

---

[9] See especially the articles by Blanks and Cruz.

ostensibly influenced by the narrators' hostility towards the people they were reporting ("England's Experiences of Islam" 544). These reports became even worse as a result of the later defeats experienced by the Europeans. This trend was commented on much later by John Selden who in *Table-talk* (published posthumously in 1696) gave an insight into his countrymen's unflattering and exaggerated narratives:

> When our Country-men came home from fighting with the *Saracens,* and were beaten by them, they pictured them with huge, big, terrible Faces (as you still see the Sign of the *Saracen*'s Head is) when in truth they were like other Men. But this they did to save their own Credits (Selden 182).

The other form of early narratives on Muslims and their lands was brought home by pilgrims to the holy land. These pilgrims' reports on the lands they visited were a natural result of the voyage they were taking as they more often than not saw the landscape through the eye of the New Testament. This trend seems to have continued in the Renaissance. William Biddulph while travelling in the Levant in the early seventeenth century had his Bible in hand and thought of Old Testament travellers all the time (MacLean 78). Sleeping in the open air reminded Biddulph of Jacob:

> The second night, in our trauell from *Scanderone,* we lodged at a place called *The gardens,* in the open fields, hauing the ground to our bed, a stone to our pillow (as *Iacob* in his trauell had) and the skie to our couering (Biddulph 41).

Thus, as Schmuck has noted, attachment to the ritualistic nature of their journeys made pilgrims' reports less about Muslims and more about the Bible ("England's Experiences of Islam" 545).

One of the earliest and most influential works of travel was *Travels of Sir John Mandeville* (c.1356 and reprinted several times). The book was "the most widely read travel narrative of the medieval and early modern world" (Loomba and Burton 70). That a real person did all these travels and wrote the book is highly doubtful. The work comprises material from several sources and perpetuates myths and legends without discretion as it does, for example, with the tales of semi-human hybrids in Ethiopia (Loomba and Burton 6). About Islam, Mandeville mentions some of the most recurrent themes of anti-Islamic polemic: the prohibition of wine, the sensuous Islamic Paradise and Mahomet's epileptic seizures.

While observing the landscape surrounding Bethlehem, Mandeville notices the abundance of vineyards and expresses astonishment at the

amounts of wine the Christians possess. The Muslims, Mandeville notes
do not drink wine because:

> their Book that *Mahomet* gave them, which they call *Alkaron* ... forbiddeth
> them to drink any wine: for in that Book *Mahomet* curseth all that drink of
> that wine, and all that sell it. And some men say that once he slew in his
> drunkenness a good Hermit whom he much loved, and therefore he curseth
> the wine, and them that drink wine (Mandeville 16).

Talking about Muslims' religion, Mandeville tackles the issue of
Paradise first. He portrays a sensuous image of the Islamic Garden as
abounding with "Fruits at all times, and Waters and Rivers running with
Milk and Honey, Wine and fresh water" (33). As for sexual delights,
Mandeville reports that a Muslim man in Paradise "shall have ten Wives[10]
and Maidens, and he shall every day once have to do with them, and yet
shall they still be maidens" (33). The biography of the prophet of Islam is
presented briefly. Mandeville points out the way Muhammad used to
receive revelation and likened it to the disease called "the falling Evil"
which Muhammad explained to his wife "that every time he fell so, the
Angel *Gabriel* spake to him, and for the brightness of the Angel he fell
down" (35).

This does not mean that Mandeville does not mention some positive
aspects. Mandeville mentions, for example, that the Quran "forbiddeth
Murther and Theft" and "commandeth them to do so to others, as they
would have others do to them" (33). However, he only makes this
observation to follow it by the fact that "Sarasins" are close to Christianity
and may thus be easily converted.

Thus, as an early example of travel literature, Mandeville's *Travels*
stands out for its stress on the exotic sides in the cultures and countries he
purports to have visited, so much so that it was later heavily used by
writers "to embellish their own tales" (Loomba and Burton 70). As far as
Islam is concerned, Mandeville views negative aspects first and foremost.
When bringing up a commendable trait, he is too preoccupied by his own
Christian heritage that he only sees this as a Christian-like feature. This
self-centred view on Islam will recur with other writers and is just another
example of the influence of local preoccupations on the representation of
Islam.

English trade with the Muslim states did not start until the sixteenth
century. Although Gregory O'Malley argues for merchant contacts as

---

[10] In another version of the book, a man will have no less than "four score wives all
maidens" (see Loomba and Burton 70).

early as the 1460s (157), sustained contacts with the Sublime Porte were not perceptible before the 1570s (Schmuck "England's Experiences of Islam" 544). England mostly imported natural produce from Muslim lands, things like currants, cotton, wool, spices, oils, chemicals, silk, carpets and even wines (Matar *Islam in Britain* 10–11; Andrews 93). Traders and merchants brought with these exotic goods more exotic tales and fantasies about the Orient especially about "the luxury of the Muslim rulers and their way of life" (Obaid 21–22). The abundance of goods in Muslim and exotic lands was used to lure merchants to venture into these lands. William Bullein's *A Dialogue bothe Pleasaunte and Pietifull* satirized these exaggerations through the following description of a journey by a character called Mendax, an inveterate liar:

> Wee sailed to the great Isle, called *Madagastat* in *Scorea*, where wer kynges, Mahumitaines by religion, blacke as Deuilles: Some had no heddes, but yen [eyes] in their breastes. Some when it rained, couered all the whole bodie with one foote. The lande did abounde in Elephantes teethe: the men did eate Camiles and lions flesh. Muske and Zeuet [civet] in euery place did abounde: and the mother of perle the people made their platters, to putte in their meate, thei dwelle emong spice, the ground is moist with oile of precious trees. Plentie of wine out of grapes as bigge as this loffe [loaf]: moche Peper, thei can not telle what to do with suger (74).

It is evident from the excerpt how exaggerated the description of the island's natural resources is. Stress is being intentionally placed on the valuable goods that the English imported from these countries. Travellers portrayed Muslim lands as phantasmal islands whose rulers are disparagingly called "blacke as Deuilles," and whose inhabitants are portrayed in subhuman terms. Thus, they hardly deserve the riches they enjoy.

1.2.3.2. Religious writing

While travel sources dealt with the Muslims and their lands, the ideological basis of Islam was approached via another form of writing. Christian polemical and apologetic writing was the main sources of knowledge about the doctrine of Islam for the medieval and early Renaissance readers. These works expectedly demonized the Muslim faith as well as its tenets, founder and holy book. Lack of original information was compensated for by misinformation, unfounded allegations and outright falsehood. Later on, although Martin Luther called for more authentic sources on the Turk's religion, the demonising tone did not diminish but rather kept in line with twelfth century polemic (Tolan xix, 275).

One of the earliest and most comprehensive polemic works was the corpus of texts compiled by Peter the Venerable, abbot of Cluny, and other authors in the 1140s and 1150s (Tolan 155–65). This collection included a Latin translation of the Quran by Robert Ketton, a translation which William Percy might have read for the writing of *Mahomet and his Heaven*. Peter the Venerable and his co-authors depended on earlier Spanish Christian polemic against Islam. Overall, the works were refutations of Islam and apologetics for Christianity. As John Tolan puts it, these works "viewed Islam as a heresy, an illegitimate deviation of the true religion. The culprit was Muhammad, portrayed as a scoundrel and trickster" (xxi).

As for England, one of the first publications on Islam in English was *Here Begynneth a Lytell Treatyse of the Turkes Lawe Called Alcaron* (1519?). The anonymous work included a woodcut of "a Muslim preacher standing in front of the figure of a horned beast-like devil" (Matar "Britons and Muslims" 217). It also featured another woodcut of a preacher holding a "naked swerde in his hande" which is held by the preacher "as longe as his sermon shall endure & last," as the anonymous author claims (*Here begynneth* 1–2). The *Treatyse*, which calls Muhammad a "nygromancer," adopts a demonising view and repeats stock issues taken against Islam like the Islamic view of paradise pointed out above (See Dimmock *Mahomet* 220 n. 40).

The English also read translations of continental polemics against Islam, such as *Here after Foloweth a Lytell Treatyse agaynst Mahumet and His Cursed Secte* (c. 1530) and Paolo Giovio's *A Shorte Treatise vpon the Turkes Chronicles* (1546) (Matar "Britons and Muslims"). The 1565 Book of Common Prayer, issued by the Elizabethan government, also had a paranoid interest in the Muslim Other. In one prayer, worshipers invoked God

> in his great mercy to defend and deliver Christians professing his holy name, and in his Justice to repress the rage and violence of Infidels, who by all tyranny and cruelty labour utterly to root out not only true Religion, but also the very name and memory of Christ our only Saviour, and all Christianity; and if they should prevail against the Isle of *Malta*, it is uncertain what further peril might follow to the rest of Christendom (Clay 519).

In 1566 another common prayer was used "every Sunday, Wednesday, and Friday, through the whole Realm: To excite and stir all godly people to pray unto God for the preservation of those Christians and their Countries, that are now invaded by the Turk in Hungary, or elsewhere" (Matar "Britons and Muslims" 217).

Christian religious writing on Islam was hostile in the vast majority of cases and it promoted a sense of enmity and paranoia towards the Muslim Other while at the same time using little or no authentic information on this religion. Even in cases where original sources were sought, the aim was still along the lines of "know your enemy" rather than interest in knowledge and better understanding.

1.2.3.3. History books

Another major source of information about Islam for the Elizabethan intellectual was chronicles and books of history. More inclined towards the narration and listing of historical facts than ideological judgment, these books generally adopted a relatively more ambivalent approach than religious writing and polemic despite using elements from them at times. Again, these works often displayed interest in local issues as they discussed Islamic history, a trend which we have already witnessed in travel writing and which will come to a fuller bloom in literary works.

The earliest history books on Islam and Muslim states came to England through translation of continental works, and they were mainly interested in the Ottoman Empire. The year 1542 witnessed the publication of three works on this topic in English. These were: Theodore Basil's[11] *The New Pollecye of War*, Theodorus Bibliander's *A Godly Consultation vnto the Brethren and Companyons of the Christen Religyon*, and Antoine Geuffroy's *The Order of the Great Turckes Courte*. As Dimmock notes, the three books are marked by a profound hostility towards the Ottomans (*New Turkes* 43).

As an example of these three books, Geuffroy's tone is primarily dismissive of Ottoman and Islamic culture despite certain exceptions, which still play into the main negative image. *The Order of the Great Turckes Courte* incorporates typical polemical discourse demonizing the teachings of Islam and its prophet. Geuffroy invites his reader to:

> Reade Mahumettes actes … and he shall fynde suche pryde and arrogãcie suche ambicion, such bloudynesse and crueltie, suche hypocrisye and supersticion, briefely suche a mynde to deface, abholyshe and destroye the kyngdome of the sonne of the lyuyng God (3).

---

[11] Theodore Basil was a pen name used by Thomas Becon (c. 1511–1567).

Linda McJannet points out instances of impartiality in Geuffroy but these can also be seen as a tool used to impress the Christian readers and implore them into abandoning sins. Thus, when he notes the strength of the Ottomans he links their victories to Christian laxness

> Wherfore, it is to be thoughte that hys strengthe is permytted of God, whyche for oure synnes sufferethe thys estate so farre swaruynge [swerving] frome all good pollycie: so to preuayle and not that it is maynteyned by their wisdom, strength, or virtue (44).

In another local reflection, the Ottoman state is seen through a Christian lens: it is the embodiment of Christian sinful life and the more righteous the Christians the weaker their enemy.

John Foxe's *Acts and Monuments*, first published in 1563, was one of the most popular books in Elizabethan England and contained a special section on "History of the Turks." The book was a main source for many writers and was used, for example, by Marlowe in writing *Tamburlaine* (King *Foxe's Book of Martyrs* 302). Like Luther and other protestant thinkers, Foxe saw the Turks as one manifestation of the antichrist, a coin whose other side was the Pope (Freeman and Evenden 82).[12]

Richard Knolles's *Generall Historie of the Turkes* (1603) is worthy of mention here despite its later publication date. The work is relevant to the works under discussion here because it was a survey that collected previously-available information from "various continental sources" of the "present terror of the world" (1) and showed how many communities of Christians had been at the mercy of the Turks since the beginning of the dynasty (Matar "Britons and Muslims" 219).

Like other sources of information available to the English reader at the time, the book is written about the Turks but through a localized and topical prism. Like many European nations, the English were at the same time terrified of the Turkish threat and fascinated by the empire's civilization. This is properly reflected in Knolles's description of the Ottoman Empire. According to him, this enemy state is both "admirable" and "strange." While its "greatnesse" is "magnificent," its military threat is "dreadfull" and "dangerous" and its main "persuasion" is to "rule ouer all" (5).

The book does not deny virtues inherent in the Ottoman society. However, like many English and European writers who always had their local audience in mind, Knolles praised the Ottomans with the aim of enticing the local community to become better.

---

[12] For more on this notion, see "Schism and Unity" in Chapter Two.

> The two strongest sinewes of euery well gouerned commonweale [are]
> Reward propounded to the good, and Punishment threatened vnto the
> offendor; where the prize is for vertue and valour set vp, and the way laied
> open for euery common person, be he neuer so meanely borne, to aspire
> vnto the greatest honours and preferments both of the Court and of the
> field, yea euen vnto the neerest affinitie of the great Sultan himselfe, if his
> valour or other worth shall so deserue (Knolles 5).

The rigid class system in Europe must have been in Knolles's mind when
he wrote this excerpt in praise of the Ottoman society's equal
opportunities and social mobility.

This is not to ignore the book's overall disapproving tone against the
Turks. After all, the book was published under the reign of King James I
and was actually dedicated to him. Aware of James's anti-Turkish stance,
Knolles praised in this dedication the king's *Lepanto* poem where the king
did "adorne and set forth the greatest and most glorious victorie that euer
was by any the Christian confederat princes obtained against these the
Othoman Kings or Emperors" (3).[13]

1.2.3.4. Literature

As one would expect, whatever little interest in Islam was in Medieval
English literature, this interest did not work towards a positive image.
According to Nabil Matar the demonization of Muslims meant that they
were anachronistically present in many locations and stories that originally
did not involve them:

> In mediaeval poetry, church plays and romances, English readers and
> audiences met with allusions that both misrepresented and demeaned
> Muslims: 'Mahound' was the god who sent Pharaoh after Moses across the
> Red Sea (York Plays); he was instrumental in the Massacre of the
> Innocents, since Herod was a 'Mahumetan' and dressed in Saracen clothes
> (Coventry Mystery Plays); and Muhammad took part in the crucifixion of
> Jesus, and both Caiaphas and Pilate were his followers (Coventry Mystery
> Plays) (Matar "Britons and Muslims" 214).

According to Metlitzki, "Medieval romance saw the Moslem through
the distorted prism of four stock figures: the enamored Moslem princess,
the converted Saracen, the defeated emir or sultan, and the grotesque
Saracen giant" (Metlitzki 161). One common theme of Medieval Romance
included a love story between a Christian knight and a Muslim princess
who helps him capture her father's castle. The princess converts to

---

[13] See section 6.3.1. "James I and Islam" for more on the King's poem.

Christianity and marries the knight while her father either converts or gets killed (Vitkus "Early Modern Orientalism" 216). Vitkus asserts that although Medieval images of Islam were mostly negative and fictitious, they were still perceived as true even in the sixteenth and seventeenth centuries (Vitkus "Early Modern Orientalism" 207, 09).

As for Elizabethan drama, there was a relatively high level of interest in Islamic figures and themes on the stage. From Marlowe, Kyd and Peele to Shakespeare, around forty-seven plays were produced in England with themes, settings or characters involving Islam and Muslims (Wann 166–7). Louis Wann further notes that interest in the Islamic world was so widespread that at least 1,600 items of source material (poems, ballads, histories, etc.) were printed between 1500 and 1640 in all European languages including English (170). Thus, it can be safely said that there was no lack of literary source material regarding Islam and Muslims when our two plays were written.

In Shakespeare, for example, there are many references to Turks and Muslims especially with a Crusade-related rhetoric. In *Richard II* (1595), the Bishop of Carlisle refers to Mowbray as such:

> Many a time hath banished Norfolk fought
> For Jesu Christ in glorious Christian fields
> Streaming the ensign of the Christian Cross
> Against black pagans, Turks and Saracens. (IV.i.92–5)

These lines show how fighting the Muslims was a commendable trait that brought praise and worth to its possessor. Similar references occur in *Henry IV* parts I (I.i.24–7) and II (IV.ii.340–3).

For the purposes of supporting the proposals set out for this work, I shall concentrate on plays that were written around the time of my plays and which had Muslim motifs and characters. These plays are seen as influences on my plays due to their subject matter as well as theatrical success. Throughout this work, reference will be made to these plays where necessary, but a brief overview of them is needed at this stage.

Tamburlaine

For a start, Christopher Marlowe's *Tamburlaine* needs no introduction. It is considered by many critics as a major milestone of the literary phenomenon known as Renaissance Drama. The character of its hero, its unprecedented spectacle and language together with Marlowe's "mighty line" (Jonson 288) made it a huge success through time as well as an inspiration to many works that followed. The events of the play take place in regions known to be inhabited by Muslims. Throughout the play, and almost repetitively, Tamburlaine's army storms through kingdom after kingdom and he humiliates his enemies in huge spectacles that had great impact on Elizabethan literary memory.

The protagonist of the play is the epitome of overriding ambition, high-flown language and ruthlessness. A low-born Scythian shepherd, Tamburlaine rises to become a formidable conqueror who subjugates the most powerful nations of the East. Throughout his journey, his cruelty manifests itself in many acts like the slaughter of the virgins of Damascus. Tamburlaine's ruthlessness, however, attracted admiration rather than fear or loathing on behalf of the Elizabethan audience. Some critics saw this admiration as a reaction to the Ottoman threat that Europeans, including the English, felt throughout the fifteenth and sixteenth centuries. Thus, from a topical point of view, Tamburlaine gave the audience a sense of revenge against the Turks and the extravagant acts of humiliation directed at the Turkish Bajazeth and the other Eastern kings are good examples of this.

Tamburlaine is relevant to my two plays in more ways than one. Peele's *Alcazar* is considered one of the literary aftershocks to the earthquake that was *Tamburlaine*, or a weak son of *Tamburlaine* as Peter Berek would have it (Berek 58). This is due to the similarities found between the two plays, especially in the pompous use of language, although Peele's version is hardly original and never as impressive. This is especially clear with Muly Mahamet's use of language.[14] On another level, Tamburlaine's trademark overriding ambition is reflected in the character of Thomas Stukeley who is presented as an ambitious hero, albeit unwise and ill-fated.

As far as *Mahomet and his Heaven* is concerned, the two plays meet on the grounds that both are seen as carrying hidden messages about the Elizabethan regime. Marlowe has always been associated with dissenting views on religion and politics. One example of this in *Tamburlaine* is the strong challenge to prevailing notions of social order and hierarchy where Tamburlaine tells his followers that "Your births shall be no blemish to your fame;/For virtue is the fount whence honour springs" (*I Tamburlaine* IV.iv.130–32). Such views would have been deemed unacceptable were they to be presented in an English setting. Shakespeare's less problematic *Richard II*, where the king is dethroned and replaced by another aristocrat not a low-born shepherd, is an attestation to this view with its history of censorship. Similarly, Percy's *Mahomet* abounds with seditious messages

---

[14] This idea is explored in Chapter One, Section 4.3.2.2 on Muly Mahamet.

about religion, gynaecocracy and magic, issues which Chapter Two discusses fully.

Titus Andronicus

The play is relevant to Peele's *The Battle of Alcazar* in more ways than one. First of all, Peele most likely co-authored the play himself. In an extensive study on Shakespearean co-authorship, Brian Vickers singles out Peele as Shakespeare's co-author. The play had long been thought of as a collaborative work, but Vickers' study brings together available scholarly work as well as new methods to prove the point that Peele wrote at least Act I of the play, if not scenes II.i, II.ii, and IV.i as well (Vickers 243). As for the play's date, critics do not have a consensus and their views locate it between 1588 and 1593.[15] Thus, the play was written around the period in which *Alcazar* was written, or no more than four years later. Another factor that brings the two plays together is the presence of a Moor in both plays: while *Alcazar* has more than one Moorish character, *Titus* only features Aaron.

The black Moor of Titus is remarkably Machiavellian and evil in a one-dimensional manner. Aaron is Shakespeare's first Moor and many of his negative qualities are seen as foretelling of Othello. Stephan Schmuck notes that Aaron is "sexually transgressive, jealous and violent; indeed, he is, as Lucius refers to him, 'the incarnate devil'" (Schmuck "From Sermon to Play" 6). This description is true but it neglects the fact that Aaron fails to gain sympathy as he lacks Othello's redeeming qualities like bravery, integrity and honesty. The result is a totally evil creature with few or no positive features. In fact, there seems to be an effort made to deprive him of any sympathy from the audience. When he is asked to reveal his evil acts, he says

> … I must talk of murders, rapes, and massacres,
> Acts of black night, abominable deeds,
> Complots of mischief, treason, villainies
> Ruthful to hear yet piteously performed, (V.i.p.653).

Later, when he is given the chance to repent or regret anything he did, he says he regrets only that

---

[15] In the *Cambridge Shakespeare* edition, Alan Hughes argues for an early date of composition, even before Shakespeare's arrival in London, of c. 1588 (Hughes 6). On the other end of the date debate, Jonathan Bate in the *Arden* edition argues for late 1593 as a date of composition (*Titus Andronicus* 66–79).

But I have done a thousand dreadful things
As willingly as one would kill a fly,
And nothing grieves me heartily indeed
But that I cannot do ten thousand more. (V.i.p655)

It is worth noting here that Aaron, although a Moor, is identified as a pre-Islamic Moor. He is described as pagan or atheist when Lucius says to him: "Who should I swear by? Thou believest no god" (V.i.653). However, this would have little impact on the image of the Moor due to the confusion of Islam, paganism and other non-Christian systems of belief described in the section above on terms used in reference to Islam and Muslims.

The play features a remarkable xenophobia in its depiction of the Others. Aaron the Moor and the Goths are seen as evil characters whose integration into Roman society brings about its disintegration. Kept at bay by Titus in Act I, they are helpless and can only beg for mercy. However, when they are given the opportunity to play a role in society it is a destructive path that they follow. They rape, murder and mutilate the Romans. As the play draws to a close, Gothic intervention is so obvious in Rome that the new Emperor takes over with their support as they symbolically stand aloft while he is crowned (Bate *Titus Andronicus* 38). Within this picture, the Moor is the mastermind of evil schemes and the play ends with his unrepentant self-condemning words: "If one good deed in all my life I did / I do repent it from my very soul" (V.iii.668). This point about xenophobia is to be contrasted with the approach adopted by Shakespeare's next play with a Moor which is the subject of the next section.

The Merchant of Venice

Shakespeare's second Moor is almost the opposite of his first one. The Prince of Morocco is everything that Aaron is not. He is gentle and civilized as opposed to Aaron's violent impudence; he is religious while Aaron is not; he a welcomed and appreciated guest unlike Aaron, who intrudes on the society in a destructive manner. Most importantly, he is treated as an equal peer not despised, and rightly so, as a criminal and a villain.

Nabil Matar finds topical echoes for this change. The Prince of Morocco has a few characteristics reminiscent of the actual king of Morocco at the time, none other than King Ahmad Al-Mansur, Peele's Muly Seth. According to Matar, in the early 1590s, Moroccan activity in the Mediterranean turned their country into "an eldorado of gold." Also, in 1591 Al-Mansur had conquered the region of sub-Sahara Niger with its rich gold mines. Hence he became known as *al-dhahabi*, or the Golden (Matar *Britain and Barbary* 22–3). In commenting on Morocco's casket selection scene, Thoraya Obaid had noticed the link earlier: "on one level, the Moorish prince describes the casket in front of him, but on another level he reveals his natural relation to gold. He is a Moorish prince whose land monopolized the gold trade for a long time" (Obaid 258). However, what Matar adds is the contemporary political significance of the King of Morocco to English politics. He also notes that Morocco's welcome presence in Europe reflects Elizabeth's relationships with Al-Mansur and her reception of his ambassadors (Matar *Britain and Barbary* 22). Obaid sees in linking the Moorish prince with gold an undermining of his character: "the identity of the Moorish Prince is then formed in terms of material wealth" (Obaid 259).

However, Matar's and Obaid's views disregard the passionate character portrayed by Shakespeare. "Mislike me not for my complexion" the prince says before he goes on to describe the passionate nature of his love which he wants to prove through the redness of his blood (II.i.1–7). His passion is thus seen through an exotic lens as it is contrasted with his dark skin which the prince hopes does not distract Portia from seeing his true feelings. The exotic manner in which Morocco expresses his love is reminiscent of Peele's Muly Mahamet and his flesh on a sword scene. The prince swears by his "scimitar" that he would "Pluck the young sucking cubs from the she-bear, / Yea, mock the lion when a roars for prey, / To win thee, lady" (II.i.29–31). Similarly, Muly Mahamet brings the flesh of a lioness on his sword to his fainting wife. In both episodes, violence is seen as intrinsic to the Moorish character, although the two playwrights use it to serve different purposes. While Shakespeare keeps his character interesting though his exoticness, Peele's exoticizing of Mahamet serves alienating purposes.[16] This scene from *Alcazar* seems to have impressed contemporary playwrights so much that, apart from its influence on this scene in *Merchant*, it was ridiculed in Ben Jonson's *The Poetaster* and Shakespeare's *2 Henry IV* among others (Edelman *Stukeley Plays* 27).

There is another point in Shakespeare's play that meets with *Alcazar* and it is relevant to the issue of the religiosity of Moors. Jack D'Amico rightly notes that although the Prince of Morocco goes to a temple to pray before choosing the caskets, he is presented as non-religious as he displays no religious affiliation (D'Amico 170). This could be understood as an attempt to accommodate the Moor within Europe by stripping away any alienating features. Similarly in *Alcazar*, Peele makes an effort at blurring

---

[16] See Ch1. section 4.5 for more.

the religious identity of his favourite group of Moors (Elizabeth's friends) in order to brighten their image in front of his audience.

The above selective survey of works with Islamic themes and characters will hopefully place the plays in their proper contexts. It is no possible feat in this book to cover all available knowledge on Islam and Muslims and it is an even more thorny issue to generalize about this knowledge.[17] However, ignorance, stereotype and negative images were the most recurrent elements in the works discussed above. The odd occasion when this rule was broken was used with aims like imploring local readers to appreciate their religion and improve their faith. The two plays thus conducted their cultural work against this background and the way they dealt with it will be dealt with in the two chapters below.

Before we delve into the plays themselves, it is important to place this study within the critical heritage of the general topic of Islam and Muslims on the early modern English stage. While my work has benefitted greatly from previous works in the field, I have found that there is still more to be done on these two plays especially regarding the topicality of the plays and its relationship to their claims to representation.

1.3. Literature review

The field of literary studies on early modern representation of Islam was perhaps inaugurated by Louis Wann in his article "The Oriental in Elizabethan Drama" in 1915. More a survey than anything else, Wann's study lists all plays with an "oriental" character in the *dramatis personae* and finds forty-seven plays in total (423). Of *Alcazar* Wann skimpily and mistakenly notes that it is a play about the "glorification" of the exploits of an Englishman (429).

In 1937, a landmark work in the field, which is still the starting point for any student of England and Islam, was written by Samuel C. Chew. *The Crescent and the Rose* has chapters on "Moslems on the London Stage" and the figure of Mahomet in western thought. Again more survey-like than critical, Chew's work attempts to scan a big number of plays in one chapter. Moreover, regarding *Alcazar*, his views move between the play and historical events without reflection on the influence and representations. This seems to be a pattern he intentionally follows for the

---

[17] A good number of works has been, and continues to be, written on this topic. The works of Nabil Matar, Matthew Dimmock, Daniel Vitkus, Bernadette Andrea, Kenneth Parker, and Matthew Birchwood have been developing new and interesting material in the area of Early Modern Britain and Islam and may be consulted for more in-depth coverage.

resulting picture is, in his own words, "composed of multitudinous fragments: it is a mosaic, not a painting. To neglect hundreds of bits of evidence because they are false, trifling, or absurd would be to omit part of the pattern; the effect is cumulative" (Chew 543).

Then, interest in Islamic themes fell out of fashion for a lengthy period of time. Except for sporadic unpublished American PhD theses, nothing of the same nature as Chew was published.[18] It was not until 1998 that the field started receiving sizeable attention. The year witnessed the publication of the first instalment of Nabil Matar's trilogy on Anglo-Muslim relations. In his *Islam in Britain, 1558–1685* (1998), Matar investigates the impact of Islam on Britain in the period between Elizabeth's accession and the death of Charles II. Special chapters are dedicated to the phenomenon of conversion between Islam and Anglicanism with an overview of the theme of conversion in English writings including literary works. Matar's second book, *Turks, Moors, and Englishmen in the Age of Discovery* (1999), juxtaposes Britain's encounters with Muslims vis-à-vis her encounter with inhabitants of the new world focusing on cases of Britons caught in Muslim captivity and Muslims in Britain. In 2005, Matar published the third book entitled *Britain and Barbary 1589–1689* in which he focuses on the relations between Britain and the North African states dedicating a special chapter to the study of "The Moor on the Elizabethan Stage."

One general reservation against Matar's works, seminal as they are, is his use of literary material. Matar does not show the necessary critical rigour when analysing literary texts and often uses them as means to prove overall theories. Moreover, he moves between literature, theatre and captivity narratives with little or no accompanying discussion of the differences between these genres of discourse. Matar's assertion that "not a single play about the Muslim Levant and North Africa that appeared in the Elizabethan, Jacobean, or Caroline periods showed the Muslim in a morally heroic and favorable light" (Matar *Turks, Moors* 14) strikes us as a bold overstatement. We shall see later in this study that Peele's Abdelmelec and Percy's Geber are not only positive but more complex than Matar's account would allow. This study hopes to prove that, apart from the easy-to-find examples that disprove Matar's view,

---

[18] These unpublished theses include Mohammed Fuad Sha'ban "The Mohammedan World in English Literature, 1580–1642" Duke University, 1965; Warner G. Rice "The Turk, Moor, and Persian in English Literature from 1550–1660, with Particular Reference to the Drama" Harvard University, 1972; Thoraya Ahmed Obaid "The Moor Figure in English Renaissance Drama" Wayne State University, 1974.

representations of Islamic figures were far from stereotypical and were part of a restless dialogue between the text and its cultural milieu. Because this milieu was never settled and one-dimensional, similarly the representations could not have been settled and one-dimensional.

The works of Daniel Vitkus have also been pioneering achievements in the field. He covers the Islamic dimensions of Othello in several articles and books starting in 1997 with his "Turning Turk in Othello" where he studies the play as a "drama of conversion" in the light of Othello's famous lines "Are we turned Turks, and to ourselves do that / Which heaven hath forbid the Ottomites?" (II.iii.161–2) ("Turning Turk in *Othello*" 145). He further develops his approach to include more plays in *Turning Turk: English Theater and the Multicultural Mediterranean, 1570–1630* (2003). Vitkus studies canonical plays (*Othello, Tamburlaine, The Merchant of Venice* and *The Jew of Malta*) and non-canonical works (Thomas Kyd's *Soliman and Perseda*, Thomas Heywood's two-part *The Fair Maid of the West*, Robert Daborne's *A Christian Turned Turk* and Philip Massinger's *The Renegado*). Vitkus's analyses draw on a wealth of historical source material, including captivity stories and travel narratives as well as legal, religious, political, and economic documents. It is unfortunate therefore that his book ignores *Alcazar* despite being particularly pertinent to the theme of Mediterranean multiculturalism. The play is a site for Moorish, Turkish, English, Spanish and Portuguese intermingling and debate with many topical themes that would have enriched Vitkus's book.

In a study that traces orientalist tendencies in early modern England, Richmond Barbour makes some valid points about the representation of the Orient especially the Mughal Empire of India. He also makes a good choice by including royal and civic spectacle into his study. In *Before Orientalism, London's Theatre of the East 1576–1626* (2003), Barbour is careful to distinguish "domestic constructions" of "the East" from those "strategic and economic relations" that produce a more complex and less polemical picture of foreign cultures (5). This distinction is of importance to the present study because it indirectly presents the role of ideological political attachment in forming a representation. Thus, for Barbour, what is produced for domestic consumption is quite different to what is written in, say, diplomatic correspondence. My approach, however, takes the idea further by suggesting that even works produced for the English audience at home were not free from political/ideological influences and were mutually shaped and reshaped by them.

Matthew Dimmock has made more than one valuable contribution to the field especially in his book *New Turkes: Dramatizing Islam and the*

Ottomans in Early Modern England (2003) which has a special chapter on *Alcazar*. Dimmock tries to explore the dimensions of the term "turke" in early modern English writing, especially in relation to the Protestant/Catholic schism. Trying to find a connecting thread of anti-Turkish demonization through his texts, Dimmock notes that his examples "reveal how profoundly ingrained the central tenets of a dominant idea of the 'turke' in English culture remained, complicated by political and mercantile circumstance yet broadly unchanged from that cultivated by More and Tyndale in the 1520s" (Dimmock *New Turkes* 195). In general, Dimmock's approach presents valuable arguments but there are certain points of detail in his analysis of *Alcazar* with which I find issue and which will be referred to in their due place.[19]

In *Traffic and Turning* (2005), Jonathan Burton attempts to move beyond the Saidian binary opposition of East and West noting that even critics who find fault with Said's *Orientalism* do not leave the confines of the same two-sided discourse. He tries to establish that early modern English drama was "more multiple, fluctuating, and susceptible to Eastern influence than has been previously recognized" (15). Focusing on English plays (*Tamburlaine, Lust's Dominion, Othello, A Christian Turn'd Turk*, and *The Renegado*), Burton posits that Arabic and Ottoman sources and texts found their way into English cognition producing an image that was not necessarily polarized or demonized. By way of finding texts that might have influenced his plays, Burton mentions the story of Thomas Dallam who went to Istanbul in 1599–1600 to assemble an organ sent as a present to the sultan. Dallam is used to show that "English discourse was not only permeable, but also permeated and influenced by Muslim voices" (52). The problem lies in the fact that Dallam wrote his account long after Marlowe wrote *Tamburlaine* (to which Burton links Dallam) and his work remained in manuscript until 1893 (Bent i). It is problems like these that this book avoids by using New Historicist methods of linking literary works to a contemporary current of thought rather than certain texts that may or may not be at the writer's disposal at the time of producing their work.

As will be clear from this brief review of the work produced over the last few years, the "representation" of Islam on the English Renaissance stage has been subjected to a detailed and comprehensive analysis, but much remains to be done. In particular, I argue that my two plays present prime examples of the importance of topical reading in understanding the way the Muslim Other came to the English stage. Some of the works that

---

[19] See Ch.1, section 1.2.

tried to cover "representations" of Islam on the English stage fell into the trap of surveying rather than analysing. By trying to cover a large number of works that had Islamic themes or figures, the critic is more often than not prone to fall into two problems. First, there is the problem of lack of depth, which results from limitations of time and space. This shortcoming is what makes works like Chew's and Matar's (especially *Britain and Barbary*) lack the necessary depth expected of a critical study of such a complicated issue. Second, the critic using these methods is prone to fall into looking for a non-existent "uniting thread" among the works he/she attempts to study. This tendency leads to an attempt to find in the plays what does not actually exist in them. An example is Emily C. Bartels' analysis of *Alcazar* based on a non-existent view of multiculturalism, a view that leads to ignoring the importance of the person of the playwright in studying the play, as well as overlooking vital textual evidence.[20]

The other problematic concept I try to avoid in my work is the mishandling of historical information. Adopting New Historicist methodology, I view the text and its history as a nexus or hub of interacting relationships. Thus, the literary text and a given historical document need not be in a direct connection manifested in, say, clear borrowing by the playwright from the historical document. Rather a collection of historical documents is seen as expressive of a general air of the period, or a *zeitgeist*, by which the literary text is influenced and which it recreates. An apt example of this relationship is the figure of the Muslim magus in *Mahomet and his Heaven*. In brief, Elizabethan views on magic were different to ours and the very word magic had different connotations that stretched to include science and mathematics. Thus, any reading of Percy's depiction of Geber the alchemist needs this historico-cultural awareness before any conclusions can be made.[21] The following part discusses the critical and theoretical background to the approach adopted in this work.

1.4. Theoretical background

This study gives special attention to the importance of the moment in time when the work of art is produced. It is the view of this work that the representations of Islam in my two plays were both born from, and contributors to, current debates on several topics in the Elizabethan worldview, including, but not restricted to, views on the Muslim other.

---

[20] See Ch.1, section 1.1.
[21] See Ch.2, section 4.

The historical moment when a new form of presentation is created cannot be divorced from the ambience to which it belongs. In this brief account of the theoretical background to this study, I will be outlining the critical debate that roughly informs and corresponds to the views adopted in this work. The school of thought this work most corresponds to is New Historicism, and its non-identical-twin Cultural Materialism.

1.4.1. New Historicism, Cultural Materialism and Renaissance studies

New Historicism has been an undeniable force in renaissance studies since the early 1980s. The term was coined by Stephen Greenblatt in an attempt to describe the critical activity at the beginning of that decade which had a special interest in politics, power relations and literary works. The "new" part of the name distinguishes it from earlier, less philosophically sophisticated historicisms which did not envisage any interaction between literary texts and their historical contexts but stressed influence instead (S. Cohen 405). Traditional historicisms, prominent in the early twentieth century, are criticised for being "constrained by the reflectionist model implicit in the binary opposition of literary text and historical context" (Mullaney "After the new historicism" 21).

Therefore, early definitions of New Historicism tried to distance the theory from this view. In discussing literary works, Greenblatt describes them as "fields of force, places of dissension and shifting interests" rather than "as a fixed set of texts that are set apart from all other forms of expression...or as a stable set of reflections of historical facts that lie beyond them" (qtd. in Mullaney "After the new historicism" 21). For Greenblatt, "the work of art is the product of a negotiation between a creator or class of creators, equipped with a complex, communally shared repertoire of conventions, and the institutions and practices of society" ("Poetics of Culture" 12). The movement borrows its philosophical framework from the ideas of French philosopher Michel Foucault, especially his assumptions that social relations are by their nature relations of power (Bertens 142).

New Historicism treats history itself as a text needing interpretation similar to that of literary texts, because the production of any text is subject to power relations. Foucault posited that power manifests itself in discourse and that, like ideology, power makes the subject feel that compliance with power is the natural thing to do, or an autonomous decision (Bertens 143). This means that the autonomy of the authors as a *subject* and an *agent* tends to be played down. New Historicism has thus been marked by a tendency to undermine the aesthetics and cohesion in literary works while at the same time promoting an interest in the work's relationship to the "dominant ideology" (Forker 47).

Some example is due here to show how New Historicism works. Seeing that plays exist in a socio-historical hub where discourses, established by institutions like the State and the Church, help determine their meaning, New Historicists try to understand the achievements of a playwright by mapping connections and relations between the literary text and its social and cultural context. The prime example of this practice is Greenblatt's seminal essay "Invisible Bullets" where he reads colonial texts from Virginia against the two parts of Shakespeare's *Henry IV*. The hero of this essay is no stranger to our study. A scientist and "wizard," Thomas Harriot was a member of the Earl of Northumberland's circle of intellectuals.[22] Harriot visited the colony of Virginia and dazzled the natives with European technology which they believed to be a magical or divine power. When some of them died inexplicably the Indians assumed that the ancestors of the Europeans shot them with invisible bullets, hence Greenblatt's title. The argument lies in the method adopted by the governing power in giving voice to the dissenting opposition. Greenblatt detects this strategy, whereby the possibility of subversive doubt functions to reinforce rather than undermine authority, everywhere in Shakespeare's culture. Harriot used a similar technique with the Indians, Greenblatt observed, when he gave them voice in many places of his writings. The aim is not to present their views but to reinforce his. Greenblatt then notes how the first part of *Henry IV* uncannily resembles Harriot's strategy of recording alien voices. Greenblatt quotes Prince Hal's "I am so good a proficient in one quarter of an hour, that I can drink with any tinker in his own language during my life" as an example for this policy. The prince intermingled with the lower classed in order to re-inforce his authority by understanding them better. In the same way Harriot gives the chance to native American voices to appear in his work in order to consolidate English colonial power, so does Hal's seeming openness to criminal culture support rather than weaken English royal power ("Invisible Bullets" 138–9).

Similar use of opposition can be detected in Peele's *Battle of Alcazar*. The play adopts unflinching propagation of nationalist government propaganda. However, in one scene Peele gives voice to a strong diatribe against patriotic feelings and nationalism through a speech by Captain Thomas Stukeley. The English renegade attacks the very basics of the love

---

[22] See Ch.2, 4.1 for more.

of the homeland by denying any value in being born in a certain place.[23] This instance of anti-nationalist discourse is instantly undermined by the fact that Stukeley is portrayed a traitor and a mercenary. One of his companions, an Irish bishop, criticises Stukeley's views immediately as they are uttered. More importantly, Stukeley himself seems to have been doomed by his words and as he moves towards his fall he realizes his mistake so that as he falls to his death he repents reneging on his country and asks for forgiveness.

New Historicism, however, is not as clear-cut and definable as other schools of criticism. Any reader of New Historicist literature would notice the apparent lack of unity among New Historicist critics. H. Aram Veeser, for example notes how New Historicists denied indulging in a movement of any sort (1). Louis Montrose, a prominent New Historicist, wrote that New Historicists were "actually quite heterogeneous in their critical practices" (Montrose "Professing the Renaissance" 18). Martin Coyle refuses to call New Historicism a theory and prefers to call it "a fairly diverse body of scholarship with some common attributes" (Coyle 793). Moreover Greenblatt, the grand tutelar of the movement denied being a theorist: "my own work has always been done with a sense of just having to go about and do it, without first establishing exactly what my theoretical position is" ("Poetics of Culture" 1). Nevertheless, some critics have been bold enough to come up with some recurring points in New Historicist criticism. H. Aram Veeser's list has been met with some critical approval (2). It is also a list that shares some ground with the present study and thus deserves some attention. Veeser's five-point list of New Historicist motifs includes:

1. That every expressive act is embedded in a network of material practices
2. That every act of unmasking, critique, and opposition uses the tools it condemns and risks falling prey to the practices it exposes
3. That literary and non-literary "texts" circulate inseparably
4. That no discourse, imaginative or archival, gives access to unchanging truths or expresses unalterable human nature
5. That a critical method and a language adequate to describe culture under capitalism participate in the economy they describe

For the present study, the first principle manifests itself especially in the chapter on *Mahomet and his Heaven* where the text is studied in the

---

[23] See Ch.1, 4.4.3.2 for more.

light of contemporary debates manifested in material practices like publications on royal succession, women and gynaecocracy, and religious schism. The third point is salient in both plays. In *The Battle of Alcazar*, as will be shown below, the text of the play depends heavily on historical accounts and at the same time reproduces the accounts in a new literary form that sometimes veers towards the panegyric. By the same token, the interplay between *Mahomet and his Heaven* and contemporary texts on several issues shows how permeable the boundaries between these texts were. The fifth point is perhaps better understood in the light of Martin Coyle's words: "discourse and representation form consciousness rather than merely reflecting or expressing it...Culture is therefore an active force in history" (Coyle 793). Thus, this study hopes to show how the two plays are not mere *representations* of solid ideas already present in the mind of the playwright, but rather re-productions and *constructions* of a nexus of views that emanate either from dominant ideology, as in *Alcazar*, or from a resistant minor ideology, as in *Mahomet*. In both cases, authorial agency plays an important role and this work presents sketches on the two playwrights by way of understanding their position towards political and religious issues relevant to his work. This is not in contradiction of the New Historicist idea that minimizes the role of the author as an autonomous producer. The writer in both cases plays a role but New Historicism sees this role more as a product of ideology than anything else.

The idea about resistance to dominant ideology has been a major bone of contention between New Historicists and Cultural Materialists. While Greenblatt and other New Historicists stressed the monolithic nature of dominant ideology which enables it to allow voices of dissent in order to reassert itself, Cultural Materialists saw things from a more inclusive point of view. Cultural materialism, a mainly British movement, was inspired by the works of Raymond Williams, who played a similar role to Foucault's role in New Historicism. Unlike Foucault, Williams saw culture as laden with contending structures which he classified as "dominant," "residual" or "emergent" (Harris 178). As a result, Cultural Materialists do not adopt the New Historicist assumption that subversion props up rather than challenges power. A Cultural Materialist critic like Alan Sinfield endeavours to highlight "fault lines" of dissent within dominant ideology that generate the possibility of change (Sinfield 9 and passim). Thus, this particular difference between the two movements means that, for instance, while a New Historicist would study power relations and instances of disjuncture in a specific area with an eye on showing a larger vision of power, the Cultural Materialist would "regard the text and its context as a site of struggle – riven with conflict and contradiction, sustaining alternative as well as oppositional elements" (Coyle 187).

From this viewpoint, this work shares the stance of Cultural Materialism in that power and dominant ideology in Renaissance England were not monolithic and fault-line-free. The case in point for this distinction is Percy's play. *Mahomet and his Heaven* is laden with dissenting views that criticise the Elizabethan regime on more than one front. William Percy's work shares and reproduces oppositional views on the Protestant government of Elizabeth in a way that cannot confirm Greenblatt's stance on dissent and power, as they are expressed in "Invisible Bullets," for example. More common ground can be found in this regard with Cultural Materialism, which adopts the view that "ruling culture does not define the whole of culture, though it tries to, and it is the task of the oppositional critic to re-read culture so as to amplify the voices of the ruled, exploited, oppressed, and excluded" (Dollimore and Sinfield 14). William Percy's work uses Islamic imagery and setting in order to pass unorthodox views based on Catholic ideology and thus can be seen as an example of the sort of "oppressed" voices championed by Cultural Materialists. Although Cultural Materialists would view Percy as an oppressor, being a member of the aristocracy, still what we are talking about here is his religious identity which was a minority and an oppressed ideology.

The image of the Muslim other in our two plays is seen as a component in the network of figurations relating to the relationship with foreignness in general and the Muslims in particular. Because, as Cultural Materialists agree, "representations do shape history [and] are shaped by history in turn, since they are terrains of struggle as well as of submission," (Wilson and Dutton 16), it is necessary to contextualize the plays and within their politico-religious framework.

1.5. The plays and their politico-religious background

Essential to this study is an awareness of the politico-religious milieu surrounding the plays it essays to investigate. The two plays are situated at two pivotal points in English early modern history and they were duly influenced by the historic events that took place as they were being conceived.

In trying to study the background to the two plays under study, one should be aware of the fact that religion and politics were hardly separable issues in that period. In fact, most of the contemporary issues informing this study of the two plays remarkably fuse aspects of religion with politics or vice versa. Importantly, the separation of the two concepts, i.e. "secularism," is an aspect that features prominently in Peele's *The Battle of Alcazar*, as I explain in Chapter One. Examples of this fusion of the religious and the political are the Spanish Armada and the Succession to Queen Elizabeth. The former was an essentially political event that saw a foreign country try to invade England. But the campaign was not free from connotations of a Catholic-Protestant conflict. The succession to the English throne was also a political issue. However, James's claim especially was more often than not supported or opposed on grounds relating to the established, though still relatively vulnerable, Protestantism in England.[24]

Although the discussion offered in this work will make detailed reference to these events, it is necessary here, by way of introduction, to give a preliminary account of them. The first play, *Alcazar*, was heavily influenced by two contemporary events, namely the Spanish Armada of 1588 and the Moroccan Ambassadorial visit of 1589. *Mahomet and his Heaven* was influenced by many historical events of which two aspects were the most salient. These were the revolt of the Earl of Essex (1601) and James Stuart's accession to the English throne (1603).

The Battle of Alcazar was most likely written in early 1589.[25] The most important historical incident of that period was the English victory over the Spanish Armada in the summer of 1588. The Spanish plot was a great test for English nationalism and as a result of his multiple plots against Queen and country, Philip II became the ultimate foe of the English state. Philip also became a subject of attack in government propaganda and pro-government literature. The most prominent example of this is John Lyly's *Midas* (c.1589) in which Philip is allegorized as an aggressive king with access to great amounts of gold. As Hilliard notes, lines like "Haue not I made the sea to groane vnder the number of my ships: and haue they not perished, that there was not two left to make a number?" definitely link Philip to Midas (Hilliard 247). As will be expounded in Chapter One, Peele's *Alcazar* also makes similar hints towards the evil of Philip and even threatens him with divine retribution.[26]

The other important event that helped shape the production of *Alcazar* was the first visit by a Moorish royal representative to the English capital and court. Mulay Ahmad al-Mansur (Peele's Muly Seth) had earlier turned down Elizabeth's offers of coalition against Spain but upon the defeat of

---

[24] See Ch.2 section 6.3 "James and Catholic hopes".
[25] See Ch.1, 3.1 for more.
[26] See Ch.1, 4.4.2.1.

the Armada, he changed his position. On January 12 1589, Ahmad Bilqasim, who became known in England as "Marzuq Rais," visited England as the first official ambassador from the Barbary States to England. His visit had many objectives some of which were related to trade, but a more pressing issue was an alliance for what became known as "the English Armada" of 1589. Marzuq Rais offered "aid to the English in the form of men, money and foodstuffs, free access to Moroccan ports, Ahmad al-Mansur's personal intervention in the struggle against Spain, and a supply of water for the English fleet's next expedition to Portugal" (García-Arenal 84). Marzuq Rais joined the expedition himself and boarded the same ship with the English-backed claimant to the Portuguese throne Don António (Matar *Britain and Barbary* 13–16; Ungerer 102–4). The Norris and Drake expedition of April 1589 was promised help by al-Mansur and given farewell by our George Peele in his poem *A Farewell*.[27] The relations raised uproar among European Catholics against England's Queen. They blamed Elizabeth for the defeat in the battle of Alcazar as she supplied Moors with cannons. The Papal Nuncio in Spain wrote of her "there is no evil that is not devised by that woman, who, it is perfectly plain, succoured Mulocco [Peele's Abdelmelec] with arms, and especially with artillery" (qtd. in Eldred Jones 138–9). It was in the interest of Elizabeth's foreign policy to present relations with Moors as merely political and underplay the religious and ideological connotations of allying with the infidel against Christians. *The Battle of Alcazar* aptly presents this distinction in dramatic form

On the other hand, *Mahomet and his Heaven* was written in 1601, which also was an important period in Elizabethan history. Two major concerns dominated the political scene at the time. The first event was the failed rebellion led by Robert Devereux, Second Earl of Essex, against the Queen in 1601. Essex was a young and charismatic gentleman and military man who gathered around him a group of enthusiastic supporters including three of William Percy's brothers. Essex was also the Earl of Northumberland's brother-in-law. The play makes a reference to the sad times during which it was written: "Comædyes be not for sad dayes, you seye, / Tragædyes too will not this blissed day fit" (Prol.8–9).

The other important political hallmark of the period was the problem of succession. Elizabeth was sixty-eight, unmarried and without a named heir. Both Catholic and Protestant subjects were apprehensive about the change that might happen with the coming of a new monarch. Two main heirs apparent existed: the Spanish Infanta and James VI of Scotland, and

---

[27] See Chapter One, 3.1 for more.

people were divided into two camps as a result.[28] Some hard-line Catholics supported the Infanta hoping for a return to the old religion while less fundamentalist Catholics and Protestants supported the Scottish king. As the play was being written, eyes were directed towards James VI of Scotland as the next king. James's prospective advent to London was another example of the religion/politics dialectic directly related to our two plays. William Percy's *Mahomet and his Heaven* was written while the Earl of Northumberland, William Percy's brother, was engaged in diplomatic correspondence with the heir apparent.[29] The topic of the letters was a mixture of politics and religion as they basically included an offer of political support on the condition of toleration for English Catholics. Percy's configuration of the Christian schism in his play shows awareness of such an enterprise and his allegorized call for unity among Christians is informed by James's history and the aspirations of English Catholics.

The two plays represent an apt example of the interplay of religion/politics in a form that corresponds to the contemporary double-sidedness of the issue. In other words, the two plays themselves, perhaps unconsciously, formulate their themes along the lines of the inseparable religion/politics duality that dominated the Elizabethan culture in the late sixteenth century.

On the face of it, Peele's *The Battle of Alcazar* presents a political issue charged with important contemporary questions relating to the tensions dominating England's foreign policy and her relations with Spain, Portugal, the Vatican and Morocco. However, undertones of religion are also present in the play. As the discussion below will show,[30] the parties at play in *Alcazar* are subtly divided into those who define themselves according to religious affiliation and those who use national identity as their primary character. Moreover, Peele criticises the crusade-based religious approach to war while he promotes state sovereignty and independence.

By the same token, William Percy's *Mahomet and his Heaven* is by and large governed by a religious worldview. Despite their exotic character, its themes are theological and it claims the Quran as its source material. Moreover, it contains universally-applicable satire regarding the

---

[28] James of Scotland and Isabella the Spanish infanta were the most likely claimants. Other candidates included: Lady Arabella Stuart, the two illegitimate sons of Edward Seymour, Earl of Hertford, and Henry IV of France, all of whom enjoyed little or no support for their claims to the throne (See Bailey 200–1; Croft 44–5).

[29] See Ch.2, section 5

[30] See Ch.1, section 4.2.

corruption of clerics and the misuse of religious discourse. Nevertheless, politics does feature in *Mahomet* on more than one level. As the chapter on *Mahomet* shows, the play carries special interest in a number of political motifs like the clandestine criticism of Elizabeth I, the call for unity among Christian powers as well as indicating that the Muslim Other is the real enemy.

Hence the connection between the two plays: *Alcazar* is a politics-oriented play with strong undertones of religion; *Mahomet* is a religion-oriented play with strong undertones of politics. In the same way politics and religion were two sides of the same Elizabethan coin, our two plays can be seen as two sides of the representational coin. *Alcazar* generally promotes Muslims while *Mahomet* depicts a corrupt Muslim world. However, this study shows that both plays do the same thing by incorporating topical concerns into the representation which render the whole resulting image a mere construction from contemporary ideologies.

While both plays require an historical reading that detects their source material, still both of them necessitate a topical approach. The plays need to be seen not just as reproductions of historical material, but also as "interpreters" of a specific moment influenced by topical interference.

1.5.1. The role of topicality

The question that arises here is: why is topicality an important factor in understanding early modern English representations of Islam? And how does understanding the role of topicality in this representation help in enlightening our knowledge of the field?

The otherness of the Muslim was manifested through two aspects. The Muslim was a religious Other and a political Other; and the perception of Muslims is best understood as a combination of these two sides. Interestingly, both fronts, the political and the religious, were witnessing heavyweight debates at home, debates that shaped the English conception of critical issues like self-definition, religious affiliation, nationalism and secularism.[31] As a result of the extreme otherness of the Muslim figure, it often featured as a yardstick against which political and religious differences were measured. The closer to Islam a concept moved, the more Other it became. On the political scene, relations with the infidel Muslim were signs of treason and betrayal to Christendom while on the religious

---

[31] I use the term 'secularism' with caution to refer to the idea of separating church from state, initiated in England by the Henrician reformation (See Sommerville especially 45–8).

scene, the two sides of the Reformation schism accused each other of being like the Turk in their beliefs.[32]

These contemporary political and religious tensions are reflected in our two plays on several levels. Thus, the representation of the Muslim Other suffers under contemporary influences and topical concerns to an extent that the result becomes a mixed-up image where positive or negative becomes highly debatable. The relationship of the two plays with contemporary ideology, both dominant and oppressed, determined most aspects of their composition, and the image of Islam in them is no exception. Therefore, the position of the two plays towards the government is a useful way to look into their position in relation to contemporary ideology.

The depiction of Islam can be seen as part of the greater picture of the Other in Renaissance drama. Though not the focus of this study, it is illuminating to see how other marginalized groups, like atheists, Jews and Catholics, were depicted. In his book on *Images of Englishmen and Foreigners in the Drama of Shakespeare and his Contemporaries*, A. J. Hoenselaars posits that the image of foreigners in Elizabethan drama depended on a whole host of "political, religious, social, and economic factors" (26). Most salient among these factors, Hoenselaars argues, is the religious factor, especially the repercussions of England's break from Rome. This political and religious earthquake especially affected the image of Catholicism as dislike for Rome and its version of Christianity became an essential part for any expression of national identity (26; cf. Bartels *Spectacles of Strangeness* 6–7, 85, 121).

In an article on "Patronage, Protestantism, and Stage Propaganda," Paul Whitfield White studies religious interludes in early Elizabethan England and their "advancing" of "predominant religious ideology of the Elizabethan governing class." This ideology, White argues:

> is characterized not only by sworn allegiance to the Queen as Supreme Governor of the Church, but by a distinctly Calvinistic world-view, emphasizing personal religious experience, the primacy of Scripture, God's sovereignty and man's depravity, and showing a pronounced aversion to Roman Catholicism: most notably its political doctrine of papal supremacy. (39)

It is not the view of this study to adopt the existence of a defined and clear agenda of government ideology with which a writer complies or not. In the case of Peele for example, no evidence was found that could prove

---

[32] See Ch.2, section 6 for more.

an involvement with some government official to the effect of inserting certain ideas in the plays or other works which Peele was writing. White himself admits that such works fell out of fashion after the early 1570s due to "the growing secularism and commercialism of theatre in London" (40). Thus, what I propose in this regard is not a direct and well-defined set of rules, as it were, by which the author abides. Rather, I look at the relationship with ideology as one whereby the author is influenced by an existent ideological agenda. The result is reflected in the very composition of the work of art on different levels. Motifs supported by this ideological agenda are thus highlighted and those contrary to it are criticised.

The two plays can be seen as examples that complement each other through their interplay with dominant government ideology or certain political stances adopted by the Elizabethan government in their time. In the chapter dedicated to George Peele's *The Battle of Alcazar*, the play is studied as a pro-government work that promotes characters, causes and values that run along government lines of policy and demotes those that do not. This view is evidenced by several factors like Peele's overall *opus* as well as textual analysis. Percy's *Mahomet and his Heaven*, in contrast, works in opposition to the dominating Protestant ideology as manifested by Queen Elizabeth's government and its policies. This view is supported by the playwright's familial background, his biography and his other works. Chapter two studies certain themes in the play that manifest this tendency and relates the findings to the depiction of Islam in the play.

The way the two plays dealt with their subject matter is indicative of such tendencies. Notable in Peele's work is the outright support of the government and its policies. His mouthpiece, the Presenter, has no hesitation in condemning and praising characters in manifest accordance with government views. Other characters also take part in the declamatory pro-government discourse. Sebastian is made to praise Elizabeth eloquently while a Portuguese captain prophesies Philip's imminent fall. We will also see how Peele used his sources extensively and made changes to fit his purposes. Moreover, he censored parts that could not be modified to be included in his work.[33]

Percy's play, the subject of Chapter One, has a different relationship with government views and government censors, however. Laden as it is with controversial but allegorized issues, Percy made an effort at hiding his intents from the uninitiated eye. In this context, the Islamic setting gains another, more realistic, dimension. Rather than seeing it as a purely artistic interest in the Muslim Other, this work posits that Percy's choice

---

[33] See Chapter One, 3.3 for more.

of setting, story and characters serves the purposes of passing messages which otherwise would be problematic.

Chapter Two tries to analyse three major areas of concern in the play where Percy's hand, as opposed to sources, features prominently. The three points discuss the Muslim Magus, the Muslim Woman, and the Muslim schism. In each of these areas, purely local concerns feature prominently to the extent that little source material, or Islamic material, remains to be seen.

This whole work is an endeavour in this direction: an attempt to steer the current trends in the field away from studying representation towards studying constructions; hence the words of Jean-Paul Sartre quoted above.

CHAPTER ONE

PROMOTING MUSLIMS IN GEORGE PEELE'S *BATTLE OF ALCAZAR*

Blest be the heartes that wish my soveraigne well,
Curst be the soules that thinke her any wrong.

1. Introduction

This chapter studies the first theatrical presentation of a Muslim Moor on the English stage from the point of view of the political ideology and circumstances surrounding its writing and production. These factors are believed to be the main motives behind the presentation of characters and themes in *The Battler of Alcazar*. As a result, the "representation" of Muslims in this play cannot be talked about without first appreciating the role of those external factors. It is hoped that this chapter can prove that Peele's work was less of a "representation" and more of a topical and ideological construction in the manner described in the introduction to this study.

In *The Battle of Alcazar*, we find that political ideology manifests itself through nationalistic and patriotic propaganda. This theme of pro-monarchical nationalist ideology is crucial for our understanding of in *The Battle of Alcazar* because nationalistic political discourse features very strongly in the play and that it is an essential factor in the formation of the first English dramatic discourse on Muslim Moors. The clearest indications of the effect of nationalist ideology on the play, and by extension, the representation of Muslim Moors, is the way Peele promotes the Queen's point of view on matters pertaining to the historical battle of Alcazar, as well as the historical figures related to it.[1]

I use the verb "promote" to refer to the ways used by the playwright to support certain characters and themes and by bringing them to the limelight, brightening up their image and toning down their negative aspects. On the contrary is "demote," which refers to the author's interference to blur and undermine certain characters and themes.

Promotion and demotion are most manifest in the presentation of the Queen's friends and enemies. The Armada of 1588 and the Moroccan Embassy of 1589 were events that marked England's new policy lines. The paucity of evidence about public awareness in Elizabethan England makes it difficult to make a definite statement about public views on these two events in conjunction. However, it is reasonable to assume that one question that must have bothered public awareness must have been: "why are we enemies with Christians and friends with Moors?" Peele's play interacts with this topical question from a nationalistic pro-government viewpoint through promoting government policies and demoting apprehensions and dissent, as the discussion in this chapter will demonstrate.

---

[1] See Introduction, section 1.1.

However, it is important to start by looking at some of Peele's other works where I detect the presence of one of Peele's "perennial themes:" praise of the Queen and Protestant England under her rule (Ardolino "The Protestant Context" 146). The focus on the figure of the ruler is given special attention as allegiance to the monarchical system was seen as a manifestation of national pride.

One objective of this chapter is to give a more comprehensive answer to the question: why did Peele choose to present Moors on the stage? The fact that *The Battle of Alcazar* presented the first Moor on the English stage is the main reason behind such questions. The question might be rephrased as: what were the circumstances surrounding the creation of the first Moor on the English stage? Answering such questions lies at the core of our understanding of the nature of representations of Islam on the early modern English stage. As this work seeks to prove, the plays under study, as far as representations of Islam are concerned, are more complicated than a mere artistic production reflecting a certain bias or impartiality on behalf of the writer. Rather they are influenced by a complicated nexus of mainly political and ideological circumstances.

One can argue that each presentation of Islam is a special case that should be studied separately; and indeed my approach here can be taken as an example of this. However, in the case of *The Battle of Alcazar*, it is necessary to take into consideration the importance of "precedence" in forming a general conception of something new to the theatre and developing this into a stereotype. Many habitués of the London theatre would have formed a first impression about Moors from this play, and playwrights were also influenced by it. The popularity of *Alcazar* vouches for this proposition. It was this popularity that made it a source for some Shakespearean allusions including the famous line: "Then feed and be fat, my fair Calipolis" (*Alcazar* II.iii.101) which is reproduced in Shakespeare's *Henry IV Part 2*, (II.iv.155) and Muly Mahamet's: "a horse, a horse, villain, a horse" (*Alcazar* V.i.96), which seems to anticipate Richard III's famous cry (*Richard III*.V.vii.13).

More important was the play's influence on later presentations of black people and Moors on the English stage. As explained below, critics agree on the fact that Muly Mahamet's precedence as a black villain served as a prototype for following presentations of black people and Moors on the stage, from Aaron in *Titus Andronicus* (1590–1) to the hero of *Othello* (1603–4). This point is taken for granted to the extent that no critic seems to question the idea of Muly Mahamet's influence on later Elizabethan stage Moors.

For example, when Anthony Gerard Barthelemy discusses the character of Muly Mahamet, he concludes that Peele's creation not only brought back to life the obsolete character of the Devil, often presented as black, but also that:

> [Peele] rejuvenated for the popular stage in England a metaphor which, without exaggeration, profoundly and adversely affected the way blacks were to be represented on the stage for years to come (Barthelemy 78).

Peter Hyland also indirectly identified Muly Mahamet as the source after which evil Moors followed suit (Hyland 92–93).

Eldred Jones is of the same opinion. Describing Muly's intriguing mixture of impressive language and mischievous ways, Jones notes that "This curious combination of the grandiloquent extrovert and the subtle plotter is a characteristic which other stage Moors, Aaron and Eleazer for example, were to demonstrate later" (Eldred Jones 43).

Therefore, *The Battle of Alcazar* is the obvious choice as the starting point for any study of representations of Muslims and Islam. It is, moreover, a perfect case study of the approach adopted here as it is in this play that one can clearly see how understanding the circumstances surrounding the play's production is essential to any approach to Moors and Muslims and the way Elizabethans portrayed and viewed them.

1.1. Previous critical approaches

The Battle of Alcazar is considered a major point of departure for students of Islam in English Renaissance culture. As shown in the introduction, before *Alcazar*, the image of Muslims and Islam in English writing was by and large negative, hence the importance of the play's contribution to public awareness of Islam, or its cultural work so to speak. In *Alcazar*, we find Moors of more than one type with an overall positive note. It is true that the play's major villain is a Moor but this is counterbalanced with the presence of many more "good" Moors as well as many factors to be explored below.

The questions I referred with regard to Peele's purposes in presenting the first Moor and in writing *The Battle of Alcazar* the way he did, have been recurrent in many critical approaches to the play, especially the most recent ones with their nascent interest in Islamic themes in early modern English literature. However, these approaches all seem to fall short of appreciating the significance of the ideology behind the play's production.

Peter Hyland makes a good attempt to place the play within its cultural context, taking into consideration that interpreting historical texts is a complicated process because it "needs to deal with the complex set of differences generated by temporal distance" (Hyland 86). Hyland does not give a clear definition of this set of differences but rather gives the example of the word "racist" as an ill-defined word which did not exist in the *OED* until 1933 and thus applying it to dates earlier than that must be very carefully done.

However, Hyland's comparison of Muly Mahamet with the character of the Vice is not very convincing, nor is the conclusion he reaches when he tells us that "the supposed progenitor of a line of Moor villains may have been born out of…theatrical need" (Hyland 92-93), that is, the play's need for a villain. Surely, Muly Mahamet has a lot in common with the Vice, but so do most villains. In addition, he was not an insertion into the story that Peele made in order to complete his *dramatis personae* with a villain; Muly is the real villain in all Peele's sources and Peele makes little effort to change anything about him. Hyland's view, moreover, misses the very thing he invites us to have: awareness of cultural context and temporal distance. The generic difference as well as advances in theatrical devices between morality plays and tragedy make linking the two genres, as well as Muly and the Vice, a problematic business. Tragedy is a more flexible form of theatre than the Morality, at least in terms of characters. Its *dramatis personae* are not a clear-cut organization-chart with pre-set positions to be filled by characters. In fact, the richer the tragedy, the more open is the assignment of "villainy" and "heroism" in it. For example, in one of *Alcazar*'s main sources of inspiration, Marlowe's *Tamburlaine*, it would be a reductive reading of the play to assign to characters tags that are borrowed from an older, less advanced theatrical form. Even if we accept the controversial epithet "villain" in relation to Tamburlaine, we would be immediately faced with the problem of lack of "heroes" in the play. Tamburlaine's victims are most of the time less fortunate tyrants (Bajazeth) or secondary characters that do not reach the status of heroes/heroines (the virgins of Damascus). Thus, the versatility of the literary genre that is tragedy sets the author free from having to inherit ready-made stock characters that may or may not fit in the scheme he has in mind. In other words, Peele did not have to have a black-hearted villain of the type of Muly Mahamet just because the literary tradition supposedly runs this way. There are other reasons for this negative presentation and they are closely linked to political circumstances more than anything else.

A more recent approach by Matthew Dimmock has shown more awareness of the nuances of the play's composition, although he does not directly discuss the question of why Peele wrote this play. Dimmock's view is focused on Turks more than Moors but he still makes many valid points about the Moors in the play. For example, the details he gives about English trade with Morocco and rivalry with Portugal for this market are indispensible for an understanding of the play's geopolitical context. At some points, he does refer to some political motives that might be behind Peele's work but they do not crystallize into a unified theory that puts all the points and remarks he makes about the play into one convincing perspective.

One point Dimmock makes is that despite a clear anti-Spanish spirit and "crude nationalism" in Peele's previous works, in *Alcazar*, this is replaced by a more ambivalent approach, a "fictionalized consideration" of Sebastian's war (*New Turkes* 114). Valid as it is, this view of the play still misses some of the points I make later when I study some of Peele's previous works, then move on to the play itself. It is true that in *Alcazar* the expression of patriotic feelings is less "crude" than, say, the mayoral pageants, but this is undermined by the fact that the whole play was written in order to promote nationalistic purposes. The more "refined" nationalism in the play can also be related to the topic of the play and the nature of theatre itself. The play is about a battle in Barbary and is so packed with action that it would not suit its coherence to insert a royal panegyric. Nevertheless, in a rare incident which seems to offer the opportunity for crude nationalism (when Sebastian praises the Queen in II.iv), Peele inserts a long-winded praise of the Queen which could easily be seen as a digression. Hence the assumption that Peele's nationalism has faded in the play falls short of the circumstances of the play's writing and the way nationalism is expressed therein.

An attempt to formulate a theory about the writing of the play is exactly what Nabil Matar does in his book *Britain and Barbary 1589–1689*. In an impressive effort to connect historical events at Elizabeth's court in London with the play, Nabil Matar informs us that it was in the wake of the first Moroccan embassy to Queen Elizabeth that George Peele wrote his play. The Moorish ambassador visited London on 12 January 1589 (Matar *Britain and Barbary* 14) while the play was most probably written between August 1588 (Yoklavich 225) and February 1589 (Edelman *The Stukeley Plays* 18). In brief, Matar's view is that the scene of Moorish ambassadors walking in the streets of London was particularly impressive and had a great impact on the cultural imagination of Londoners. This topical allusion is at the heart of the current study, but I find it hard to concur with the conclusions drawn from it by Matar.

Matar argues that the play is dominated by negative images of Moors and formulates his approach around the idea that Peele was trying to warn the Queen against her involvement with the Moroccan King Mulay Ahmad al-Mansur. One point he tries to establish is that:

> The spectacle of Moorish fratricide and the triumph of Moorish deception signal the danger of the Moroccans in London: what happened ten years earlier to the Christian king could well happen to the Christian monarch of England, and the same kind of deception that was practiced by Muly Mahamet on Sebastian could well be intended by Mulay al-Mansur's delegation to the queen. (Matar *Britain and Barbary* 17)

Matar's clever linkage of the play with the Moorish embassy is undermined by these speculations which lack the textual support as well as historical and contextual proof. Again, Matar's approach fails to convince as a coherent theory: as the following discussion shows, the premise is right but the conclusion is not.

One phrase that stands out of the text quoted above is "the triumph of Moorish deception," a statement which shows lack of awareness for the basic themes of the play. George Peele depicts the failure of one Moor's deception and the triumph of another Moor's honesty and right to rule. Muly Mahamet's villainy is not only condemned throughout the play by most other Moors, it also never achieves any results. Moreover, the play adopts a very clear stance that distinguishes between a rightful throne claimant and a deceiver and murderer of kin and kind. Moreover, the ambassadors in London were the representatives of al-Mansur, the play's Muly Mahamet Seth and the heir of Abdelmelec. In a play where major characters strike us as villainous, foolishly ambitious or young and rash, Abdelmelec can fairly be seen as the only honourable and praiseworthy character and if anyone in the play seems to inherit his characteristics it is his heir Muly Mahamet Seth, or al-Mansur. Therefore, when Matar describes Seth as "dangerous," he seems to be putting into the play what is not actually there. The part dedicated to discussing the character of Muly Mahamet Seth (entitled "Heroes") gives a more detailed perspective into this point. Peele does not make disparaging remarks against Elizabeth's ally but on the contrary lauds him (directly and through his brother) as a noble, Christian-loving, and honest Moor as well as a legitimate monarch.

Matar makes similar inferences in his discussion of Captain Thomas Stukeley's involvement in the action, representation of the Turks as well as other points most of which tend to miss significant evidence from text and characterization in the play. For him, the killing of Englishmen led by Stukeley at the hands of Moors is a sign by Peele of the menace of those Moors because not only is he an Englishman but also the English public admired him and built legends around him (Matar *Britain and Barbary*

17). Stukeley's death in *Alcazar* is not that straightforward: he is not quite simply an admirable Englishman killed by Moors. On the contrary, Peele seems to make an effort at absolving the Moors from blame through several means. First, we are shown that Stukeley's whole participation in the battle was not his idea but Sebastian forced him to join, thus Sebastian shares a good deal of the blame. The second important factor that led to Stukeley's downfall is his waywardness and the fact that he lived on the edge of similar danger all his life. This is displayed in *Alcazar* in such a way that it leads to a divorce between admiration for his heroic and adventurous nature on the one hand and his principles and actions on the other. On the other hand, Abdelmelec is shown as making every effort to avoid the battle and spare Christian blood. Finally and more importantly, Stukeley is not killed by Moors but rather by his Italian Catholic followers. Thus, if any danger is highlighted by his death, it is the danger of disloyalty, rebellion and the danger of mingling with Catholics as well.

Therefore, close as Matar gets to figuring out the important link between the writing of the play and the politics of Elizabethan England, still his theory fails to convince as it builds its conclusions on several misreadings of the play. Throughout the play, as will be shown below, Peele complies fully with a rule he seems to have set for himself according to which he promotes the friends of his nation and demotes her foes. Textual evidence from Peele's other works, as well as historical events, strongly support this idea so any inference that runs against this view, like Matar's, must have a strong textual backdrop but unfortunately Matar's does not.

Another critic who asks similar questions of the play is Emily C. Bartels in her book *Speaking of the Moor*. Bartels rightly notes the diverse nature of the figure of the Moor in early modern representations describing the Moor as "a dramatic subject uniquely poised to negotiate, mediate, even transform the terms of European culture" (15). Peele's representation of Moors fits neatly into this view. As the discussion below shows, traditional English conceptions of Self and Other are challenged in the play through the presence of a heroic Moor, a villainous Christian and a wrong-doing but sympathetic Englishman.

However, in regards to *Alcazar*, Bartels extends this view to what becomes an enforced and almost irrelevant interpretation that lacks textual evidence. Muly Mahamet is, according to Bartels, an isolationist while Abdelmelec presides over a regime promoting "global politics" (*Speaking* 34). It is true that Abdelmelec established serious political relations with the Ottomans and later with the Spanish, but this is counterbalanced by Muly's dependence on Portuguese intervention which in turn included

Italians, Irishmen and Englishmen. Moreover, Abdelmelec's aim was to establish a sovereign state which is not a satellite to any of the regional powers, while Muly promised to become Sebastian's "contributary" in Morocco (II.iv.16). Thus, Abdelmelec is more of an isolationist in this sense than Muly is.

Moreover, although Bartels admits the vital political events that surrounded the play's production, like the Moorish Embassy to London, she chooses to undermine them for the sake of promoting other, currently modish and textually unsupported, views on "globalisation" and "global politics" (*Speaking* 17, 34). Moreover, she misreads Sebastian's panegyric for England and Elizabeth as a warning to the audience: "Sebastian's vision of an inviolate, impenetrable England should give pause to spectators who have just seen where isolation leads Muly Mahamet: to a debilitating despair, impotence, regression, and retreat" (*Speaking* 37). Built on the previous inapplicable assumption, this interpretation ignores the crystal clear message of the speech which praises Elizabeth and runs along the lines of Peele's general interests in his other works.

1.2. The missing link

The above critical survey tries to point out how keen certain critics have been on making *The Battle of Alcazar* perform an ideological role of their own, or fit within a general frame they are trying to establish, especially Bartels and Matar. This tendency has had a negative effect on understanding the cultural work carried out by the play which, in my view, rests on a topical basis. The play takes existing notions on Moors and Other and toys with them by passing them through the prism of topical events and nationalistic ideology.

In other words, the representation of Moors in the play needs to be approached through the extremely important political and historical incidents surrounding its writing as well as the nature of the playwright's interests. Although previous approaches, especially Dimmock's and Matar's, do refer to the political milieu and Peele's political interests, they do not produce a comprehensive vision of the play in which separate details from the play are joined by historical evidence to fill in their appropriate places, like pieces of a puzzle, in order to give a fuller picture of an historic moment in English dramatic history: the moment when the first Moor mounted that step and appeared on an English stage. This is important because it is one of the foundations of this work that representations of Muslim and Moorish characters cannot be studied in isolation from contemporary political ideology. In fact, "positive" or "negative" representations in the play, for any character, can be seen as an outcome of a political agenda. Thus, it is delusional to assume, upon seeing a positive representation in the play, that Peele was breaking an abiding stereotype, i.e. the evil Moor, only for the sake of breaking it. The same applies to negative stereotypes; they are not simply inherited images from past representations or prejudiced views on Islam expressed in theatrical form. In other words, there is more to the representation of Islam in *The Battle of Alcazar* than the mere judgement of positivity or negativity. The play's interaction with contemporary cultural awareness of Islam and Muslims runs in parallel with its topicality. Peele was most likely not interested in breaking or confirming stereotypes and preconceived ideas but rather wanted his play to please the government including its presentation of Muslims.

A key point about the play is its relationship to the contemporary tensions regarding the relationship between state and religion. In this play, curiously enough, we witness the end of a historical phenomenon and the start of a literary one. The historical battle is generally accepted by historians as the last European crusade against the Muslims, or in other words, the last religious war.[2] The play itself initiated the Moor on the stage. One aim of this chapter is to connect the two facts together in an attempt to show how the presentation of the Moor in *Alcazar* is politically motivated. The end of the crusades came about because it was no longer viable for European states to commit themselves to a religious agenda that might or might not serve national interest. By the same token, it was not viable for Peele to commit himself to the stereotype of the evil Moor while it might or might not serve the interests of his nationalistic tendencies.

In the rest of this chapter, I shall give evidence supporting the argument for the role played by topicality in *Alcazar*'s presentation of Muslims. I will also expand the idea of the effect of nationalistic ideology on the representation of Moors in *Alcazar*. I will start with a look at the author's life, his social background, upbringing and education. The aim is to trace points in George Peele's life and social background that define his position within Elizabethan society and the implications of this in relation to popular ideology and conceptions of monarchy and social order. For example, the fact that Peele was a university wit who belonged to the middle class,[3] but still died a poor man, contributes to our understanding

---

[2] See section 4.1 for more.

[3] I use the term "middle class" in the sense proposed by Louis B. Wright when he divided the Elizabethan society roughly into three major divisions. Apart from the highest class of "titled nobility, or landed gentry" and the lowest class of "unskilled labourers...and those small artisans whose trades required little training

of the kind of life he led. After setting out these preliminary observations about the author's background, it becomes necessary to look at relevant examples from his *oeuvre*, especially city pageants and his only play which enjoyed a courtly performance, *The Arraignment of Paris*. Then I make a short study of nationalistic elements in these works with the aim of proving Peele's attachment to this ideology of pro-government nationalism.

Next comes the discussion of *The Battle of Alcazar* itself as a pro-government work of literature. In this part, focus will be shifted towards the play itself starting with a general background study of the historical incident upon which the play was based, with special focus on England's point of view of the events, supported with a look at the sources used by Peele in writing the play. Studying the sources reveals places where Peele significantly alters his source material in order to serve his overall purposes.

What follows is the discussion of *Alcazar* itself. In this part, discussion will cover certain areas of import in the play where the nationalist and royalist themes feature prominently. I start with the play's approach to the relationship between state and religion. The important issue of self-definition in the play occupies the next section in the discussion and reveals significant issues regarding how characters in the play are made to present themselves. I also show Peele's attempt to emphasize or de-emphasize the exoticness of Moors in the play. The depiction of characters, especially promoting and demoting certain characters, is also given a special section which is supported by sections on the use of significant keywords and epithets in relation to certain characters.

2. Peele's life and works

2.1. Life

George Peele was born in 1556 and died in 1596. A Londoner by birth, Peele also lived all his adult life under Queen Elizabeth I, the monarch to whom he dedicated a good amount of attention in his works. He was the son of a well-to-do hospital clerk, James Peele. Alongside his career as

---

and whose rewards were meagre," the middle class, Wright posits, was the one that lay between these two extremes. This was "a great class of merchants, tradesfolk, and skilled craftsmen, a social group whose thoughts and interests centered in business profits. They made up the middle class, the bourgeoisie, the average men" (2).

clerk, James Peele wrote two works on book-keeping and, interestingly, he also wrote two city pageants, a gene he seems to have passed on to George who also wrote pageants for the Lord Mayor.

In 1572, Peele, then sixteen, went to Oxford's Broadgates Hall, then to Christ Church where he took a BA and an MA in 1577 and 1579 respectively. In Oxford, he kept the company of men of letters and he was noted for his love for the classics. He was reported to have "neglected his logic and philosophy for poetry and antique fables" (Cheffaud qtd. in Horne 36).

Whilst at Oxford, Peele was recognised as "a most noted Poet in the University" (Wood qtd. in Horne 41). Moreover, his main acquaintances included young men with literary interests. David Horne gives details of three scholars with whom Peele kept company: Richard Edes, Leonard Hutton and William Gager. All three had literary interests and Hutton and Gager actually wrote plays that were presented before the Queen in one of her visits to the University. One of Peele's first poems, *The Tale of Troy*, was probably written after his MA but in his last years of residence in Oxford, about 1580–81 (Reid Barbour). This poem would become the basis for his royal encomium *The Arraignment of Paris*. In 1580, Peele married a sixteen-year-old girl named Anne Cooke. He was widowed in 1587 and married another woman named Mary Yates (or Gates) on 26 December 1591, five years before his death. It is believed that he spent the last years of his life in poverty and misery. He was buried at St James's on 9 November 1596.

George Peele had a fluctuating financial situation throughout his life. His father was a middleclass man who was able to send his son to Oxford so he must have had healthy finances. However, once on his own, Peele seemed to have had trouble in self-maintenance. A look at his biography shows how his financial situation depended on his work and vice versa, i.e. his literary output on his finances. For example, even though in 1580 he was "certainly not in need" (Horne 55), after the writing of the *Arraignment of Paris* (c. 1581), his funds "were running low and he found it necessary to turn to a form of writing which would produce less prestige but more bread and butter" (Horne 71). This was achieved through writing pageants for the Lord Mayor's show. Of Peele's three known pageants, two are extant and these are: *Device of the Pageant Borne before Woolstan Dixi* (1585) and *Descensus Astraeae* (1591).

Like many of his contemporary young men, Peele's marriage had financial purposes (Horne 50). His first marriage provided some income and for many years after his marriage, he was embroiled in a number of lawsuits because of his wife's inheritance. By 1592, shortly after his second marriage, Peele "had been driven to extreme shifts. His troubles ... may have been primarily financial" (Horne 82). Later in life, his financial and physical fortunes took a downward turn. On 17 January 1596 he sent via his elder daughter a presentation copy of *The Tale of Troy* to William Cecil, Lord Burghley. In the dedication, Peele complained of a long, enfeebling illness and attributed his boldness to necessity (Reid Barbour). Burghley neglected the letter and Peele died later that year.

This short overview of Peele's life shows that his quest for financial security was never over. Throughout his career, he struggled to use his pen to achieve social recognition: first by entertaining the Queen directly through *The Arraignment*, then through dedicating a lot of his work to praise her person, promote her policies and sing the English nation under her reign. Unfortunately, his desperate efforts never achieved the recognition he was after and he died a poor man. *The Battle of Alcazar* is best understood in this light: a work by a playwright who is struggling both financially and socially to make a name, and who used his literary output as a means to achieve fame and recognition.

2.2. Works

Facing financial problems throughout his entire life, George Peele made continual attempts to present his literary output as an intellectual creation that runs along the lines of government propaganda which mainly focused on praising Elizabeth, valorising national sentiments, and, more importantly, supporting state policies.

The above-mentioned facts about Peele's life prompted critics studying the works of George Peele refer to the notable relationship between his works and the Elizabethan politics of his days. For example, in an article about *The Old Wives Tale* (1595) Frank Ardolino notes that "the primary theme of all of Peele's works is the praise of Protestant England under Elizabeth," and that as a "courtier poet" Peele demonstrated through his art, in various forms and genres, "the rightness of Elizabeth's reign" (Ardolino "The Protestant Context" 147).

Ardolino's description of Peele as a courtier poet is perhaps not quite accurate, as Steven May's specialised study of Elizabethan courtier poets states clearly that Peele "was not a courtier nor in any demonstrable way a member of the court circle" (May 9–10). However, Ardolino's claim presents two valid points upon which it could have been based. One of them is mentioned in the article and it relates to the general theme that can be found in most of Peele's works, the praise of the Queen. The second point relates to the fact that one of Peele's plays was actually a "courtly text" and this was *The Arraignment of Paris* (Montrose "Gifts" 433).

Ardolino's observations about the themes of Peele's plays have a good amount of validity in them, although they strike the reader as bold statements. Peele might not have been a courtier in the proper sense of the word, but notable in his works is the aspiration to be closer to the exclusive circle of intellectuals surrounding the Queen. Another possibility is that he aspired to get himself into the limelight for the crucial moment when the Queen might take an interest in him and recommend him to a post. The earlier episode in his life when two of his Oxonian friends, Leonard Hutton and William Gager, wrote plays for the Queen's visit indicates that, early on in his career, Peele kept company with people who were eager to engage with courtly literature and performance.

Peele's literary career is further proof to this early tendency. *The Arraignment of Paris* and other examples of Peele's earlier works indicate his intent on running along the literary lines defined by the social and political elite. Trying to place *Alcazar* within a context of the playwright's oeuvre, I will be analysing Peele's courtly play and two of his city pageants in which nationalistic themes feature prominently. Then I shall apply a theoretical approach on nationalism to these works. Nicola Royan's model for 'myths' of nation formation will serve as the basis for this discussion. The aim is to show how Peele conformed to these theories by adhering to the basic tenets of national formation.

2.2.1. *The Arraignment of Paris* 1583–4

In his first major work, *The Arraignment of Paris*, Peele blended together material from three different sources to produce an admirable work that served the purpose of entertaining and complimenting Elizabeth through inserting the character of the nymph Eliza, "our Zabeta fayre" (l. 1236), into the classical tale. However, certain aspects of the play indicate that, in his eagerness to write for the Queen, Peele was more the emulator than the originator. The story he used comes mainly from Greek antiquity; the characters also derive from myth. Even the themes and aims he adopts stem from earlier royal entertainments presented before Queen Elizabeth. This is an important observation because, in both *The Arraignment* and *Alcazar*, Peele has done the same thing: using sources extensively while still making modifications and additions that serve patriotic purposes.

Peele's three source-models, as Braunmuller explains, are legend, mythology and the pastoral (Braunmuller 30). The legend of the Trojan War is where the eponymous hero comes from; Greek mythology provides ancient gods, like Venus, Jupiter and Diana, to the play; and pastoral is behind the setting of the play. The three elements are carefully blended by Peele to reach the final scene of his play where he adds his personal touch by inserting praise and dedication to the Queen as the resolution to the conflict that arose in the play.

The term "Zabeta" seems to come from the shows that took place in the Earl of Leicester's Kenilworth castle in 1575 and were documented partly by George Gascoigne in his *Princely Pleasures at the Court at Kenilworth* (Frye 70–71). Susan Frye points out how these eighteen-day festivities were an "unprecedented" event whose "length and expense [were] never again attempted" (Frye 61–62). Peele could have read about the festivities in the contemporary pamphlet on them, or in the widely-circulated posthumous collection of Gascoigne's works published in 1587 (Cunliffe 231). As a young writer, Peele perhaps wanted to emulate the best shows ever presented for the Queen and so used Gascoigne's work as a basis, but this led him into some confusion regarding the symbolism he used.

Confusion arises from the hidden messages Peele may have had in mind when writing the play. Louis Montrose seems to have fallen into this confusion. He takes the characters of Juno and Diana, representing marriage and virginity respectively, as elements suggesting marriage to the Queen:

> It is apparent ... that Peele's play belongs to a corpus of courtly texts and performances which shadowed the controversial issues of royal marriage and succession. ("Gifts" 440)

Further, Montrose explains that:

> Diana is a goddess of girlhood chastity, of princesses who live in maiden meditation, fancy-free; Juno is a goddess of womanly majesty, of marriage and matron queens. Zabeta has been a nominal follower of Juno since Elizabeth became Queen in 1558; the intent of the show is to bring the Queen to emulate Juno fully by fulfilling herself in marriage. ("Gifts" 442)

There is no doubt about the symbolic dimension of these characters in royal spectacle but their application to a later work is not appropriate. Indeed, these characters were used to convey such messages but not as late as 1583. In her chapter "Why did Elizabeth not Marry?" Susan Doran makes mention of Court masques making "petitions" to the Queen to get married: "in most of them, the goddess Diana representing virginity was trounced by Venus or Juno, the goddess of marriage" (31). However, the important difference is that these shows were presented in the mid-1560s and not later as Peele does. (Doran "Why Did Elizabeth Not Marry?")

Gascoigne's work was written in 1575 when Elizabeth was 42, i.e. almost near the end of her childbearing age, while Peele's play was written around 1583–1584 i.e. when the Queen was fifty-one and it was futile for her to try having an heir to the throne. As early as 1565, Frye tells us, Elizabeth expressed dislike of insinuations about her marriage and stressed her status as a virgin queen and sole sovereign and decision-maker in her kingdom (Frye 70). Thus, while it is undeniable that *The Arraignment* can be read as a text laden with the need for Elizabeth to get married, there is little chance that Peele intended this reading as the Queen was, first, too old for giving birth and, second, too resolute in punishing such indications. That is the reason why I think that when Peele unwittingly made this crude hint about the Queen's marriage, he was only emulating the success of *The Princely Pleasures* rather than sending his own messages to his sovereign. In other words, Peele almost copied wholesale themes from Gascoigne and did not notice the dangerous symbolism of Eliza and Juno. This was the sort of symbolism that previously led to "Philip Sidney's banishment from court, John Stubbs's amputated right hand, and Peter Wentworth's imprisonment in the Tower until his death" (Frye 70). Peele's unscrupulous assimilation of his sources in *The Arraignment* is an indication of a writer whose keenness to present material that will please the Queen sometimes overcomes the need to know the depths of what these sources indicate. It also hints at the way Peele tends to use sources. In *Alcazar*, as we shall see, Peele's hurried use of sources is an important factor of both the discussion and the date of writing the play.

The Battle of Alcazar has also received critical appraisals that run along the same lines. A. R. Braunmuller saw the central theme of the play to be the question of royal succession. He linked the Moroccan struggle for the throne to England's own succession problem and the execution of Mary. The use of terms like "rightfull" and "lawfull," according to Braunmuller, "was familiar to English audiences and would become even more familiar as the queen aged and adamantly refused to name her successor" (Braunmuller 79). Simon Shepherd also pointed out that the play presents in "diegesis" (narrative form) a political debate that could not be talked about openly, i.e. royal succession (Shepherd 146). This approach to *Alcazar* is more convincing than Montrose's approach to *The Arraignment* as the diegetic usage of concepts and ideas that occupied the popular mind is more logical than stating directly to the Queen that she should get married.

Another important point about *The Arraignment* is that Peele diverges from the classical tale only once and that is when Elizabeth is introduced into the play. In the final scene, after the dispute between the three goddesses is referred to Diana to solve it, she proposes the nymph Eliza "a figure of the Queen" (V.i.SD) as the most beautiful of them all. Diana's speech is an extravagant encomium that runs as follows:

> There wons within these pleasant shady woods
> …
> Amids the Cypres springes a gratious Nymphe,
> That honour Dian for her chastitie,
> …
> Her name that gouernes there Eliza is,
> A kingdome that may well compare with mine.
> An auncient seat of kinges, a seconde Troie,
> Ycompast rounde with a commodious sea:
> Her People are ycleeped Angeli,
> Or if I misse a lettre is the most. (1139, 1147–8, 1151–6)

These few lines are charged with nationalist themes: the praise of the Queen (as a chaste virgin), the greatness of her kingdom, the legendary link between England and ancient Troy, the country as a protected island, as well as praising the English people themselves. Not only do such themes recur in courtly literature time and again (Strong 26 n.60) but they are central to theories of nationalism which will be discussed below.

The figure of the Queen receives more than just praise. Another significant observation about the play is its promotion of Eliza as the solver of discord. Louis Montrose noted that in this play, Peele showed concern with "the establishment and maintenance of order, and with the constant threat of disorder" (Montrose "Gifts" 444). It is important to note that when Peele represents Elizabeth as the solution to the problem that could lead to chaos and discord he is also expressing a typical view of a middle-class man in the late sixteenth century (Wright 266–67).

In Peele's earliest major theatrical work, then, it is notable that he pays special attention to two major themes: praising the Queen, the country and the nation on the one hand, and the stress on the importance of the monarch as the harbinger of social harmony on the other. Peele also shows awareness for themes and modes of expression preferred by the government.

2.2.2. Pageants for the Lord Mayor of London

Since their first conception, around the year 1540 (Horne 157), the mayoral pageants were associated with royalty and politics. In Elizabethan times, they became even more so and praise of the Queen was a permanent motif in these shows. "Nowhere is the image of the Queen so sharply defined," as in these shows which reflected "not only popular but courtly concepts of the Queen" (Strong 18). Peele jumped on the bandwagon, as it were, of the Lord Mayor's shows and continued the tradition of merging the politic with the artistic in his pageants, with a special interest in popularizing nationalist propaganda, as will be shown below.

Records show that George Peele wrote at least three pageants for the Lord Mayor's shows, only two of which survived (Horne 154). As mentioned above, the period during which Peele wrote pageants (1585–1591) was marked by low funds on his part and thus they can be seen as a downward career move from the courtly *Arraignment*. However, they still share the nationalistic and royalist tendencies shown in previous works. The first of the three pageants was written in 1585 for the mayor Wolstan Dixi and is considered the earliest complete mayoral pageant extant today. In 1588, Peele is reported to have written another pageant which has been lost. The last pageant, *Descensus Astraeae*, was written in 1591. The two extant pageants will now be discussed in order to support the idea that Peele had a continuing interest in promoting nationalist and royalist ideology through his literary output. This view gains greater significance especially because the first pageant was written before *Alcazar* and the third one after it.

In these two pageants, one can notice a tendency towards stressing certain themes which serve nationalistic purposes. Most prominent among these themes are: the praise of the monarch, stressing positive aspects of the nation like "honourable" classical origins, commending unity, peace and harmony in the homeland, and the failure of enemies to harm the people of the nation. Thus, just like in *The Arraignment*, the country's safety is given high priority and is associated with the presence of the guardian monarch without whose presence discord may arise. The theme of outside threat is a common tool used by regimes to subdue dissent and opposition.

2.2.2.1. *Device of the Pageant borne before Woolstone Dixi* in 1585

Peele's first pageant is interesting for a number of reasons. Not only is it "the first printed description of a lord mayor's pageant known to exist" (Fairholt 24), it is also presented by a person who is "rid on a Luzarne

[lynx] before the Pageant apparelled like a Moore" (*The Device*, SD). Peele follows the tradition of pageantry by introducing his work through a Presenter, an idea he used later in *The Battle of Alcazar*. In his first mayoral show, Peele chooses a "strange" presenter, a Moor, to deliver the induction to the characters on the pageant. The mayoral pageant belongs to a literary genre where a speaker was often used to present the figures on the pageant and comment on their roles and significance, and the Moor aptly performs this role. However, given that the English theatre's first Moor was Peele's Muly Mahamet in 1588–9, the figure of the Moor was unknown to the drama let alone pageants. So what role does this "pre-Alcazarian" Moor play and how is he related to a Lord Mayor's show and, more importantly, to the general view of Peele's *oeuvre* adopted in this book?

It was a tradition that the pageant would be themed in relation to the guild to which the new mayor belonged (Horne 159-60). Therefore, the most immediate and valid link is the fact that the lynx was the emblem of the Skinners' Company and it featured on their arms (Braunmuller 23; Horne 277). Lynx fur was apparently making a good trade and was worn by women of high rank (M. Greenblatt 48). However, this observation only justifies the presence of the lynx, not the Moor himself. Was Peele alluding to trade relations already in place between England and Morocco which might have included leather and fur trade? This is difficult to verify. Historical sources indicate that trade relations between England and Morocco started at least as far back as 1551, when an English ship led by Thomas Wyndham (d. 1554) reached the Moroccan port of Agadir carrying canons and heavy arms and returned with precious Moroccan "sugar, almonds and gold" (Al-Ghunaimi 313; Matar *Turks, Moors* 33). Importantly, the Barbary Company was chartered in the same year this pageant was presented, 1585 (Games 50). However, there is no mention that I could come across of trade in leather or fur. Thus, it is more appropriate to look at the Moor and the lynx as two separate points Peele was trying to make.

In this view, what does the Moor signify then? The words the Moor says are significant, I think, in answering this question:

> From where the Sun dooth settle in his wayn
> And yoakes his Horses to his fiery Carte,
> And in his way gives life to Ceres Corne,
> Even from the parching Zone behold I come
> A straunger straungely mounted as you see,
> Seated upon a lusty Luzerns back.
> And offer, to your Honour (good my Lord)

This Emblem thus in showe significant.
Loe lovely London riche and fortunate,
Famed through the Worlde for peace and happinesse
…
And next, with humble gesture as becomes,
In meeke and lowly manner dooth she [London] yeeld,
Her selfe her welthe with hart and willingnes.
Unto the person of her gracious Queene,
Elizabeth renowned through the world,
Stall'd and annointed by the highest powre,
The God of Kings that with his holy hand,
Hath long defended her and her England.
(*The Device* 1–10, 35–42)

The prevalent theme of these opening lines is the exoticism of the speaker. The Moor is not only strange in himself, he is also "stangely mounted" on a lynx. One can only wonder about what the introductory "stage direction" says about him being: "apparelled like a Moor" and whether that refers to clothing only, or the colour of his skin as well. Nevertheless, the overt exoticism symbolised in the figure of the Moor is used to serve a purpose. The strange Moor, who might have been as exotic as Peele's Elizabethan imagination could get, is coming to tell the Londoners that the fame of their city and Queen has reached the furthermost regions of the world "where the Sun doth settle in his wane." London's and the Queen's fame was so widespread that even a Moor has come to acknowledge it. George Peele is using the Moor as a physical metaphor of the undiscovered and unknown world which has come to acknowledge the greatness of England's Queen and capital city.

At the time of the pageant, Elizabeth had already begun diplomatic correspondence with the Muslim rulers of Constantinople. According to Matar, "in September 1579, a Turkish envoy arrived with a letter to Queen Elizabeth in which the sultan offered 'unrestricted commerce in his country to Englishmen,'" and in 1583 the first Ottoman ambassador arrived in London (Matar *Turks, Moors* 33). Taking into consideration the little distinction Elizabethans made between different types of Muslim "Others" (like Turk, Moor, Barbarian etc), the Moor in Peele's pageant can be seen as a play on these recent political events that were likely to draw certain public attention.

Another significant point is that although the image of the Moor might well be exotic and "strange," his words are comforting and reassuring. He comes to tell the audience that remote peoples come to this city as friends who admire London and the Queen. This notion is further supported by the theme of London's security which recurs in the Moor's words.

Throughout the pageant, Peele seems to return repeatedly to the theme of the peaceful and safe city that is London. The Moor says that London is world famous for her "peace and happiness" and that the Thames provides "safe and easy passage" for her ships. Therefore, the Moor reminds London to thank "her God the Author of her peace" (10, 20, 34). When London speaks, she reminds the audience again of her "peace and calm" and attributes them to the "royal Queen" (58). Later on, with other speakers, the idea of appreciating peace and security is further reiterated. The Country reminds London: "love and serve the sovereign of thy peace" and so do the Fourth Nymph and Science (100, 126).

London's safety and peace are thus presented as major royal achievements for which the city (and in practice its dwellers) must be grateful. The character of Magnanimity encourages the Lord Mayor to protect this city and preserve its peace. The message is intended for Londoners as well who are encouraged to be "glad, and well apaid, / in readiness their London to defend" (67–68).

Predictably, praise of the Queen is found throughout the pageant and most characters take part in it. The character of London wishes that the Queen "may ever live and never die" (61) and the Thames tells the city that the Queen's "highness lengths thy happy days" (87). However, most impressive in the praise of the Queen are the Moor's lines with which he concludes his role in the pageant. The length as well as the timing of these lines is significant as the former (nine lines) indicates high importance in such a short piece of writing and the latter means that these lines have higher impact on the audience as they are the last thing they hear from this "strange" Moor. The ideas carried in these lines are traditional in their promotion of royalist values like the Queen being "stalled and anointed" by God, and being the defender of her country.

As mentioned above, notions about the greatness of the monarch and of the city of London were commonplace in mayoral shows. However, in this particular pageant, the fact that the Presenter is a Moor gives all these concepts new dimensions. First comes the highlighted "strangeness" or exoticism of the Moor which gives the notions of fame and power new far-reaching meanings. Second there is the notion of the friendliness of Moors towards the English. Not only does the Moor come to praise the city and Queen, he does so using a discourse highlighting peace and security more than anything else. In his praise to the Queen and keenness on peace, the Moor is a remarkable visitor to London, especially as a city pageant presenter. More important within this view is the fact that exoticising the Moor does not lead Peele into the minefield of religion. As in *The Battle of Alcazar*, the Moor's religion is not referred to although it could have been easily used as an exotic flavour to be added to this character. Peele perhaps knew that while black colour and exotic "apparel" might be palatable if presented in the right way, religious difference was more difficult to accept especially when the other is so vague and unknown that no common ground can be sought.

In the pageant, Peele utilizes another theme that serves nationalistic purposes. "The Children in the Pageant" speak the following words: "New Troy I hight whome Lud my Lord surnam'd, / London the glory of the western side" (54–55). The lines are a clear indication of the origins of London. King Lud was a mythical king of Britain frequently referred to as the founder of London. The name "New Troy" also relates to the mythical origin of Britons coming from the Trojan Brute or Brutus, great-grandson of Aeneas, who left Troy and came to England and established a city he called Troynovant or New Troy. Brute was the "progenitor of a line of British kings including Bladud, Gorboduc, Ferrex and Porrex, Lud, Cymbeline, Coel, Vortigern, and Arthur" (Drabble 144). It was perceived a source of national pride for the English (and British) to claim descent from Trojan ancestors. Peele utilises this source of pride in his pageant to complement a work laden with patriotic and royalist propaganda.

The Device of the Pageant of 1585 is, therefore, an interesting and primary example of Peele's concerns in his work. He presented the public with an attractive display of various characters to celebrate the appointment of the new mayor. Peele seized this opportunity to show his compliance with the government's propagandistic purposes through reminding the Londoners of the greatness of their city and monarch and the need to appreciate the blessing of security they are endowed with. Peele also shows an early interest in Moors as exotic characters, an interest that will come into full bloom in *The Battle of Alcazar*.

2.2.2.2. *Descensus Astrææ* 1591

Six years after *The Device of the Pageant*, in his third known Lord Mayor's Pageant Peele made an important change to the whole genre in *Descensus Astraeae*. Now the work has its own title derived from its theme, a tradition that seems to have started with this pageant (Fairholt 29). It is also notable that in this work Peele wanted to make pageants more of a work of art and thus produced what some considered "the most sophisticated of the Elizabethan Lord Mayor's pageants" (Braunmuller 24). In this pageant, Peele adhered to his overall patriotic tendency which ran in perfect harmony with the traditional attitude shown in mayoral pageants of stressing peace and harmony while popularizing the monarch.

The show starts with a Presenter, who introduces the pageant and the characters. Then an elevated Astraea, the "celestiall sacred Nymph," holding a sheep hook is shown tending her flock who feed "among the gladsome greene" (54). Immediately after Astraea speaks, we are shown her two enemies: "Superstition, A Friar," and "Ignorance, A Priest." The two try to poison the fountain from which the flock is drinking but they fail because of Astraea's power: "and bootlesse we contend / While this chast nymph, this fountain doth defend" (64–65). The three Greek Graces or Charites: Euphrosyne (Joy), Agalia (Beauty) and Thalia (Good Cheer) speak, followed by the three theological virtues: Faith, Hope and Charity. Then Honor, Champion and two Malcontents repeat the same theme of defeating the ill-wishers who have no ability to harm the flock. The pageant is concluded by a speech on the water (the Thames) telling the Mayor to "go in peace happy by sea and land, / Guided by grace, and heavens immortal hand" (145–46).

Peele's contribution to the art of pageantry in this work by choosing a title for his work: *Descensus Astraeae* (which is Latin for "the descent of Astraea') was loaded with pro-royalist connotations. Associating Elizabeth I with mythological figures was common practice in late sixteenth century literature (Strong 10). Indeed, in *Descensus Astraeae* Peele does mention a number of these figures:

> Our faire Astraea, our Pandora faire,
> Our faire Eliza, or Zabeta faire
> Sweet Cynthias darling, beauteous Cyprias peere. (40–42)

Zabeta, as we have seen, was previously used in *The Arraignment*. However, of all the figures Peele chose Astraea as his eponymous character and reading the text of the pageant reveals the intriguing mythological and religious symbolism behind the title, and how it was selected to serve nationalistic and royalist propaganda.

Astraea was one name for the Greek goddess of Justice who was represented also by the celestial constellation of Virgo. The story of Astraea is mentioned by Ovid in the first book of his *Metamorphoses* when telling the story of the four ages of Gold, Silver, Bronze and Iron, and how Astraea lived on Earth until the Iron Age when evil prevailed and she ascended into heavens to become the constellation Virgo (Strong 29). In Elizabethan times, Astraea became but one of the many mythological figures with whom the Queen was identified. But there is more to this symbolic identification than first meets the eye. For Astraea was a virgin goddess who stood for Justice and whose return to Earth marked the return of the Golden Age, as proclaimed by Virgil in the opening line of his

Fourth Eclogue: "*Iam redit et virgo: redeunt Saturnia regna*" (Strong 30), which can be translated as: Now the Virgin [Astraea] returns, and the reign of Saturn [the Golden Age] begins (Lewalski 683). It is interesting to note as well that Queen Elizabeth was actually born on the seventh of September under the Zodiac sign of Virgo. Thus, an appropriate combination of chastity and good rule was represented by Astraea and applied to Elizabeth as a virgin, chaste and just queen.

Peele was not breaking new ground in presenting the theme of the Golden Age as this was a recycled theme that occurred once and again long before the Renaissance. According to Roy Strong, "the return of Astraea to the earth became a never-ending theme in imperial propaganda both in antiquity and the middle ages" (Strong 30). So Peele's choice of title and main character was another instance of promoting and lavishing praise on the Queen through using material from well-established sources. This was achieved through elevating Elizabeth to the status of mythological goddesses and describing her reign as the Golden Age which brought back justice and prosperity to earth.

Symbolism in the pageant gains another level of complexity. The Greek mythological figure is given a Christian Protestant dimension as Astraea is placed in opposition to two theologically based characters: Superstition, a Friar and Ignorance, a Priest. The former urges the latter to "stir" poison into the fountain with his "beads." But the Priest says that he cannot do harm under the gaze of Astraea because her heart is "purely fixed on the law," and because she is "chaste." The two outstanding features of the Queen, her chastity and her upholding of the law both serve to praise the Queen, but the latter is a clear indication towards the importance of law and order and public obedience to them. People are told not only to abide the law but to abide the law as enjoined by Elizabeth.

Figures of Catholic clergy, and by extension the Catholic practice of Christianity, are associated with negative epithets that stem from a Protestant ideological viewpoint towards Catholicism which accuses them of ignorance and superstition. Moreover, the role of the two Catholic characters in the pageant is to try to poison the fountain from which Astraea's sheep are drinking using a rosary, another religious emblem. The backdrop of this episode relates understandably to English anxiety towards Catholic danger represented, at that post-Armada time, mainly through Spain. The presence of the Queen, whose "gaze" and vigilance stop ill-wishers, is thus stressed as a protective factor against external threats as she is represented as a shepherdess and citizens a flock. It was this part of the pageant that prompted critics to note a tendency towards showing the importance of the role of the Queen as a harmonizing and a "reforming" factor (Yates *Astraea* 60) around whom the people should rally. Instilling fear of an external enemy, an ideological enemy here, is a practice used to unify people around a ruler, especially through promoting a unifying ideology like the ideology of nationalism.

Descensus Astraeae reiterates many themes from Peele's first pageant. The mythical origin of the Britons is referred to again in *Descensus* when Astraea and the Britons are related to Jove and Brutus:

> Astræa daughter of the immortall Jove,
> Great Jove defender of this antient towne,
> Descended of the Trojan Brutus line:
> Ofspring of that couragious conquering king,
> Whose pure renown, hath pierced the worlds large eares. (14–17)

The last line also relates to the recurring idea of the fame of the country, its inhabitants and sovereign. Aglaia later describes Elizabeth as a "peerless Queen" whose name is "Enrolled in register of eternal fame" (76–77).

Peele was more interested, though, in restating and stressing the security of the country under Elizabeth. His method in the pageant was to "take a number of contemporary difficulties and blend them into a reassuring pageant" (Braunmuller 25). This is clear from the almost-symmetrical recurrence of defeating the enemies; the difference is just in the identities of the enemies: one time they are two Catholic figures and the other time they are two "malcontents." Friendly figures accentuate the idea of peace in different places. The Presenter, for a start, sings in praise of the status quo:

> O happie times
> That do beget such calme and quiet daies,
> Where sheep & shepheard breath in such content. (25–27)

Later the Champion promises to defend the flock against Malcontents and tells Astraea to "Sit safe sweet Nymph among thy harmless sheep" (104). Finally, the Water Nymph's recommendation to the new mayor is to preserve London, a city the "mortar" of whose walls is "peace" (134).

Descensus Astraeae, as we have seen, is another example of Peele's work where he uses his art to promote nationalist and royalist ideology. In this pageant, he makes a good effort at passing to his audience certain messages which centre on, but are not restricted to, the figure of the Queen. In this context, the reign of Elizabeth is promoted as a Golden Age where good will and harmony will return to earth. This reign is not unchallenged as foes, both external and internal, religious and secular

(Catholic clergy and malcontents), try to destabilize its tranquillity. Peele's acknowledgment of dangers is dealt with on two levels: first, they are dealt with effectively by Astraea; and second, they are sandwiched between an opening that praises the Queen as the chaste and just ruler and a conclusion that promotes the tranquillity and harmony represented by the status quo. It was this use of pageantry that Braunmuller was referring to when he wrote:

> In Elizabethan society—a society divided over religion, the distribution of political authority, and indeed the state's very definition—images of power and ceremonies of mutual responsibility asserted, and even seemed to "prove," the existence of a splendidly reassuring universal order. (Braunmuller 11)

The image of the kingdom presented in *Descensus Astraeae* was aimed at supporting a royalist discourse in the cause of "reassuring" harmony and stability, which in fact were far from assured. As the following discussion of Peele's works will show, his selection of themes is not that simple. It strikes many notes that relate to nationalist ideology as theorized by scholars of nationalism.

2.2.3. Nationalism in Peele's other works

The previous discussion on some of Peele's works apart from *Alcazar* raised some prominent themes pertinent to the question of the existence of ideological nationalist discourse in the works of Peele. On a theoretical level, a leading scholar on nations and nationalism, Anthony D. Smith, discusses the components of what he calls "ethnic myths" (Smith 62–68). These are six concepts shared by nationalist movements through which they try to define and differentiate themselves from others. Applying these myths to fifteenth- and sixteenth-century England and Scotland, Nicola Royan combines some of them together to narrow down the number to three: "myths of origin and ancestry, myths of national heroes, and myths of regeneration, which look towards the future. These are the areas where the figuring of nationhood takes place" (700). To find that the theories about imagining the nation feature so precisely in Peele is of some moment to this study in particular.

The following analysis of these categories is aimed at showing how Peele deployed all the necessary ideas to promote an ideology of the nation. It is noteworthy here that the idea of the nation in Peele's mind was inseparable from the government propaganda of promoting both the monarch as a person and her rule and policies. Different as these three categories are, Peele was so obsessed with praising and promoting the monarch that he seems to have implied Elizabeth in all of them. It seems that for him the nation was the Queen and the Queen was the nation.

2.2.3.1. Myths of origin and ancestry

In this category, writers and proponents of nationalist ideology present the public with stories which relate a certain community with a historical temporal origin "When We Were Begotten," as well as an ancestral origin: "Who Begot Us" (Smith 63-64). The factor of common origin instils a feeling that the nation is one big family and thus promotes a sense of belonging and togetherness. Royan furthers this definition by pointing out that "the emphasis in this view of identity is on the people, not on the territory, and on the king as a representative of the people" (Royan 701). This applies typically to Peele who sees loyalty to the monarch as the pinnacle of nationalism and any praise of the monarch a praise of the nation.

The clearest example of this type of nationalist ideology is the repeated reference by Peele in his pageants to London as Troynovant which combines both ancestral and temporal origins as it refers to the originator of the race as well as the imagined period in time when he originated it. The invocation of Brutus meant that at a certain point in time, Brutus left Troy and came to the British Isles and established the city of Troynovant and thus became the progenitor of the British. This is what Smith terms "the sacred moment of birth" (63).

In another reference to this factor of national ideology, and one that relates to the significance of the ruler, Peele combines the origin of Astraea with that of the Britons (*Descensus Astraeae*.14–17 qtd. above). Here, the ancestry of both people and ruler is stated but with a difference. The Queen, as Astraea, is descended from the mythical deities whereas her people descended from Brutus, thus granting noble origin for both but superiority to the monarch.

2.2.3.2. Myths of national heroes

Having historical or mythical figures identified as heroes is a technique, as it were, that utilizes tale-telling to give the community a sense of shared history and relate them to heroic ancestors. These heroes can be mythical or real and ancient as well as contemporary.

Peele mentions some of the heroes of old, like Brute and King Lud when he says, as well as the lines quoted above about Brutus (*Device*.54–55). However, he focuses on presenting Elizabeth as a contemporary national hero who is defending the nation and around whom the public need to gather in order to save themselves. This is most apparent in *The Arraignement* and *Descensus Astraeae* where in the former work Eliza is seen as the solution to the dispute and in the latter work the audience are reminded more than once of the external dangers from which Astraea is protecting them.

2.2.3.3. Myths of regeneration

The word "regeneration" refers to the popularization of ideas about the nation's fate in achieving a higher level of prosperity or a "golden age" as Smith terms it (67). Royan also uses the same term when he talks about Renaissance nation-writing in England, reminding us that "the most striking myth of regeneration of this period is the return to a golden age of Christendom" (705).

As discussed above, Peele's choice of Astraea as a metaphor for the Queen carries a great amount of symbolism stemming from Astraea's position in Greek mythology as the emblem of chastity whose return marks the return of the Golden Age of justice and purity to earth. This theme might seem non-Christian at first, but for an Elizabethan intellectual, like Peele, it had more connotations than that. Frances Yates points out the Christian dimension given to the Greek Goddess when Emperor Constantine said that the virgin who will return to earth is none other but the Virgin Mother of Christ (Yates *Astraea* 34–5). She also links the Golden Age to Protestantism as "Peele clearly associates the return of the virgin of the golden age with reformation in religion" (Yates *Astraea* 61).

Descensus Astraeae is the clearest manifestation of the ideology proclaiming Elizabeth's reign as the awaited Golden Age. But while the other two works do not have this symbolism at work, they still relate to this idea in indirect ways. The Golden Age is marked by the end of all disputes and problems, just as Eliza ends the discord in *The Arraignment*. It is also an age of a great nation whose fame reaches the far ends of the earth, just as the Moor in *The Device* comes to tell us. *Descensus* openly proclaims the coming of the Golden Age and the other two works show different facets of Elizabeth's Golden Age.

2.2.3.4. Call for unity and obedience

Peele employs these nationalist and mythological factors in the works discussed above but not without an addition. It is true that his vision of national unity personified in the figure of the Queen was supported by certain themes but the conclusion he implies is somewhat different to the premises. It seems to stem from an ideology of authority that calls for commitment to law and order, maintenance of status quo and obedience to authority.

In *The Device*, as mentioned above, the recurrence of words like peace, happiness, safe and welfare, stresses to the viewers the importance of these things in their lives. Having presented London's status quo as such an important matter, Peele speaks on behalf of the people "All English harts are glad, and well appaide, / In readines their London to defend" (68–69). He then asks the new mayor to do the same "Defend them Lord and these faire Nimphs likewise: / that ever they may doo this sacrifice" (70–71).

The Arraignment is more metaphorical in this regard. There is a stress on the role of the Queen in maintaining order and solving disputes, and this is clearly linked to the fact that "She giveth lawes of justice and of peace" (1157). Thus, the Queen's "laws of justice" and the maintenance of peace are inseparable ideas. If the public wants to enjoy the latter, they must accept the former.

In *Descensus Astraeae*, Peele uses similar words to those in *The Device*:

> The morter of these walles tempered in peace
> Yet holdes the building sure, as are the sprigges
> Woven from the spreading roote in knottie boxe. (134–136)

The Queen's role in this view is a provider of peace to the people "That while thy subjects draw their peace fro thee, / Thy friends with ayd of armes may succor'd be" (52–53).

It would speculative to try to know what exactly Peele meant by the Queen giving arms to her friends. However, it is noteworthy that he wrote this pageant after *Alcazar* where he must have read in the sources that his monarch supported the non-Christian Moors with arms and ammunition and continued to do so. Could Peele be justifying a possibly objectionable act by the Queen? In fact, this runs in line with the discussion of *Alcazar* below where the visit of the ambassadors is given a positive view in the literary-historic world of Peele's play. Moreover, there are hints that Peele tries to justify plans of military cooperation between Elizabeth and the Moors against Philip of Spain.

***

This part on George Peele's other works has shown us how keen he was to formulate his work along nationalistic lines which take the praise of the queen as a central theme. Moreover, throughout his career, as *Alcazar* will also testify, Peele strikes us as a writer who is highly sensitive to contemporary events. Thus, topical references in his works abound. It is also interesting how these other works by Peele adhere to the tenets of nationalistic propaganda and advocate them wholeheartedly. The conclusion of this part is that Peele was always quick to capitalize on any current event to write a work which will bring him to light as a supporter of royal policy. The three works discussed above have many elements that support the main argument of this chapter: that topical factors and government policies defined how issues, themes and characters were portrayed in Peele's work. In this light, *The Battle of Alcazar* should be no exception as the following discussion will show.

3. The play

3.1. The historical incident and Peele's version of it

On Monday, 4 August 1578, the history of North Africa, the Iberian Peninsula and perhaps England witnessed a major historical turning point. Two great armies with a total of at least seventy thousand troops met in the famous battle of Ksar el-Kebir (sometimes spelled Al-Qasr Al-Kabīr, or Alcazarquivir in Spanish), also known as the Battle of Three Kings and the Battle of Wādī Al-makhāzin (Trim 4). The encounter led to the death of three kings (hence one of the names), the fall of the kingdom of Portugal and the failure of a papal mission to regain Ireland from English rule.

Put very briefly, the story of the battle is that a Moroccan king, Moulai Muhammad al- Mutawakkil, was deposed by his Ottoman-supported uncle, Moulai Abd Al-Malik. Despairing of returning to power single-handedly, al-Mutawakkil sought aid from Sebastian, the young king of Portugal, promising to hand over the Atlantic coasts of Morocco to Portugal upon winning his throne back. Sebastian went to war with blessings from the Pope and support from other European kings including the French and Spanish monarchs. Abd Al-Malik, on the other hand, was supported by Ottoman forces. The battle was ill-prepared on the Portuguese side and ended with an overwhelming victory for the Saadis (the dynasty to which Abd al-Malik belonged), and the invading army was almost exterminated. Sebastian and Muhammad drowned, and the already-sick King of Morocco, Abd al-Malik, died during the battle, leaving his brother Moulai Muhammad Al-Mansur to continue the battle and sit on the throne after him.

As is the case with most historical events, the reasons that led to the battle have more than one version. If we put aside the improbable idea that Sebastian was indeed interested in returning a deposed king to a "rightful" throne, what remains is either a battle resulting from the clash of interests between neighbouring countries, or a crusade caused mainly by religious fervour. Sebastian's role in the action is the key point in determining each of these two views. As will be shown later, Sebastian did not wait for Al-Mutawakkil's alluring offer to invade Morocco, but rather offered help himself and even before that received a papal bull to crusade against Barbary.

But how were these events perceived in London? The English authorities could not have watched this battle without interest. In fact, before, during and after the battle, the English played a significant role that had doubtless effect on the outcome of the battle as well as the events after it. The two contending parties, Portugal and Barbary, had special places on the map of Elizabethan foreign policy interests. The dissolving of the former and stabilization of the latter had serious repercussions on Elizabethan foreign politics. The battle of Alcazar destabilized the power balance in the region and made England more vulnerable to a Spanish attack.

Portugal, for a start, was important for England as a trade partner as well as for its geopolitical position. The Queen allowed crucial exports of gunpowder to Lisbon up to a few months before the battle of Alcazar. In *The Salisbury Papers* we read two "warrants" for gunpowder exports to Portugal: the first with "forty quintals" on 22 March 1577, the second for "fifty thousand pounds" on the sixth and eighth of May 1578 (Dimmock *New Turkes* 122). Moreover, as Spain's neighbour, Portugal was perceived as a "check to any Spanish drive northward" (Dimmock *New Turkes* 118). As a result, Portugal's fall and annexation to Philip's realm led to an inevitable clash. Indeed, the 1588 Armada sailed from Lisbon to attack England (Dimmock *New Turkes* 118). Portugal was thus not a sworn enemy of Elizabeth in the way that Spain was, and its welfare and independence from Spain was of importance to England's own welfare.

Barbary, on the other hand, was also a trade partner with England. As far back as 1551, with Captain Thomas Wyndham's voyage aboard the *Lion* of London, English cloth was traded in Moroccan markets and Moroccan sugar was bought from there (Andrews 101). Trade later took a more serious turn. For in 1577 Elizabeth dispatched Edmund Hogan to negotiate with Abd Al-Malik about buying Moroccan saltpetre, the chief component of gunpowder. The lengthy negotiations were successful and Abd Al-Malik acquired for his saltpetre English "cannon and shot" (Edelman *Stukeley Plays* 14). Edelman indicates that these cannons were used by Abd Al-Malik in his war against the Portuguese in the following year. So when Matthew Dimmock states that the English "characteristically supplied both sides in the *Alcazar* conflict with equipment: the Portuguese with large quantities of gunpowder and the

Moors with arms and especially with artillery" (Dimmock *New Turkes* 122), he puts his finger on a really interesting point. The English not only supplied both sides, but bought Moroccan saltpetre, made gunpowder out of it and sold it to the Portuguese. In other words, the Moors were being bombed with gunpowder made from their own saltpetre.

England's Protestantism was a main factor in its relationship with the Moroccans. Catholic European states were banned by the pope to deal or trade with the Muslims, but Elizabeth defied the bull by selling arms and ammunition to Barbary (Bartels *Speaking* 24). The leader of the Moors did not seem to matter to Elizabeth, who had trading relations with all three kings mentioned in *The Battle of Alcazar*: Muhammad Al-Mutawakkil, Abd Al-Malik and Ahmad Al-Mansur. However, common ground was always sought between the two parties. Abd Al-Malik was reported by Edmund Hogan, Elizabeth envoy to Barbary, to have "a greater affection to our Nation then to others because of our religion, which forbiddeth worship of Idols" (Hakluyt 289). This is almost literally the same note made by English ambassador to Istanbul, William Harborne, about the Grand Signor (Dimmock *New Turkes* 3). England was very interested in relations with the two Muslim kingdoms and was trying to find mitigating excuses for this interest.

Thus, in the battle of Alcazar and its aftermath, the English saw a historic turning point which meant that their arch enemy grew stronger and more capable to attack them. On the bright side, trade relations with Barbary became even closer. In order to undermine Philip's power surge, Elizabeth adopted the cause of Don António who claimed to be the rightful heir to the Portuguese crown after Sebastian. In 1589, she sent him aboard an expedition to reclaim his throne but the venture was a failure. It was for this expedition that Peele wrote two poems, a farewell and a welcome-back. Textual evidence indicates that Peele wrote these two poems right after writing *The Battle of Alcazar* because he mentions characters from *Alcazar* in them (see section 3.3 for more).

George Peele makes a theatrical version of these complex historical events and he comes up with a five-act tragedy that proved to be a popular success. Since the play is not well known even to experts in Renaissance drama, I will give a brief synopsis of the plot, or Peele's version of these historical events, in order to make future reference more convenient.

In Act I of the play, a Presenter briefly tells us the origin of the problem of royal succession in Barbary in a style that reflects confusion on Peele's part towards foreign names. But what can be made out is that a King called Abdallas wronged his brother Abdelmelec and installed his (Abdallas's) cruel son Muly Mahamet on the throne, who then ordered the murder of his young brothers and his uncle Abdelmunem. Abdelmelec is supported by the Ottoman Emperor Amurath and he defeats Mahamet in battle. The act ends with him fleeing from Abdelmelec's forces.

In Act II, having won the battle, Abdelmelec is sovereign over Morocco. In Lisbon, a papal expedition to invade Ireland, led by the Englishman Captain Thomas Stukeley, is forced to land and is welcomed by Portuguese leaders. On the run from his enemies, Muly Mahamet decides to resort to Sebastian and sends him ambassadors. Upon receiving the ambassadors, Sebastian agrees to help Mahamet and he forces Stukeley to join the war.

In Act III, Sebastian receives assurance of help from Philip of Spain. Preparation on both sides begins with Abdelmelec learning about Sebastian's intention. In Act IV, the battle is about to start and Sebastian presses his reluctant captains to fight. In a soliloquy, Muly Mahamet reveals his true intentions of using the Portuguese for his advantage.

The final act has the actual battle being fought offstage with different characters coming in to comment on what is happening. However, Abdelmelec dies in his bed before the battle starts. Soon we learn that the Portuguese are defeated. Muly Mahamet flees on a horse and Stukeley is stabbed by two of his followers for leading them into their doom. While dying, he soliloquizes telling his life story to the audience. A triumphant Muly Mahamet Seth, Abdelmelec's brother and heir, comes and winds up the action. Muly Mahamet and Sebastian are dead. However, while the former's body is flayed and stuffed with straw, the latter's is retrieved and dealt with in due respect and the play ends with Sebastian's funeral.

3.2. Politico-historical background

Because this study proposes giving emphasis to the political and religious factors that played a role in the creation of the first Moor in an English play, it is necessary to give a brief background study of some facts and incidents that are relevant to the topic of the play. The aim is to gain more awareness of the cultural and ideological milieu that informs Peele's work. Three main areas are worthy of focus here: first comes the discussion of the nuances of the relationship between England and Portugal; second is the question of the Elizabethan succession and its relation to Portugal; and third is the papal expedition to Ireland. The three areas are linked together in an intriguing web, and discussing these interrelations gives a better insight into *The Battler of Alcazar*.

3.2.1. Portugal and England

England's support for Don António, whose cause *The Battler of Alcazar* champions,[4] was just an episode in England's long and complicated relationship with Portugal. A look at the history of Anglo-Portuguese relations shows the pivotal role played by the battle of Alcazar in changing the course of these relations. After a period of decline and unfriendliness, the fall of Portugal triggered the English interest in restoring sovereignty to the Portuguese and they saw in Don António a good means to that end. Claiming Portugal for Antonio had many benefits for England like revitalizing the old alliance, having a foothold in the Iberian Peninsula and other overseas locations, as well as putting an end to Philip's northward aspirations.

Before and after the battle of Alcazar, Portugal had a special place on the map for English foreign policy due to several geographical, commercial and even dynastic factors that linked the two countries together. The Portuguese markets were important targets for English merchants and so were the English markets for Portuguese merchants. Moreover, the two royal families had strong ancestral ties going back to John of Gaunt (1340–99). However, in the Elizabethan era, the most important geo-political feature of Portugal was its neighbouring location to Spain, England's deadliest enemy. English diplomats believed that a friendly Portugal was an insurance against Spanish attacks from the Atlantic shores, a theory that was confirmed by increased Spanish hostility after the annexation of Portugal.

The alliance between England and Portugal stretches back to the Treaty of Windsor in 1373.[5] Up to and during the reign of Elizabeth, Anglo-Portuguese relations fluctuated between the warm and close on the one hand, and the cold and intense on the other. The two countries had vibrant relations towards the end of the fifteenth century. This was basically due to commercial reasons as the two economies complemented each other as one country produced what the other needed and vice versa. Later in the early sixteenth century, Portugal was so occupied by her colonial enterprises little importance was given to her European relations. In addition to Spain, Portugal was one of the world's two major colonial powers at the time. Under Charles I of Spain, the two Iberian powers had a strong alliance, and this distanced Portugal from England. The reformation schism also helped widen the gap (Prestage 77–8).

---

[4] See section 4.2 for more.
[5] The alliance has been described as the oldest alliance in the world which is still in force (see Caldwell 149).

Before Elizabeth came to power, English merchants upset the Portuguese and Spanish authorities when they tried to trade with newly discovered regions controlled by these two countries. Susan Doran notes that in the 1550s "some London merchants ... opened up traffic with Guinea in West Africa ... but the government of Mary I ... banned commercial activities there in response to protests from Philip II" (*Foreign Policy* 28). Of course, Philip's influence in England died with Mary I.

The accession of Elizabeth I to the English throne changed the political scene drastically. First of all, the two monarchs, Elizabeth and Sebastian, were hard to conciliate: "the hot-headed leader of a last crusade and the wary, intelligent woman, untroubled by moral scruples, could have little in common" (Prestage 81). Elizabeth did not see in Portugal a trustworthy political ally especially because Sebastian's policy was seen as pro-Spanish. The English were worried by Sebastian's zealous nature and feared that Lisbon would be used as a base to attack them or Ireland. Even Sebastian's expedition against Barbary, which ended in Alcazar, was feared to be headed towards Ireland (Chapman 145).

Under Elizabeth, the English revolt against Spanish influence meant more enterprise for English merchants and pirates, and thus England became a threat to Portuguese interests as well. Elizabeth gave promises of reining in the pirates but few of her words materialized into action. As for trade, she saw that the English had the right to trade in Portuguese controlled regions as much as the Portuguese had right to trade in England and Ireland. In 1567–8, the Portuguese actually captured some of William Winter's ships. The English retaliated by capturing Portuguese ships in Falmouth and Elizabeth seized the goods of the Portuguese in England and all trade was suspended (Chapman 138–40). Prestage also documents the exchange of strong words between Elizabeth and Sebastian in 1567 because of these incidents (84). However, trade relations were too important to give up easily and they were restored in 1571 (Prestage 86).

Morocco was an important factor in these tumults in Anglo-Portuguese relations as one reason for Portuguese indignation against the English, apart from piracy and illegal activities with Africa, was the particular case of Barbary. The English trade with Barbary was said to be worth more than that with Portugal. In 1575 Burghley negotiated with the Portuguese ambassador, Giraldi, the matter of trade with Barbary at length, and conceded that no arms trade should be involved but rejected a proposed Portuguese inspection of English ships (Chapman 143, 4).

It was not long after these incidents that the battle of Alcazar took place. Sebastian's death led to the accession of his old uncle Cardinal Henry who was not married and who died two years later. As a result, three major claimants were seeking accession: Philip II of Spain, the Duchess of Braganza and António, Prior of Crato (Chapman 147). Elizabeth was warily trying to fathom the situation in Portugal and she dispatched a special envoy who was instructed to address himself to the governors who were supposed to settle the matter of succession and to each of the three claimants giving them good wishes but committing England to nothing (Chapman 147). Philip did not hesitate and claimed the throne by force reportedly saying "I inherited it, I bought it, and I conquered it" (Birmingham 33).

Philip's menacing powers were doubled by this union which brought under one ruler the two halves of the world that had been divided at Tordesillas (Newitt 87).[6] These new acquired dominions had great repercussions on England especially later in 1588 when the Portuguese fleet, ports and resources proved vital for Philip's great Armada (Newitt 92). But things did not run smoothly for Philip as Don António, having lost his claim to the Portuguese throne, escaped to France and later staged a failed revolution against Philip in the Azores (Newitt 90). When he finally came to England (c. 1585),[7] the English government saw in him an opportunity not to be missed.

Elizabeth adopted António's cause due a good number of political goals that could be achieved by this move. At least, Elizabeth would be able to exert pressure on Spain and threaten to destabilize Philip's rule in Portugal. A greater achievement, however, would be to plant António back in Lisbon and win greater influence in Iberia than the Anglo-Portuguese alliance ever brought. A. R. Disney explains that António:

> promised his allies a one-off payment of five million gold ducats, subsequent payments of 200,000 gold ducats a year in perpetuity, permission for the English to sack Lisbon and garrison the Tagus forts at Portuguese expense and freedom to trade in Portuguese overseas possessions (211).

These submissive conditions by António would have made Portugal "an abject English dependency" (Disney 211).

---

[6] The treaty of Tordesillas (7 June 1494) divided the newly discovered lands outside Europe between Spain and Portugal (See Brotton 72).

[7] Upon António's arrival in England a pamphlet arguing for his claim was printed. The title of the anonymous pamphlet was *The explanation of the true and lawfull right and tytle, of the moste excellent prince, Anthonie the first of that name, king of Portugall, concerning his warres, against Phillip king of Castile for the recouerie of his kingdome* (1585) (Escribano 114).

Convinced of Spain's weakness after the Armada, Elizabeth started preparing for a counter-Armada to claim Portugal back for António. The expedition, "one of the worst fiascoes of Elizabeth's reign" (Chapman 149), was not successful due to several reasons not least among which was Elizabeth's wary tardiness.[8]

However, the English were not unanimous in supporting António. Because Philip kept his protection for their trade in the territories he ruled, English merchants saw in António's cause a risk. After all, Portugal represented only one sixth of the trade with Iberia as a whole and risking the Spanish market for the Portuguese did not make good commercial sense (Chapman 147–8). Nevertheless, António had on his side the anti-Catholics represented by Walsingham and the explorers represented by Drake (Chapman 148).

In Portugal, first and foremost, António's ancestral claim to the throne did not have very valid grounds. Not only was he an illegitimate son of Don Luis, brother of Don John III,[9] a fact that greatly undermined his claim, but also his mother was a New Christian or "a Jewess in the eyes of many orthodox Portuguese" (Newitt 86). His main support in Portugal was among the nationalists who saw that, as an anti-Castilian candidate, António was the only option to repel the Spanish. António lost this important public support by resorting to the English. As Prestage notes, when António was sent aboard English ships in 1589 to claim Portugal: "the citizens of the capital did not rise in favour of the invaders, probably because while they had little love for Spaniards, they had less for heretics and felt resentment towards the nation which had intruded itself into their colonies" (88–9). The result was that England's hope in gaining a foothold in Iberia was denied and António left England for France where he died in 1596 (Griffin 106).

Thus, at the time when Peele wrote *The Battler of Alcazar*, (between late 1588 and early 1589), English foreign policy saw in António an important asset that was exploited in order to keep Spain's control of Portugal in a state of instability with the ultimate aim of planting him in Lisbon one day. As will be expounded later,[10] George Peele's play garners up sympathy for the cause of a lost kingdom whose valiant but rash leader perished in a battle which he was encouraged to join by Philip of Spain.

George Peele seems to have been particularly interested in the cause of Don António and England's involvement in it. Shortly after writing

---

[8] See section 4.3.5 where I discuss Elizabeth's tardiness as referred to by Peele.
[9] See Fig. 1-1.
[10] See Section 4.4.3.1

Alcazar, we see him writing a special poem titled *A Farewell to the Famous and Fortunate Generals of our English Forces* (1589). In this poem, Peele celebrated the English expedition to Portugal which carried Don António aboard in an attempt to plant him as king. Moreover, when the failed expedition returned home, Peele wrote another poem welcoming the troops back, *An Eclogue Gratulatory* (1589). One element of Peele's interest in Don António's cause manifested itself in the play's depiction of, and relationship towards, royal succession themes. In the following section, I try to trace the theme of royal succession in *Alcazar* and in the history surrounding it.

3.2.2. The succession to the throne in the 1580s

The Battler of Alcazar displays a genuine interest in issues pertaining to royal succession through portraying the dangers associated with conflicts over such an issue. These tensions are presented in the play in different forms. Present in the actual text of the play is the description and commentary on a succession problem in Barbary. However, the historical moment the play describes, as well as the cultural milieu it was conceived in, both relate directly to another succession problem in the kingdom of Portugal. As a result, the topical association with English anxieties over Elizabethan succession can hardly be escaped.

The play does not sit on the fence concerning the Moroccan succession question. Using elements of characterization, language, and mime (*inter alia*), Peele makes it quite clear with which party he wants his audience to sympathize. Muly Mahamet loses his claim to the Moroccan throne for reasons relating to his hereditary claim as well as his personality. In a remarkably brief style, the Presenter tells us that Muly Mahamet's father breached the inheritance laws of Barbary and killed his brothers in order to install Muly on the throne. As king, the Moor discredits himself through his actions as he perpetrates the murder of his own young brothers. His claim to power is further undermined by his inability to keep hold of the throne despite his tyranny. He is easily deposed by Abdelmelec and he fails repeatedly to regain his throne. Thus, legally, ethically and politically Muly Mahamet is presented as an unworthy ruler.

The succession to the Portuguese throne receives little direct commentary in the play. However, it lurks strongly in the background to the play's writing and performance. *Alcazar* presents the case for a misfortune experienced by Portugal that resulted in the death of an heirless king and the near extinction of the nobility. It also criticizes Philip's unethical behaviour towards Sebastian and thus undermines his eventual annexation of Portugal to his empire. Don António is the benefiting party of all these efforts and his claim to succession is given major boost in the play.

As noted elsewhere,[11] A. R. Braunmuller pinpointed strong links between the play and the political atmosphere of the late 1580s. Mary Stuart's plot against Elizabeth and her eventual execution in 1587 must have been strongly present in the public mind when *Alcazar* was written. Thus, terms like "rightfull" and "lawfull," according to Braunmuller, were of paramount importance in this context (Braunmuller 79). Royal succession became more and more urgent as Elizabeth aged and refused to get married or name a successor. In this respect, the play is also topical by being related to the two Iberian countries who have dynastic links to the English royal family and thus to potential heirs to the English throne.

In *Alcazar*, Muly Mahamet stands for the danger of a traitor from within the royal family. His claim to the throne is undermined by his actions and crimes. Later on, he even brings in enemies of his state in order to gain a throne. As Braunmuller noted, at the time of the play's composition, Mary Queen of Scots was in a very similar position. She had been accused of plotting the assassination of the Queen as well as planning foreign intervention by Spain and France (Warnicke 233–45). The extension of this similarity of situation between Muly Mahamet and Mary to a complete identification is not likely to be what Peele meant. The approach adopted by this study caters for a better understanding of such situations. The play interacts with an existing cultural milieu and its themes and characters cannot be detached from this milieu. Thus, the strong presence of ideas about succession in the time of the play's composition is playing its part in its formulation of relevant ideas. Peele, being a patriotic author, sees these issues from the government's point of view. As a result, and by return to the main concern of this work, the representation of Islam in the play has to be seen in this light. In the particular situation, the demonization of the Moor Muly Mahamet is more a denouncement of treason to the country than a biased view of Muslims.

3.2.2.1. Dynastic links

In addition to the geopolitical importance of the Anglo-Portuguese connection, genealogical factors linked the two ruling houses. The link between the house of Tudor and the House of Aviz stretches back to John of Gaunt (1340–99) who was the father of three important figures in this relation. His son was Henry IV who became father to Henry V and

---

[11] Section 2.2.1

grandfather to Henry VI. John of Gaunt had another son, John Beaufort, First Earl of Somerset, whose great grandson became King Henry VII the founder of the Tudor dynasty. John of Gaunt's daughter, Philippa married King John I of Portugal, the founder of the house of Aviz. Both Philip II of Spain and Sebastian of Portugal descended from King John and Philippa. Thus, Queen Elizabeth was Sebastian's fifth cousin once removed and King Philip's fifth cousin (see Fig. 1-1).

During the succession controversy surrounding Elizabeth's early commitment to celibacy, various candidates existed, some of whom were not English. One argument against "aliens" inheriting the crown despite superior hereditary claims was the case of Elizabeth's grandfather, Henry VII. Elizabeth's grandfather inherited the throne despite the fact that King John II of Portugal descended from John of Gaunt's marriage to his first wife, while Henry VII descended from John of Gaunt's third wife "called his concubine by Froissart" (Levine 106). Levine notes that if it had not been for this rule against alien inheritance, John II should have been the king of England. Thus, Portugal was also present at the heart of one of England's hottest political debates, the succession to the crown, no matter how small this presence might have been. The fall of Portugal also contributed indirectly to the power of Philip who, in addition to his expansionist and military attitude towards England had a claim to the English throne through his descent as well as his marriage to Queen Mary. Had his Armada been successful, he would have also been in a position to say about England: "I inherited it, I bought it, and I conquered it."

3.2.3. The Irish Expedition

One reason that made the battle of Alcazar especially important for English politics was that, among other things, it put an end to a serious threat to England that was manifested through the papal expedition led by Captain Thomas Stukeley to liberate Ireland from English rule. Pope Pius V had already excommunicated Elizabeth in 1569 and his successor, Pope Gregory XIII, was even more hostile towards the Protestant queen as he engaged in many plots to overthrow her. The papal expedition heading towards Ireland was nothing more than a reduced version of an originally larger plan to invade England, involving Rome, Austria, Spain, Irish rebels and our man Captain Thomas Stukeley.

As early as 1570, while at the Spanish court, Stukeley played a key role in Spanish plots and political manoeuvres to invade Ireland (Holmes "Thomas Stucley"). The planned invasion never materialised due to several reasons like Philip's attempts to improve relations with England

and Stukeley's unreliability (Tazón 103–4). When he went to Rome, Stukeley's calls found receptive ears. After Pope Pius V's bull of excommunication against Elizabeth, the Holy See started an effort for what became known as the "Enterprise for England," a crusade to win England back into Catholicism using any means possible, including military action (Campbell 139). When he became Pope, Gregory XIII adopted the "enterprise" with keenness (Tazón 203). Promoting the invasion of England, the Pope encouraged Philip II to take on the enterprise describing it as "a duty that lay upon [Philip's] conscience" (Meyer 262). The Spanish king was not against the principle, as proven by the years ahead, but he was aware of the difficulties accompanying such an enterprise and adopted a policy of postponing and delaying action (Tazón 203–4).

Deciding to take action on his own, the pope started putting together a plan for action. A memorial was presented to him in February 1576 outlining the details for military action against England. The proposed army was to consist of five thousand men who would land on English soil in one body, with Liverpool as the preferred port for landing. The expedition would also use the Pope's name to incite English Catholics into action. A plan to free Mary Stuart and install her as queen was to be kept secret in order to save her life (Tazón 205–7). Later, a meeting was held in Rome discussing the invasion of England and Captain Thomas Stukeley was among the prime nominees to lead the invasion (Tazón 207).

However, political, financial and logistic difficulties meant that the expedition was still too hazardous to be undertaken. Thus, the plans were modified to an invasion of Ireland instead. Ireland was to become a thorn in England's side and Philip might be interested in paying Elizabeth in kind for the troubles she was causing him in the Netherlands. More importantly, the invasion of Ireland "could be handled with a very small investment" (Tazón 216).

Having acquired blessings and a few titles from the Pope,[12] Stukeley started collecting men for his mission. Not only were his men mercenaries, but a great number of them were Pope-pardoned ex-bandits (Simpson 126). He left Rome with less than a thousand men and stopped at Cadiz then landed in Lisbon where he was supposed to team up with the Irish rebel Fitzmaurice so that "they in concert may do all the mischief they may to that wicked woman" (Tazón 219). However, that never happened because Fitzmaurice had lost most of his mission's men and resources on

---

[12] Stukeley was named "Marquess of Leinster and Baron or Earl of Washford" (Simpson 130).

the way to Lisbon and needed time to build up his mission again. Meanwhile, Stukeley was persuaded by the Portuguese king to join him for his African enterprise, which ended in the battle of Alcazar.

Stukeley's Irish expedition might seem to us petty and harmless to English power in Ireland, but it was not viewed so by Elizabeth's government. The scale of the expedition was not known for sure, and thus fear of its real abilities was increased. The Spanish Ambassador in Paris reported Elizabeth's anxiety at hearing the news of Stukeley's departure and the English army's extreme preparations for war (Tazón 223–4). Thus, the expedition was seen as a real menace against national sovereignty and Sebastian was perhaps viewed positively for diverting Stukeley into Africa, all the more reason for Peele to portray him sympathetically in *Alcazar*.[13]

The last two sections, "Historical Incident" and "Politico-historical background," work closely together. While the first is purely historical the second is topical. In other words, historical events remain in books of history and are unlikely to trigger a writer's interest until something at the present makes them useful. Peele's catalyst for digging up the material on the battle of Alcazar was politically topical, and so his writing of the play was part of this topicality.

To summarize these historical and topical events, in 1578 the Portuguese fought against the Moors and lost. King Sebastian died in the battle and his throne became the subject of a succession crisis that ended up with England's archenemy, Phillip II, annexing Portugal. Together with other factors, the power gained by Philip helped him in his hostilities against England which culminated in the 1588 Armada. On the other side of the story, the Moorish king that one the war became Elizabeth's ally and sent his first diplomatic mission to London in January 1589. Peele, an aspiring playwright was perceptive of the recent events and their dramatic usability and must have checked some recent historical sources to know more about the Moors. Alcazar was a very good topic due to the presence of Spanish and Portuguese motifs alongside Moors. However, Peele's use of sources was not completely innocent.

The way Peele worked with his sources is studied below with the aim of establishing the basics of Peele's approach to his subject matter. Through the playwright's process of inclusion and exclusion, it would be possible to detect what he deemed fitting for his purpose and what he deemed harmful.

---

[13] See section 4.3.3.1.

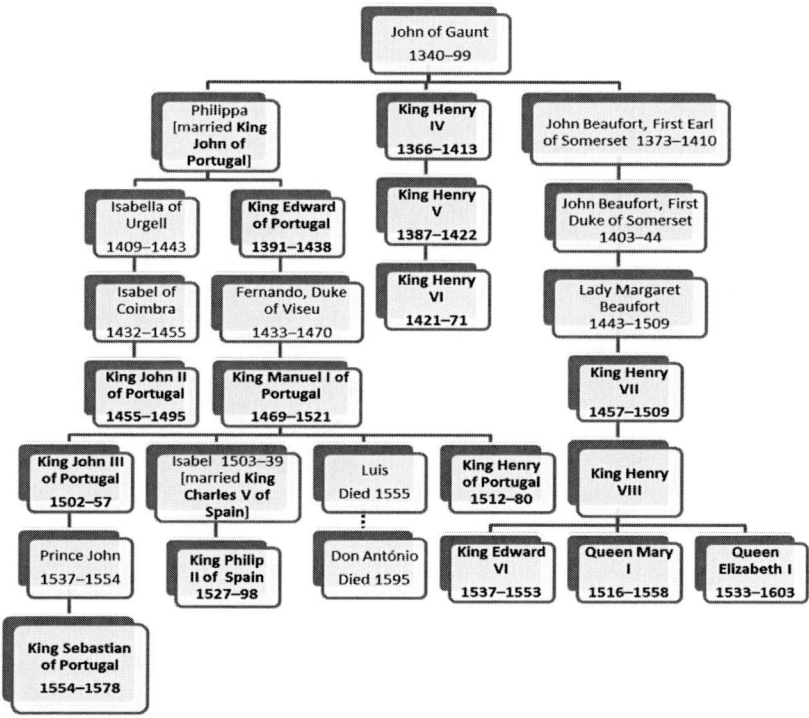

Fig. 1-1. John of Gaunt's descendants

The chart shows the genealogical relationship between the English, Portuguese and Spanish royal families. Monarchs, set in bold, are of England unless otherwise stated.

3.3. Sources

Part of the importance of *The Battle of Alcazar* is the fact that it is a literary work about a historical incident which was well documented in non-fictional forms. This fact opens the door to an interesting area of research which focuses on the dramatic text and its sources and how the playwright used or misused his sources. While it is not the focus of this study to do an in-depth study of Peele's sources, it is still important to know how he dealt with his source material and how he changed it to fit in the overall purpose from writing the play, as this study sees it. In the same way that written sources provided the author with material for the making

of the play, politico-historical background provided, or dictated, the way
these sources were used/misused and how they were transformed into a
literary work.

The importance of the battle and its far-reaching consequences meant
that as soon as the action finished, a great deal of stories, hearsay and
legends were created around it. Thus, in order to satisfy a popular need to
know more, pamphlets, booklets and books were written claiming "true"
relation of the action of the famous battle. However, no official Portuguese
or Spanish accounts of the battle were released and it was not until late in
the nineteenth century when the Spanish archives were opened that
something like that happened (Bradley 131). Thus, the playwright had
quite a few sources from which he could draw material but none of which
was official. Moreover, according to David Bradley, it seems that Peele
used his material intensively:

> Of the 1,590 lines of text, 342 can be traced verbatim in the sources. At
> least as many more are mere commentary on this material or repetition of it
> in other ways. We can thus assign just under half of the play with literal
> certainty to the source-materials. (131)

This source-based half of the play, Bradley maintains, covers the "sum
total of the information presented on any subject in the text" (131). *The
Battle of Alcazar*, from this view is a very source-based play which raises
questions about the reasons behind this high dependence on behalf of the
playwright on raw material. If we accept Matar's proposition of the
occasion that prompted the writing of the play then Peele must have had
little time on his hands to write. In fact, Bradley does mention that Peele
was writing "probably very rapidly, a popular pot-boiler" (130). He also
tries unsuccessfully to pinpoint the reason behind this "rapidness" in
writing the play by relating it to the importance of the event as "recent"
and more important than other, similarly recent, incidents. The eleven-year
gap between the battle (1578) and the play (1588–9) does not provide
evidence for writing a play in haste. Rather, an immediately recent event
that is closely connected with the battle would be a more convincing
reason. Bradley briefly mentions the Portugal Expedition of 18 April 1589
led by Norris and Drake. But this is against the textual evidence we have
of Peele mentioning a character from *The Battle of Alcazar* in his poem
Farewell which he wrote on the occasion of the expedition:

> Bid Mahomets Poo, and mightie Tamburlaine,
> King Charlemaine, Tom Stukeley and the rest
> Adiewe (21–23)

These lines first confirm that Alcazar had already been performed, and second they show how Peele took the opportunity of this national-scale event to publicise his dramatic achievement alongside the well-established *Tamburlaine*. By this time, *Alcazar* must have been in performance and thus Peele must have written it before the expedition. Moreover, the Norris and Drake expedition, or the "English Armada" as it is also known, had little to do with Barbary and more with Spain and Portugal, quite the contrary to *Alcazar*. Therefore, the visit of the Moorish ambassadors to London on 12 January 1589 is still the most convincing suggestion as the prompting factor that made Peele rapidly gather material from different sources to make his play. Taking all these factors into consideration, I think that the play was written between 12 January and 18 April 1589.

According to David Bradley's masterful study of the text and sources of *Alcazar* entitled *From Text to Performance in the Elizabethan Theatre*, at the time Peele wrote his play there were at least four or five main sources (there are others that depended on them) which told the story and he is likely to have used three of these (Bradley 131). These sources are:

1. *Les Voyages et Conquestes des Roys de Portugal* (1578). This is the earliest known account to be published on the battle. Bradley deems this "inaccurate" and full of "invented" details. He believes that, even if he knew this work, Peele hardly ever used it.

2. Luis Nieto's *Histoire Véritable des dernières Guerres en Barbarie* (1579), from which Thomas Freigius made a Latin version *Historia de Bello Africano* (1581) which was then translated by Polemon and used in his *Second Booke of Battailes* (1587). Peele certainly knew both the English and Latin versions (Bradley 132). Critics unanimously agree that the Latin and the English versions were the most important sources for Peele's works (Bekkaoui 16; Bradley 132; Nicholson 107; Rice). In fact, in some places, Peele even copies literally from the English version by Polemon (Rice).

3. *Dell' Unione del Regno di Portogallo alla Corona de Castiglia* (1585) by Hieronimo Conestaggio, or probably by Juan di Silva, the Spanish ambassador in Sebastian's court. Seen as the "most authoritative source" on the battle, the work was obscured by its overtly pro-Spanish mood. So Peele perhaps was not attracted to this source and only used it where Polemon's translation failed him (Bradley 132).

4. *A dolorous discourse of a most terrible and bloudy battle, fought in Barbarie* (1579). Peele seems to have used it to check the time-scheme. It might have been also the source for Peele's description

of Muly Mahamet as a Black Moor because it calls Muly "the blacke Kinge" throughout (Bradley 133).

Of these sources, the two English ones will be discussed in this study i.e. Polemon's *Second Booke of Battailes* and the anonymous *Dolorous Discourse*. In the discussion below, it will be shown that despite the play's heavy dependence on its sources, Peele meticulously picks and chooses certain details and discards others. This process of including and excluding details is the core point of the discussion as it is a clear indication of Peele's nationalistic strategy in *The Battle of Alcazar*.

3.3.1. *A Dolorous Discourse* 1579

The purpose of the pamphlet, as the introduction seems to imply, is the condemnation of pride:

> For surely there is not in the whole world a more pestilent evil, or a thing that breedeth so much mischife as doth the cankred and most accursed vice of ambition … For from whence springeth bloody warres so much, as from this roote of Ambition. (2)

This theme is applied in different places to Sebastian who is described as "a lusty young Gentleman peradventure pricked forwarde by a vaine hope and ambitious desire of gaine and glory, not respecting the perill and depeded [sic] theruppon." Thus, the whole "discourse" on the battle is used to serve a didactic purpose of denouncing pride and overriding ambition.

The pamphlet starts with a very brief description of "the orders and customes of Barbary." This section focuses only on the religions of the people therein: being Muslims "a barbarous people observinge the lawes of Mahomet, geven (for the most part) to idleness & sundry supersticions," as well as Jews, described as controlling "the most parte of the trafique of the Country, being the onelye Marchantes of Sugers, Mallases, and other riche merchandise" (7). Peele ignores the religions of the people of Barbary in his play. As will be shown in a separate section, he never mentions Islam or Muslims (or Mahometans) explicitly nor implicitly but prefers national and regional epithets like Barbarians and Moors. This is an attempt by Peele to demote the extremely different religious identity of the Moors with whom the Queen is making contact. Another example of this is a passing note made by the anonymous author of *Dolorous Discourse*, where he says that in Barbary "they maye have as manye wives as they wyll" (8). Again Peele ignored this detail about Muslim life which, if mentioned, could raise a lot of eyebrows as to the religious identity of these Moors.

When the anonymous author praises Abdelmelec in the following words, Peele only follows suit:

> Mulla Maluca ... was well-beloved of his people, being a man very active, and of great agillitie, skylfull in warres, wherein from his youth he had alwayes ben trayned to: and as men report, ministred Justice with equitie, much favouring Christians, and specialie our Nation. (12)

Everywhere in the play, we find Abdelmelec's gentleness, even towards his enemies. At one point, we are told, Abdelmelec felt sorry for the young Sebastian and did not want to kill him: "I have in pity to the Portugal / Sent secret messengers to counsel him" (III.ii.10–11). This is the ruler whose brother and successor is Elizabeth's ally and whose ambassadors were walking in the streets of London perhaps as the play was being performed. Thus, his image was being brightened up by Peele.

3.3.2. Polemon's *Second Booke of Battailes* 1587

In 1875 Brinsley Nicholson was the first to point out two important sources for *The Battle of Alcazar*. The two were Luis Nieto's *Histoire Véritable des dernières Guerres en Barbarie* (1579), and Thomas Freigius's Latin translation of it as *Historia de Bello Africano* (1581). However, it was only in 1943 that Polemon's work, a compilation of battle stories in English which included a translation of these two sources, was established as a "principal source" for *Alcazar* by Warner G. Rice. As Polemon's work is the major source for the play, reading it in juxtaposition with *Alcazar* gives a unique view into the process of selection practiced by Peele in his work.

One shocking detail that seems to have gone unnoticed by critics, and which serves this study very well, is where Polemon talks of the sons of Muley Mahamet Al-Sheikh (Xeque). He says:

> But although he [Al-Sheikh] had a great number of them, as well lawfull as bastards, yet we will speake in this place onely of them, which were cause of troubles and strives in this kingdome ... the youngest of all was a *bastard*, called Muley Hamet [Seth], who doth at this day possesse the kingdome. (Polemon 62, italics mine)

Peele ignores this piece of information and prefers not to talk about Seth's birth. It goes without saying that in Elizabethan England the word "bastard" held a great deal of negative connotations associated with it, especially when it came to inheritance and royal succession. Instead, Muly Mahamet Seth's ascension to the throne is accompanied by every possible approving gesture. For instance, as soon as Abdelmelec defeats his nephew and is secure on the throne, he declares:

> Hark to the words I speak, and vow I make,
> To plant the true succession of the crown,
> Lo, Lords, in our seat royal to succeed
> Our only brother here we doo install,
> And by the name of Muly Mahamet Seth
> Entitle him true heir unto the crown. (II.i.14–19)

As a brother and as an heir to the throne, Seth is as legitimate as they come.

In the same way Peele ignored information in order to brush up the image of those chose, he modified other details to demonize the villains. One of the clearest examples is related to Muly Mahamet, Peele's black-hearted villain. While Peele's sources "treated Mahamet with reasonable objectivity, commenting on his insignificant stature and indolent nature" (Bradley 134), the playwright made an extremely demonized villain of him. Part of this demonization was to make Muly Mahamet a "traitor to kin and kind" (II.Prol.12). The historical Moulai Muhammad Al-Masloukh was surely responsible for killing his brothers, as Polemon clearly states that it was Muly's father, Abdallas, who killed three of his brothers, Muly's uncles, to secure his son's access to the throne: "Abdallas privelie compassed the murther of his brothers, that he might safelie leave the kingdome to his sonnes," (Polemon 70). However, Peele in his dumb shows tells us both verbally and in mime that Muly Mahamet first killed his young brothers then his uncle.

In another instance related to demonizing Muly Mahamet, and the grooming of Sebastian as well, Peele made it very clear that Muly Mahamet instigated the fatal battle through lobbying and luring a rash Sebastian into serving his own purposes. This part of the story can be seen as a deliberate change of the material in Polemon, who mentions that Sebastian was the one who sent to Muly Mahamet offering help and assistance before the latter succumbed as a result of a series of defeats. Thus, Polemon states that before Muly's first battle against his uncle the following happened:

> At the same moment that Mahamet did set forth with his armie against Abdelmelec, there came unto him a noble man Ambassador from Sebastian the King of Portugall, who promised him in his master's majesties name, aide against the Turkes, and his Unkle. But Mahamet being made more

proude for that he saw so great an armie and so strong under his command, contemned the benefit of the king of Portugall. (Polemon 72)

Once again after Mahamet's defeat in first battle, and as he was preparing for the second battle:

> But it happened that also at this second muster the king of Portugal sent againe an Ambassador unto him, with Letters, & again offered him aide against Abdelmelec his unkle. But he made the very same answere to the second Ambassador that he did to the first. (Polemon 73)

To a student of history it is no new discovery to say that Sebastian, as many Iberian monarchs before him, had a keen interest in controlling his southern trans-Mediterranean neighbours. In fact, in 1573, one year before the real Muly Mahamet even became king, a papal Bull for the Holy War against Barbary was issued. Polemon is thus very clear on this: Sebastian did have an interest in Barbary before Muly's intervention. However, although Peele shows Sebastian's burning desire to win new territory and prove himself, this is mitigated with a general discourse of religiousness and an overall rashness of youth which makes his shortcomings less objectionable. Sebastian's two offers of help to Muly are ignored by Peele in order to absolve him of blame. This modification, manifested in covering Sebastian's prior offers of help and stressing Muly's role in tempting Sebastian, plays an important role on portraying Portugal's present state as a sad plight which needs to be corrected by restoring Don António, Elizabeth's pawn, to the Portuguese throne.

The point I referred to when discussing Peele's use of *A Dolorous Discourse*, where he ignores the religious identity of the Moors, comes to a fuller and clearer manifestation with the use of this source. Peele seems intent on secularizing his Moorish heroes while at the same time "de-secularizing," in a manner of speaking, their enemies. This is a reflection of Elizabeth's relations with the Moors which were a secular act of politics that put aside religious difference for the sake of mutual benefit. Thus, while Polemon shows that both sides were in fact deeply religious in their discourse of war, Peele presents Abdelmelec and Seth as unreligious and Sebastian religious.

In Polemon, we are told how before the battle begins, Abdelmelec uses religious sentiment to encourage Moors to fight:

> he [Abdelmelec] commaunded Tents to be set up in a fielde a league from Marocco, and warres to be openlie proclaimed through his kingdome against the Christians: the which thing highlie pleased the Moores. (Polemon 77)

On the other side of the struggle, when Muly Mahamet wanted to fight Abdelmelec, he deceived his people into believing that his enterprise was against the Christians "because the Moores doe desire no warres more, than those that are kept against Christians" (Polemon 72).

Both incidents are ignored by Peele who, as mentioned above, does not want the Moors to be exoticised on the basis of their religiosity. To say, as his source here does, that war against Christians is something that generates burning enthusiasm among the Moors is to risk causing apprehensions among his audience towards the visitors of the royal court, something which Peele surely does not want to do.

On a different level, Polemon's praise of Abdelmelec was welcomed by Peele who integrated it into his play thoroughly. The same idea of Abdelmelec's reluctance to fight and kill the young Christian prince occurs in Polemon who tells us that Abdelmelec:

> was very sorrowfull therefore, not so much because he feared the king of Portugal his forces, as for that he being well affected towards men of the Christian Religion, did foresee in minde that Africa would be the grave of the king of Portugal. (Polemon 76)

In *The Battle of Alcazar*, there is every indication that anything Abdelmelec stands for is transferred almost automatically to his brother and heir. Thus, this chivalrous nature of Abdelmelec helps in showing that the Queen's ally is the inheritor of a line of gallant monarchs who have a special respect for the Christians of England and therefore deserve praise and mutual reverence.

Thus, it seems reasonable to conclude from Peele's use of his sources that despite the haste in composition, Peele had an alert mind that enabled him to make many subtle but important changes to his sources. Peele modified some pieces of information, deleted others and made unfounded additions. The common theme of these interventions on behalf of Peele was his aim to make his play run smoothly alongside government views on the parties involved in the play. However, there is more to the play's relationship with its political milieu than this, as the following detailed discussion shows.

4. *Alcazar* as nationalistic propaganda

Having studied the play's historical and political background and its source material, what remains is to turn to the text of the play. The five-part discussion views the play as a pro-government work that propagates state ideology on more than one level. The first three parts give an overview of the play's approach to nationalistic propaganda. The first part locates the play within the contemporary ideological tensions surrounding state and religion and the relationship between them. In a similar vein, the second part looks at the way characters in the play define themselves with regards to ideological commitment, in other words, how characters prioritize religion and nation. Part three discusses the issue of exoticism in the play and shows how episodes of exoticism are linked to the overall concerns of the play and are in line with Elizabeth's foreign policy. The aim is to show that the image of Moors in the play is constructed from pre-conceived views of the playwright that abide by government interests and support them. The following two sections demonstrate that Peele's interest in this propaganda purveys the whole of his work. This is absolutely clear from the way he conceived his characters. Part four discusses the characters and how characterization reinforces government propaganda regardless of whether this means breaking stereotypes or confirming them. This interest by Peele also works at the very level of vocabulary. Peele uses vocabulary in conformity with his ideological commitment. Thus, part five takes an in-depth look at the use of keywords in relation to characters in a manner that creates collocations emphasizing the play's message.

4.1. The state/religion dialectic

At the heart of *The Battle of Alcazar* lies a delicate dialectic that needs to be discussed in order to advance the argument of this work. Embedded within the play are the complex tensions between state and religion, Protestantism and Catholicism, and, importantly, crusade and state-led war. The play clearly takes sides on these issues for the sake of promoting a Protestant pro-government view of separating religion from politics. It is of high importance to study how the play does that and in what ways Peele promotes one cause to the disadvantage of the other.

From an English viewpoint, the battle of Alcazar was fought by Christian Europeans, supported by enemies of England, against non-Christian Africans who were friends of the English monarchy. The situation was further complicated by the presence of a band of Englishmen, led by a Catholic renegade, nevertheless a folk hero, who was planning to invade English-controlled territory and win it for the Pope. So how do all these complex factors feature in the play and how does Peele portray them in a way that reflects his nationalist tendencies?

The battle of Alcazar was undoubtedly a landmark in early modern European history. The paramount historical importance of the battle has always been noted by critics and historians alike as an event that had great repercussions on the histories of Morocco, Portugal, Spain and England (see for example Bovill; Dimmock *New Turkes*). However, the battle of Alcazar has another very important facet to it, and that is the fact that it was one of the last crusades, an historical event that helped mark the end of religious wars and the start of state wars and colonial campaigns. In other words, Alcazar is placed at a crucial turning point in history during which the final blows, so to speak, were dealt at a Europe unified by religion and loyalty to the Pope; and at the same time nation-based colonialist enterprises were thriving in what led two centuries later to the realization of the concept of nationalism proper.

That Alcazar was in fact *the* last Crusade is a position held by Norman Housley in his book *The Later Crusades from Lyons to Alcazar*. In personal correspondence, Housley explains that Alcazar's claim to be the last crusade rests on two criteria: "(1) it was the last act in a long process of Iberian expansion southwards and westwards which was regarded by contemporaries as fitting into a crusading framework, in religious, strategic and cultural terms; and (2) it was the last major encounter between Christianity & Islam in the Mediterranean world in which crusading instruments and mechanisms (forgiveness of sins, Church taxes, the military orders, etc) played a significant role" (Email to the author 16 Jul. 2009).[14]

Another important backdrop to understanding the significance of the battle is England's Protestantism. It hardly needs mentioning that England at the time of the battle, and the play, had made major steps towards becoming a Protestant nation. The Henrician reformation was an important move in the direction of realizing England as a separate entity from Rome and, in effect, Catholic Christendom. What is important and relevant to note here is that the way English foreign policy was conducted under Elizabeth indicated that religion was "controlled in the interest of national policy" (Wernham *Elizabethan Foreign Policy* 21). This trend can be traced back to Germany where Lutheran teachings held the belief that, instead of calling for a new crusade to stop the Turkish threat on Germany, the war against the Turks should be fought by the state (Setton 141; Vitkus "Early Modern Orientalism" 212). The move from Pope-endorsed crusades to state-led wars was a fundamental shift in European thought and politics throughout and after the Reformation. It was one of the

---

[14] See also p.144–5 in Housley's *The Later Crusades*.

important chapters of the state-church breakup as it put an end to the crusades and opened the gates for European states to seek national, rather than religious, interests including expansion, commerce and colonialism.

The Portuguese enterprise against the Moors was conceived as a crusade. The Pope endorsed it and supplied it with men and ships from other Catholic European monarchies. In *The Battle of Alcazar*, the idea of a crusade is present strongly. Sebastian's rhetoric is deeply religious. Despite the political imperialistic aims he has, he insists on using the "Christian" label in descriptions of his campaign. He wants to "plant the Christian faith in Affrica" (II.iv.165) through launching "holy Christian war" (II.iv.66). On the other hand, rhetoric of Holy War is absent on the Moroccan side of the story. It might be true that the Ottomans supported their fellow Muslims against Christians but Peele chooses not to show any hint of religious rhetoric on the part of the Ottomans or Moroccans. It is this party that wins the war; and thus the religious concept of war is dealt a major blow.

Another important issue is England's commercial interests in Barbary which were a major source for official as well as public attention to the region. After the Reformation, as Kenneth Setton notes, there was "a significant shift from the medieval world where even businessmen and politicians put God before profits" to a world where pragmatic "worldly" gains were put first (qtd. in Blanks and Frassetto 36). This was the case in English relations with Barbary. Elizabeth and London merchants did not heed papal bulls against dealing with "infidels." On the contrary, they supplied the Moors with arms and artillery (Dimmock *New Turkes* 122). Catholics actually believed that Elizabeth was responsible for Sebastian's defeat in Alcazar (Dimmock *New Turkes* 112 n.63). Seen from this point of view, and taking into consideration the substantial commercial gains Elizabeth I received after the battle, the English were big winners in the battle of Alcazar both commercially and politically.[15]

Reading *The Battle of Alcazar* as a reflection of English popular conceptions of Muslim Moors rests on the unstable assumption that the author merely represents these formations without any interference by contemporary ideology or topical factors. But this is not the case. The representation of Moors in the play comes within the general framework of Peele's career which focused on currying the Queen's favour and championing court policies. The historical incident remained in books for eleven years before topical factors brought it back to life. These factors

---

[15] At least temporarily because the battle led to an increase in Spanish power after it annexed Portugal.

played a role in fashioning the "representation" of Muslims in the play as
well. Due to the playwright's ideological stance, topical influence is
manifested primarily through portraying events, causes, characters and
even countries from the government's viewpoint.

This viewpoint necessitates presenting England's friends in a positive
way and her foes in a negative way, which in turn leads to a whole list of
characters and issues that need to fit into a grid of favourable versus
unfavourable, or good versus bad, categories. This eventually means that
certain Moors should be presented positively, while other negatively; the
war against the "good" Moors deemed unjust and their war just; and the
cause of Elizabeth's protégé, Don António, must be supported. But this
leads to discrepancies that are difficult to settle especially in the case of
Sebastian: on the one hand, he be presented as a victim in order to gain
sympathy for Don António; but, on the other, his war should not be
supported because it was launched against friends of the English
government. Elizabeth's allies, moreover, must be cleared from the
negative connotations of their "Moorishness." To resolve these issues,
Peele adopts a subtle approach that runs in harmony with his nationalistic
tendencies and serves the above purposes. The following discussion tries
to show Peele's method and relate it to the overall argument of Muslim
representation in the play.

Bearing in mind the contemporary tension between state and religion,
and the above-mentioned presence/absence of religious discourse in the
warring parties, we can see that *Alcazar* dramatises the Portuguese crusade
against Muslim lands in a way that polarizes the involved parties into
religionists[16] and non-religionists. In the religionist field, we mainly find
the Portuguese in addition to their supporters who include Spain, Rome
and even Muly Mahamet. Their cause, to start with, is judged from the
beginning of the play as unjust and unlawful. Muly Mahamet's claim to
the throne is mooted in the first dumb-show by the Presenter who also
keeps on reminding us of Muly's villainy and dishonesty. Thus,
Sebastian's support for Muly is lacking any grounds as restoration of right.
What remains to it is the crusading and religious side which becomes the
subject of Peele's criticism. Thus, Peele's disapproving presentation of the
Portuguese side is also aimed at the religionist approach to warfare.[17]

---

[16] The *OED* defines religionist (n) as "One addicted or attached to religion; one
imbued with, or zealous for, religion. Sometimes in bad sense, a religious zealot or
pretender." I will be using this term in this sense, alongside two derivates "non-
religionist" and "co-religionist," throughout this work.
[17] See the section on the Irish Expedition above for a contemporary negative
example of a religious military campaign.

Another element of the religionist approach to war is represented by the papal expedition against Ireland. Sectarian motivations are behind the Pope's effort to attack another Christian country that refused to recognize his supreme authority. Stukeley's mission is roundly condemned in the play and by more than one person. Upon learning the goal of the expedition, Diego Lopes, Governor of Lisbon, gives a disapproving evaluation of Stukeley's venture:

> Under correction, are ye not all Englishmen,
> And longs not Ireland to that kingdom, Lords?
> Then may I speak my conscience in the cause,
> Sans scandal to the Holy See of Rome:
> Unhonourable is this expedition,
> And misbeseeming you to meddle in. (II.ii.20–25)

Diego Lopes is speaking his conscience and is, in effect, criticising the "Holy See of Rome" although he says he does not intend to. Making a Catholic leader judge papal-sponsored attacks on Elizabeth's territory is more effective and frames the Pope as a transgressor and the expedition as treasonous.

Moreover, the religionist side is criticised through Sebastian, the champion of Christian chivalry, who is portrayed very much like a Quixotic hero who is anachronistic in his quest and unrealistic in his handling of real-life issues. This is most evident in his attitude towards his "allies," Muly Mahamet and Philip, both of whom give him nothing more than words and empty promises. For example, Muly Mahamet's messengers convince Sebastian of their honesty by burning their hands in fire which is not very different from hollow words in that it does not mean a lot on the ground. When Muly Mahamet and his son come to Sebastian, no treaties or pacts are signed and the father and son use their usual high-flown discourse to win his support. Philip, on the other hand, deceives Sebastian by his promises and leaves him at a critical moment to face the Moors single-handedly. Sebastian is too naïve to fathom Philip's hypocrisy:

> I know our brother Philip nill [will not] deny
> His furtherance in this holy Christian war. (II.iv.65–66)

This naivety is clearly connected to religious fervour in these two lines. Sebastian takes Philip's pretence of religious zeal at face value and believes his kinsman will put religion above everything else. Philip does not. He only uses religious discourse to achieve political goals. Thus, according to Peele, only naïve leaders believe religious discourse and fail to see the politics behind it.

On another occasion, Sebastian, as a representative of the religionist party, is accused, perhaps indirectly, of practising oppression against his inferiors. Stukeley's anchorage in Lisbon is exploited by Sebastian to use the papal expedition in his Barbary adventure. Stukeley and his followers are reluctant and only accept under pressure and indirect threats which makes them more like mercenaries than faithful soldiers. Peele made this part of the story up in clear contradiction to his main source, Polemon, who states that Stukeley "being arrived in Lisbon, offered his service to the king and promised to follow him in the journey" (Polemon 76). This is to be contrasted with the Ottoman help sent to Abdelmelec. The Turkish Janissary leader, Calsepius Bashaw, declares early in the play that they come not "As mercenary men to serve for pay, / But as sure friends" (I.i.22–23).

The religious approach to war in *The Battle of Alcazar* is thus undermined through various means. First, it is presented as supporting an unjust war. Second, its representatives are demeaned in various ways: Sebastian as a wistful and quixotic Christian knight who practises the occasional tyranny; Philip as a deceiver and tempter whose schemes help the demise of his Christian "brother;" and the Pope as the religious leader who abuses his position to settle sectarian and personal differences. Third, the religious discourse is marred by worldly preoccupations and its users display ulterior motives. This is especially true of Sebastian who is not covert about his aims in propagating "the fame of Portugal" (III.i.7), and Stukeley who becomes so convinced in the new enterprise he joins that he declares: "I cannot sell my blood / Dearer than in the company of kings" (IV.ii.69). Putting religion first leads to a disastrous end and destabilizes states. The induction to Act V portrays the fall of crowns from a tree placed on the stage associated with a spectacular display of "Lightning and thunder," a "blazing star" and "fireworks" which is further highlighted by the Presenter's sigh: "Ay me, that kingdoms may not stable stand" (V.i.22). The stability of kingdoms is more important than anything else, including religious purposes, Peele seems to imply.

Champions of religious wars are denounced as their approach is seen as a threat to national security. On the other hand, preserving national security by a nationalist war is praised and promoted. The state/religion dialectic is thus a present motif throughout the play in which the nationalism is promoted over religious sentiment that contradicts national interests. On another level, characters are divided into those who put religion first, and those who put nation first. The latter party wins Peele's support every time as the following section shows.

4.2. Self-definition

George Peele's presentation of the idea of war is important in the extent to which it helps in figuring out how characters and states define themselves through their motives for launching war: religious motives or state interests. Peele's underlying argument in the play is that nation comes first and if religion is to play a role in war, it is only to support national interests. The play shows how those who define themselves in terms that contradict those rules lose all. The war is heralded by two different means on the two sides. Members of the religionist side of the war are those who prioritize the cause of religion over the cause of the nation, while the nationalists are the opposite. The starting point for the discussion below is the notion that in *Alcazar* the Portuguese and the Spanish have remarkably religious rhetoric while the Moors' discourse is patriotic; hence the two parties are discussed as religionists and nationalists below.

4.2.1. Religionists

Peele adopts several means to accentuate the religious inclinations of the European side in the war. Apart from the play's reflection of the historical fact that the battle was a papal crusade, their rhetoric in the play is marked with a religious tone in addition to their use of certain keywords and expressions related to religion and crusade. Their aims are shown as expansionist rather than defensive, and they are on the unjust side of the war. One scene where these ideas are highlighted is the meeting between Muly Mahamet and Sebastian which gives an enlightening insight into the religionist approach to war.

This meeting is depicted in III.iv. Upon receiving his Moorish allies, Sebastian shows them a good deal of hospitality and Muly returns similar sentiments. Impressive in their dialogue is the overt stress on religion by both parties. Given that one of the major political inhibitions Muly Mahamet had when resorting to Portuguese support was that he was seeking Christian help against his co-religionists, it would seem appropriate that Sebastian should avoid mentioning his religious inclinations at least in front of Muly Mahamet. But Sebastian clearly tells Muly that the Portuguese are fighting for "our Christ" in order to "enlarge the bounds of Christendom" (14–15). Muly Mahamet remarkably makes no comment on these expressions and proceeds to his usual fustian rhetoric pledging allegiance to Sebastian. In his words we find that the discourse of religion is still present although not clearly. Muly prays that Pluto "Ding," or beat, his soul down to hell unless "I perform *religiously* to thee / That I have *holily* erst underta'en" (28–29, italics mine). Muly Mahamet's Son also praises Sebastian and asks for help "agreeing with your wholesome Christian laws" (47).[18] Thus, in showing the religious nature of this side of the battle, Peele deploys two different levels of expression. While Sebastian can show his religious motives clearly and unashamedly, Peele finds an indirect way for Muly's discourse to be presented as religion–based.

On another level, just as sympathy is evoked for Sebastian as a result of his presentation as a rash and deceived young man, he is given a religiously-appealing sobriquet. In the same way Philip monopolizes the title "the Catholic king," so does Sebastian with the title "the Christian king" which is used exclusively in reference to him three times in the play.[19] These three times are never associated with negative epithets and no one uses a formula like "he that is called the Christian king" to describe Sebastian. Thus, he is clearly portrayed as a truly religious person not a hypocrite like Philip.

4.2.2. Nationalists

On the other hand, the Moroccan side in the battle is presented as the rightful defendants of the throne of their king and the sovereignty of their country. Having established in the first prologue Abdelmelec's right to the throne, Peele moves on to support the Moroccan side through various ways, most of which have been discussed above. One subtle and important point about the Moroccan side, however, is that they are presented as a nation not a religious entity, sect or faction. This mainly stems from the fact that the Moroccans are not given religious epithets throughout the play and are mainly referred to as Barbarians, a word stripped from negative connotations in *Alcazar* through the distinction in use and context between it and the word *barbarous* which carries all the negative

---

[18] There is a missing line directly before this expression. However, the meaning referred to can be deduced to be in accordance with the previous lines in the son's speech.

[19] Historically speaking, the King of France exclusively held the title "Roi Très-chrétien" or "most Christian King." The title was given to the French King by the Pope as early as Charlemagne (742–814) and became hereditary with the reign of Charles VII (1403–1461) (Potter 18).

connotations. Thus, the Moroccan side is defined through national affiliation and "barbarian" becomes equivalent to English or Portuguese as a mere ethnographic name not a pejorative adjective. Another factor is that the Moroccans do not use religious rhetoric to propagate the call for war. Any religious references in their speeches are no more than opaque prayers supplicating various classical deities (or simply "gods") of the kind: "Called for is Abdelmelec by the gods / To sit upon the throne of Barbary" (I.i.128–129). This view is supported by the fact, noted above in "3.3. Sources", that Peele ignored any religious markers related to Abdelmelec and Seth.

Through this division of different parties in his play, Peele cleverly gives stress to royalist-serving ideas of how peoples and countries should define themselves. Catholic monarchs like Philip use religious façade in order to achieve political goals but they fail because of their dishonesty. On the other hand, honest monarchs, like Abdelmelec and Elizabeth, defend their country by promoting national feelings amongst their subjects while avoiding the false use of religion except for morale lifting purposes. The Moors are thus made more acceptable through defining themselves as a nation rather than a religious entity. Peele makes more effort at naturalizing the Moors as the following section shows.

4.3. Naturalizing and exoticizing

As Queen Elizabeth's allies were exotic Moors with whom the English would not find much common ground, Peele's Moors had to be brought closer to the English. To achieve this goal, Peele employs means relating to theme, characterization and action all of which make Elizabeth's friends more familiar, or more "like us," so to speak.

To start with, the whole story behind Muly Mahamet's dethronement and banishment would not have been known to an average Englishman at the time and it was the job of the playwright to introduce it to his audience. The question of royal succession is therefore highlighted in the introduction to the play in a way that befits the English mind. This is because the method of succession in Morocco was different to that in England.[20] Primogeniture was not the main method of succession in Morocco at the time; rather, the throne passed to the eldest male member of the ruling family even if the deceased king had male children (Bovill

---

[20] Despite complications in Henry VIII's will, primogeniture was still the basis for English succession in the sense that sons of the king had the right to inherit before his siblings (see Tennenhouse 23 for more).

22).[21] However, what often happened was that once this eldest person took power, he wanted his sons to succeed him and so he assassinated any male rivals i.e. his own brothers, uncles and nephews. Although supposed to clarify this code of inheritance, Peele's induction to the play through the Presenter makes a mess of it (Yoklavich 240) by confusing foreign names and presenting incoherent information. The Presenter says that Sebastian wanted to help:

> The Negro Muly Hamet that withholds
> The Kingdom from his uncle Abdelmelec,
> (Whom proud Abdallas wronged),
> And in his throne installs his cruel son,
> That now usurps upon this prince,
> This brave Barbarian Lord Muly Molocco.
> The passage to the crown by murder made,
> Abdallas dies, and deigns this tyrant king,
> Of whom we treat, sprung from the Arabian Moor. (I.Prol.7–15)

If we take into consideration that within four lines the same character is referred to using two names (Abdelmelec and Muly Molocco), it becomes clearer to us how hard it was for an audience to get through this labyrinth of foreign names that sounded confusingly similar (Abdelmelec and Abdallas, Muly Hamet and Muly Molocco) and understand who was a rightful heir and who was not. Thus, Peele gives his audience a shortcut to what they need to know in this dumb show by telling them clearly who was good and who was not. The clarification of this system of succession comes later in I.i. Had Peele made the story clearer in the Prologue, the audience would have struggled to comprehend why a son is wrong in succeeding his father. Thus, this vagueness in the important first induction might be deliberate and can be seen as an example of Peele trying to assimilate Moorish habits for an English viewer, or even substitute English customs for Moorish ones as he does later in Act V when he makes Seth sit on the throne in an English fashion with a crown and a diadem (Bradley 170).

Peele tries to familiarize the two "good" Moors further. On one occasion related to promoting Muly Mahamet Seth, Peele makes the foreign hero speak the mind of an English patriot. In his first appearance, Seth is pushing Abdelmelec to go on and "chastise" Muly Mahamet after the latter's defeat in the battle. Seth's words can be seen as an invitation to

---

[21] This principle of inheritance is known as "agnatic seniority."

Queen Elizabeth after the armada to capitalize on Spain's defeat and "chastise" Philip:

> And why is Abdelmelec then so slow
> To chastise him with fury of the sword,
> Whose pride doth swell to sway beyond his reach?
> Follow this pride then with fury of revenge. (I.i.105–108)

This reading of mine has its background in the preparation for the Portugal Expedition of 1589 which happened very closely after the play was written. In other words, the preparation was going on at the same time that Peele wrote *Alcazar*. R. B. Wernham notes that "[Queen Elizabeth's] timidity and hesitations so hindered its fitting out that its departure had to be fatally postponed from 1 February until 18 April 1589" (Wernham "Queen Elizabeth" 2) i.e. the same time the play was written. Katherine Eggert notes similar sentiments in some factions of the Elizabethan government who criticised Elizabeth's and Burghley's cautious approach to military action (46–7). This expedition was seen as an excellent opportunity to deal a fatal blow to England's archenemy due to his relative weakness in the aftermath of the Armada and it would be understandable for a patriotic author like Peele to put such a cry into the mouth of one of his characters. The passage is also indicative of Peele's "hawkish" military attitude towards England's enemies. In a manner of speaking, Peele was so eager to run along government policies that at some points he outran them. In this particular incident, Peele looks *plus royaliste que le roi*.

Bearing in mind the Armada, it is proper here to note the suggestive nature of the word "swell" in this context as it somehow brings to mind the word "sea" with which it collocates (in *Alcazar* also in III.Prol.4: "swelling seas"). Philip's pride has swollen, like the sea, beyond his reach and the Queen must not postpone his punishment. It is also of some significance to see that Seth is the one who utters these words taking into consideration that it was with him that the Queen was plotting an attack against Philip (Matar *Britain and Barbary* 18).

On the other side of the equation, Peele makes a big effort to exoticize and outcast Muly Mahamet as well as his few followers. Two incidents have generally been identified by critics as primary examples of this effort by Peele. Importantly, both are restricted to Muly Mahamet and his followers and both are the work of Peele's imagination and cannot to be found in his sources (Bradley 131).

In II.iii when Calipolis, Muly's wife, says that she is fainting of hunger, Muly exits briefly and comes back "with [raw] flesh upon his sword" (69 SD) which he says that he: "forcèd from a lioness" (71). This scene has been often referred to as a manifestation of Moorish exoticism (see for example Eldred Jones 45; Bradley 152–53) where a Moor is depicted as capable of fighting and forcing food from a wild beast then feed the raw meat to his wife. Peele is borrowing this metaphor from Marlowe's *Tamburlaine*. Tamburlaine addresses his horses thus:

> To make you fierce, and fit my appetite,
> You shall be fed with flesh as raw as blood,
> And drink in pails the strongest muscadel:" (*2Tamb* IV.iii. 12–19)

Peele could have been influenced by this episode and used it to depict Mahamet as a savage Moor. However, Peele's use of bombastic language and his unfortunate use of pun, "Meat of a princess for a princess meet" (III.ii.72), seem to have had such a remarkable effect on Elizabethan audiences and dramatists that it was mocked in Ben Jonson's *The Poetaster* and Shakespeare's *2 Henry IV* among others (Edelman *Stukeley Plays* 27).

In Act II, scene iv, we see Sebastian welcoming the ambassadors of Muly Mahamet with a good deal of respect. Asked for a proof of their master's good intentions, they put their hands into a flame proclaiming:

> We offer here our hands into this flame,
> And as this flame doth fasten on this flesh,
> So from our souls we wish it may consume
> The heart of our great Lord and sovereign
> Muly Mahamet king of Barbary,
> If his intent agree not with his words. (II.iv.32, 37)

Sebastian accepts this proof of honour and promises Muly "aid and succour" (43). This is the second of the two exoticizing episodes added by Peele to his narrative. Here, we see a weird form of pledge being practised by the Moors in order to convince Sebastian of their truthfulness. In analysing these two incidents, one could go along the lines of the exotic and the spectacle that Peele might have wanted his audience to enjoy, and this element cannot be denied. This is especially important when we notice that the use of flames is reminiscent of Dido's suicide in *The Aeneid* or perhaps in Marlowe's *Dido* whose probable date of composition is 1587–93 (Logan and Smith 24-6) and thus could be prior to that of *Alcazar*. Dido's strange and exotic way of committing suicide by throwing herself into the flames is unique among classical figures (Edgeworth 129) and thus could have been associated with north African characters. In fact, Peele does use Dido's death in the induction to Act V where he likens

Fame ending the suffering of the combatants in the battle to Iris finishing "fainting Dido's dying life" (V.Prol.10).

However, it is of paramount importance that both incidents of exoticism are attributed by Peele to Muly Mahamet and his party and not to Elizabeth's friends, Abdelmelec and Seth. The latter party is given "domesticating" attributes that make them look more familiar. The exoticism of the Moor was not something that Peele could discard altogether. In fact, he did use it in one of his pageants as discussed above. Therefore, what he does in *Alcazar* is that he keeps this aspect of strangeness but he does not apply it to the "good" Moors and restricts it to the "bad" Moors i.e. England's friends and foes respectively. The result is a feeling of identification with the "good" Moors, which means further justification for the government's dealing with them. For Peele, being strange and other was a negative characteristic that he did not want his audience to associate with government allies. Therefore, he was doing his best to portray Abdelmelec and Muly Seth as familiar as possible while restricting incidents of otherness to the enemies of these two Moors, Muly Mahamet and his followers. In addition to these efforts by the playwright, he also portrays his characters along lines that arouse either sympathy or loathing depending on the government's point of view as the following section reveals.

4.4. Characters

As we saw above, Peele's nationalist propaganda made it necessary to divide his characters into good and bad. A study of the way in which the play presents certain characters leads us to some interesting results regarding Peele's message in his work. The playwright utilises many subtle strategies to promote and demote certain parties and characters in the play. The most obvious examples are Abdelmelec and Muly Mahamet but a closer look shows that the same applies to almost all other characters and parties in the play: friends and foes.

Because England's friends in the play were Moors, one of Peele's main tasks was to make them more familiar to the English audience. The basic level of familiarization would simply be to present them in the roles of heroes rather than villains. Peele employs subtler methods to make his audience more comfortable and welcoming towards the Moors. These methods fall under two categories: the use of epithets and naturalization of foreignness. These are discussed in detail below.

4.4.1. Heroes

Certain characters receive Peele's endorsement because of their position within the outlook of English foreign policy. These characters are mainly Abdelmelec and Muly Mahamet Seth who were Elizabeth's allies; a minor recipient of praise is the Ottoman Sultan Amurath who was also a friend of the English Government.

Abdelmelec is portrayed as the old and wise monarch who reclaims his rightful throne and presides graciously over it. The play actually opens four of its five acts with Abdelmelec on his throne, which helps establish his image as the rightful king of the realm. Act I, scene i, starts with a victorious Abdelmelec celebrating with his followers and supporters after defeating Muly Mahamet in a battle. This is the first time we see Abdelmelec and an effort is made to present him as a good leader whose graciousness in victory is manifested by his acknowledgment of the efforts of all those who helped him. Abdelmelec pays tribute to Zareo, the Moors, Great Amurath and Calsepius Bashaw. The tribute is especially important in the case of praising "Great Amurath, great Emperor of the world" (I.i.9) as a partner in this victory. His troops are also praised in that they are presented as honourable fighters who did not come as mercenaries. This scene also presents Muly Mahamet Seth, or Ahmad Al-Mansur, who strikes us as an energetic character urging for the fight to continue.

Abdelmelec's appearance in II.ii is almost identical to his first one. We see him and his train celebrating victory over Muly Mahamet in the second battle between them. Abdelmelec also declares Seth his true heir. Apart from showing more of Abdelmelec's and Seth's magnanimity, one thing strikes us about this scene and that is the fact that the dialogue digresses almost completely to become a panegyric of Amurath for his help in this battle. This link between the two monarchs helps establish them as trustworthy partners in international affairs and thus becomes a way of justifying England's relationship with them.

One major concern held by Londoners about the Moors would have been the fact that the Moorish kings actually fought and caused the death of a Christian prince, Sebastian. This concern is dealt with carefully and is alleviated through stressing Abdelmelec and Seth's integrity. This is especially true of the episode in III.ii when an important message is delivered about Elizabeth's friends in a rather short scene. In an attempt to support the image of Abdelmelec as an ethical ruler with sympathy towards Christians, Peele shows us Abdelmelec telling his captains how he has "in pity to the Portugal / Sent secret messengers to counsel him" (10–11). This seems to be Peele's own insertion into the story although there are similar hints in the sources (Bradley 197). Abdelmelec ends the scene with a disclaimer from guilt as he says these words:

> Sebastian see in time unto thy self,
> If thou and thine misled do thrive amiss,
> Guiltless is Abdilmelec of thy blood. (28–30)

This becomes Abdelmelec's characteristic attitude which he expresses again before the battle when he sighs "Alas good King, thy foresight hath been small" (IV.i.14) (see Braunmuller 81). The implication, of course, is that, Elizabeth's allies do not like to kill Christians.

The effect of Abdelmelec's noble-natured attitude towards his enemies is shown, perhaps indirectly, in III.iii. In this scene, which mainly reveals Philip's deception, both Abdelmelec and Amurath are referred to by the Portuguese captains discussing Philip's actions. Peele makes the Portuguese captains show respect to Abdelmelec even though he is their enemy, "When Abdelmelec got the glorious day, / And stalled himself in his imperial throne" (7–8). His victory is thus a glorious day and his throne imperial. This view of Abdelmelec is contrasted with that of Amurath who is described as "angry" and is blamed instead of Abdelmelec for chasing Muly Mahamet "from his land" (11). It is understandable to see the captains describing their enemies in negative terms but Peele makes an additional effort for sparing Abdelmelec any disparaging remarks which might smear his image even by his enemies. Even describing Amurath as "angry" falls short of the ability shown by the playwright to defame other characters like Muly Mahamet and Philip. Moreover, the concept of anger itself was not even a smear in itself if it was "righteous" and related to defending honour.

The mime scenes introducing acts III and IV are of some interest here as well. In both cases we are presented with shocking scenes of ghosts, shouting Furies, death and dismemberment. In the induction to Act III, the Furies "first fetch in SEBASTIAN and carry him out again, which done they fetch in STUKELEY and carry him out, then bring in the Moor and carry him out" (III. Ind.11 SD). A "bloody banquet" is served in the induction to Act IV and the attendants are "SEBASTIAN, MULY MAHAMET, the DUKE OF AVERO, and STUKELEY" who are then joined by "Death and three Furies, one with blood, one with dead men's heads in dishes, another with dead men's bones" (IV.Ind.8SD). Although four major characters die in the battle, the three kings and Stukeley, only Sebastian, Stukeley and Muly Mahamet are brought in and are associated with Devils. Abdelmelec is thus excluded from this horrible scene of death, vengeance and devilish torture. Peele chooses to dissociate

Abdelmelec's afterlife from the hellish imagery of damnation that accompanies the other dead people, and thus he avoids presenting a negative image of Abdelmelec which might harm the Moors' general positive picture he is trying to present.

Abdelmelec is also portrayed as the heroic leader who is capable of engaging in warfare when the need arises. In IV.i. Abdelmelec is shown mustering his forces and discussing the preparations with the leaders. As noted above, Abdelmelec does this with a note of pity towards the young Portuguese monarch whose "unconstant chance" (23) led him to the city of Alcazar. Introducing Sebastian's army plan to Abdelmelec, Celybin describes him as "The brave and valiant King of Portugal" (24), which indicates that not only did Abdelmelec feel sorry and express respect for the Christian prince, but so did his men. Even in war, these Moors are honourable and respectful of worthy enemies. So their friends and allies, like the English, should not fear them. In addition, the Moors are capable of winning wars against Iberians, so an alliance with them is advisable in order to neutralize Philip's aggression and win Don António a throne.

Abdelmelec's (and Seth's) heroism is given the final touches in Act V. The whole act revolves around the battle which begins with an initial setback to the Moorish army due to the bravery of "The valiant Duke, the devil of Avero" (V.i.12). Sorrowful for hearing this piece of news, the chivalric Abdelmelec dies with these last words: "Farewell, vain world, for I have played my part" (30). However, Abdelmelec's "part" is carried over by Muly Mahamet Seth who steps in immediately as Abdelmelec dies and takes charge of the events of the battle to turn it round to his favour. The battle's outcome has been known since the beginning of the play but this fast turnaround of events from defeat to victory is designed to portray Seth as a clever and courageous leader who knew how to turn defeat into victory and hide news of the death of his brother in order to avoid defeat caused by low morale.

The last few minutes of the play are dedicated to portraying the magnanimity of Muly Mahamet Seth. With all the major characters now dead, Seth takes centre stage and has the chance to shine. First he pays tribute to the dead body of Abdelmelec conveying news of victory to his "soul's joy" (186) then he orders his body "embalmèd as is meet" (194). Upon receiving the body of Sebastian, he expresses grief over the death of the "mighty King of Portugal" (223) and as a reward to the Portuguese soldiers who found him, he sets them free. The opposite happens with Muly Mahamet's body which is met with scorn and disrespect. Apart from all the negative epithets used throughout the play to attack Muly

Mahamet,[22] more derogatory terms are used in the last few lines of the play. The soldier who found him describes him as the "ambitious enemy, / That squandered all this blood in Africa" (229–230). Seth orders that the "beastly, unarmed, slavish, full of shame" body of this "damnèd wretch" be flayed and "stuffed with straw" (236, 246, 252). Finally, Seth turns back to pay even more tribute to Sebastian's body and orders the soldiers to:

> tread a solemn march,
> Trailing their pikes and ensigns on the ground,
> So to perform the prince's funerals. (258–260)

These are the final lines of the play and the action very likely ends with the body of Sebastian being carried off the stage in a solemn funeral similar to the end of *Hamlet*. This would be the last impression the audience would take with them as the action ends: that of Sebastian's tragic death and Seth's magnanimous victory. The way all these corpses are treated is of paramount importance as a moral judgment as it were. In a study of the similar scene in *Hamlet*, Mariko Ichikawa notes the importance of the way Hamlet's body is carried away by four soldiers in a respectful manner while the corpses of Claudius and the others are left "sprawled on the stage" (Ichikawa 212). The way dead bodies are dealt with was a clear sign of how they were meant to be perceived.

The final moments in the play thus summarize how major characters are to be remembered: Abdelmelec and Sebastian respected as noble dead kings; Muly Mahamet despised as a traitor and a coward; and Muly Mahamet Seth remembered as the chivalrous king who restored justice and stopped an aggressive attack on his nation. And Stukeley ignored, strangely enough.

4.4.2. Villains

Conformity with government propaganda necessitated the vilification of at least two characters. One is a character presented actually on the stage, Muly Mahamet, who is the enemy of Elizabeth's friends, and the other is England's main enemy at the time, Philip II. Although not a character in the play, Philip's villainy is essential to the action and it is with him that I start.

---

[22] See section 4.5 for more.

4.4.2.1. Philip II of Spain

The general anti-Spanish mood in the play is well-noted by most critics dealing with the play and it gains special importance when combined with the fact that the sources Peele used lacked this anti-Spanish spirit (Dimmock *New Turkes* 112-3). In post-Armada England, it was difficult for a writer like Peele to ignore the stance of his queen towards Philip II.

In real life, Muly Mahamet did not represent such a threat to England. The arch-enemy was rather Philip II of Spain. Phillip was the king of Spain when the battle of Alcazar took place. His relationship with Elizabeth's England could hardly be any worse. He had been king consort of England when his wife Mary I of England was queen. However, after his wife's death and when the Protestant Elizabeth I assumed the throne, Philip despaired of adding England to his Catholic empire. Thus, he resorted to hostility and military action later on. Although many attempts at invading the island did take place, the most prominent military offensive launched by Philip II was the infamous Armada of 1588. The serious repercussions of this naval enterprise were felt on many levels. In one area, English nationhood, the result was a heightened feeling of national unity and patriotic enthusiasm (Ardolino *Apocalypse & Armada* 83). Another natural result was a public feeling of unease, to say the least, towards the Spanish and their king. It can be said, therefore, that Philip II had an extremely negative image as an implacable foe and serious menace to both the sovereign and the people of England. The triumph over the Spanish Armada was a major reason that led Peele to write his play and thus *Alcazar* cannot be separated from the anti-Spanish spirit of 1588–9.

Christopher Highley documents an important current of thought in Elizabeth government towards Philip and other Catholic enemies. According to Highley, William Cecil, the Queen's chief minister, gave orders to playing companies to deride Philip of Spain and make him "odious unto the people, [by permitting] certaine players… to scof and jest at him, upon their common stages. And the lyke was used in contempt of his religion" (Highley 57). This is very similar to the case in *Alcazar*, as the discussion below shows.

In *The Battle of Alcazar*, Philip II never appears on stage. This does not mean that he is in any way less of a menace than he was in real life. An unseen force can sometimes be more threatening and suggestive of fear than a clear force. Looming behind the scenes, Philip's remarkable effect on the action manifests itself in convincing Sebastian of going on in his adventure. In Act III scene i, not only does he promise an ambitious Sebastian support of "men, munition, and supply of war" (14), but he also offers him marriage with his daughter Isabel. Through adding this piece of information which is non-existent in his sources, Peele is trying to indicate what is more than straightforward political support. From his point of view, which was likely to be held by other Elizabethans, Philip was trying to push young Sebastian into this dangerous war for reasons that become clear only some time after the battle (Ardolino *Apocalypse & Armada* 89). Definitely by the time the play was written and performed the results were well-known. After Sebastian's fall, the Portuguese throne was easily claimed by Philip, thus further endangering English sovereignty. One critic sees in Philip II "the true dark villain of this play, who never appears... who stands silently outside the play but whose influence is felt everywhere in it" (Hyland 99). Peter Hyland's approach might be taking the point too far by implying that Philip II was the real villain of the play, but it cannot be denied that the dark image of the real-life Philip was cleverly reflected in *The Battle of Alcazar* despite the lack of a character by the name of Philip.

Philip's absence from the play needs some clarification towards which two points are particularly helpful. First, in a post-Armada context, Philip was strongly present in English apprehensions and an onstage presentation was perhaps not possible. For example, when John Lyly wanted to attack Philip he did it indirectly through allegory in his play *Midas*. As a courtier poet, Lyly was better acquainted with the government's view on issues of foreign policy, and it seems that he was reluctant to present Philip himself on stage and preferred to use an indirect way. In this play, based on classical mythology, Lyly is thought to have presented Philip of Spain symbolically through King Midas, whose golden touch was comparable to Philip's huge resources of American gold and his plans on the island of Lesbos were linked to Philip's plans against England (Bond 109–10; Pincombe *Eros* 113). Interestingly, the play shares with *Alcazar* a possible date of composition of "between May and September 1589" (Bond 110).

Another significant aspect of the offstage position Peele reserved for Philip might be related to the Elizabethan concept of tragedy. A general look at famous theatrical representations of monarchs, villains as well as heroes, shows that the vast majority of them were dead princes. Obvious examples are Shakespeare's histories and Marlowe's *Tamburlaine*. In a famous work of Elizabethan literary criticism, *The Art of English Poesy* (1589), George Puttenham mentions that poets tend generally to avoid criticising princes while they are in power (Whigham and Rebhorn 123–4). Thus, Philip can be called as an offstage villain, a description that gives him a secondary position, in theatrical terms, to that of the main villain who is no doubt Muly Mahamet.

In the induction to Act III, after scenes of Furies, Ghosts and Devils, the Presenter does not forget to remind the audience of King Philip's treachery for "There was nor aid of arms nor marriage" to Sebastian (III.Prol.21). Strangely enough this happens right before III.i where Sebastian welcomes the Spanish ambassadors bringing messages about Philip's promise of logistic support and offer of marriage to one of his daughters. At this stage, pathos is intensified through an acute sense of dramatic irony caused by the succession of these two glimpses into the Spanish help to Portugal.

Later in the same scene, III.i a cynical and down-to-earth Stukeley is the one who reveals to the audience, after Sebastian exits, what he thinks of Philip's promises. To him, the Spanish king's "faith will not be firm" (53). Asked by the Duke of Avero what he makes then of "Those numbers that do multiply in Spain," Stukeley says correctly that they are headed to Flanders and that "Spain means to spend no powder on the Moors" (56, 62). The scene ends with a speech that can be taken to be a commentary on contemporary politics, similar to the one delivered by Seth in I.i (see section 4.3 below). These words sound like they are spoken by an English patriot at the time of the play:

> Philip if these forgeries be in thee,
> Assure thee king 'twill light on thee at last,
> And when proud Spain hopes soundly to prevail,
> The time may come that thou and thine shall fail. (63–68)

Avero's speech closes the scene and it is written in a proclamatory tone that perhaps requires the actor to speak it facing the audience rather than in dialogue with Stukeley. If true, in addition to the sense of dramatic irony, this will make it easier for the audience to identify with, especially with the post-Armada sentiment (Edelman *Stukeley Plays* 100 n.67,8). As the speech promises Philip retribution for his actions, his defeat one year before the play's date would seem an inevitable divine visitation that was fulfilled through an English medium. Philip's treachery is confirmed later (III.ii) by Abdelmelec who explains how he has made a pact with Philip to make sure Sebastian does not get help from Spain in return for "seven holds"[strongholds] (18).

The final touch on Philip's treacherous plan is portrayed in III.iii when we see the Portuguese captains discussing the delay of King Sebastian's arrival in Tangier. The Portuguese fleet arrived in Cadiz and remained there for fifteen days waiting for Philip's promised support only to be turned down as the Spanish King "pretends a sudden fear and care, to keep / His own from Amurath's fierce invasion" (III.iii.37–38).

Philip's actions in the play are presented as threefold deception. First he supports Sebastian's war which is surely presented in the play as an unjust enterprise, and while Sebastian can be justified on grounds of youthful zeal and lack of political acumen, Philip can hardly be seen in this light. Second, he cheats his way out of supporting Sebastian with men and ships by allying with Abdelmelec, thus pushing Sebastian towards confrontation then leaving him to face it almost alone. And finally, as people in the time of the play knew, he was a winner from all that happened by annexing a weak Portugal to his possessions two years after the death of Sebastian.

Queen Elizabeth's archenemy is thus condemned as a Machiavellian ruler who will not stop at anything, including pushing his own kin, Sebastian being his cousin, to death in order to expand his realm. Thus, supporting Don António's claim to the Portuguese throne gains a moral high ground as it will depose an evil and undeserving usurper and restore a rightful king.

4.4.2.2. Muly Mahamet

The arch-villain of the play is, no doubt, Muly Mahamet. His crimes run throughout the play and the flashback-like dumb shows tell us about more of his "heinous stratagems" (I.Prol.22). He is presented as a traitor to his people and country who caused the deaths of thousands of people starting from his own young brothers and uncles to the numberless soldiers killed on the plains of Alcazar. Peele makes little effort to change any of the historical facts from his sources and adds to them some theatrical elements that intensify them. This is mainly the result of the playwright's need to polish the image of the "good" Moors, the Queen's friends. Abdelmelec and Seth, like every hero, need a villain against whom they can shine. This is not to say, however, as Chew and Hyland argue, that Muly is a villain that just happens to be a Moor (Chew 526; Hyland 95). Nor does it serve the purpose of understanding the relationship of the play to its political background to do as Eldred Jones and Emily Bartels do when they talk about Muly Mahamet as being black in direct contrast with his uncle Abdelmelec. Jones also distinguished between black Moors and white Moors (Eldred Jones 14, 49), and Bartels quotes a contemporary description of king Abdelmelec where he is called the Christian King (Bartels "Making More" 439).

The stereotype of the evil Moor was not a thing that Peele could deal with easily. Before Peele, the black villain has long been an established figure in Western literary tradition. This figures was present since the antiquity and Christian literature (Ham's curse), up to Medieval and

Renaissance stage shows (Barthelemy 3ff). Thus, an audience of *Alcazar* would have expected dark skinned characters to be villainous and Peele does not flatly contradict this expectation. Rather he modifies, restricts and indirectly challenges black villainy in a way that redeems his favourite Moors from the stigma of blackness. This is achieved through presenting two completely opposite characters under one stereotypical category: Abdelmelec and Muly. A stereotypical conception can possibly be inferred from any other representation in the play: renegade (Stukeley), young Christian knight (Sebastian), Catholic leader (Philip and the Pope), but not from the category Moor. Thus, essential to the promotion of Abdelmelec's magnanimity was stressing Muly's negative attributes. So what are these attributes?

i. Weak and pompous

On two separate occasions, we see Muly Mahamet defeated by Abdelmelec. In both cases Muly Mahamet's, and his son's, reaction is to lament the situation they are in, a characteristic that shows him as a weak and defeated villain who is capable of nothing more than using grandiloquent rhetoric that comes to nothing after all:

> Boy, seest here this scimitar by my side,
> Sith they begin to bathe in blood,
> Blood be the theme whereon our time shall tread,
> Such slaughter with my weapon shall I make,
> As through the stream and bloody channels deep,
> Our Moors shall sail in ships and pinnaces,
> From Tangier shore unto the gates of Fez. (I.ii.54–60)

The same type of language is used by the son:

> And of those slaughtered bodies shall thy son
> A hugy tower erect like Nimrod's frame,
> To threaten those unjust and partial gods
> That to Abdallas' lawful seed deny
> A long, a happy and triumphant reign (I.ii.61–65)

Both father and son use rhetoric that features two unpopular traits: desperation and ruthlessness. They are thus stripped of any possible sympathy by showing that if they had the power they would become heartless tyrants.

This image is to be contrasted with Tamburlaine. The Marlovian larger-than-life hero uses similar grandiose language:

Zenocrate, were Egypt Jove's own land,
Yet would I with my sword make Jove to stoop.
I will confute those blind geographers
That make a triple region in the world,
Excluding regions which I mean to trace,
And with this pen reduce them to a map, (*1 Tambu.* IV.iv.75–80)

While Muly Mahamet and his son do little more than these speeches throughout the play, Tamburlaine actually goes on to conquer kingdoms and subdue whole regions. The ironic effect of hyperbolic language with no effect on the ground results in more contempt for Muly Mahamet.

The same routine of bombast recurs in Muly's last scene as if to emphasize this image. Trying to flee the battle he is losing, Muly shouts at his servant: "A horse, a horse, villain, a horse" (V.i.96). His last long speech is yet another rambling rant in which he blames everything else for the outcome of his actions:

Where shall I find some unfrequented place,
Some uncouth walk where I may curse my fill,
My stars, my dam, my planets and my nurse,
The fire, the air, the water, and the earth. (V.i.75–78)

He even curses himself and expresses nihilistic suicidal wishes similar to Hamlet's famous "O That This Too Solid Flesh Would Melt" soliloquy, albeit with a huge difference in the context and character

Ye Elements of whom consists this clay,
This mass of flesh, this cursèd crazèd corpse,
Destroy, dissolve, disturb, and dissipate,
What water, earth, and air congealed. (V.i.89–92)

Muly's pompous finale is to be clearly contrasted with Abdelmelec's death and last words. In their final words the two Moors are absolute opposites: while Muly is fiery, treacherous and self-centred, Abdelmelec is calm, altruistic and concerned mainly about the fulfilment of his role in this world.

ii. Double-dealer

Muly Mahamet's double-dealing is a running theme in the play. In II.iii, after losing the second battle with Abdelmelec, Muly is cursing the elements of nature that caused his defeat and he attributes Abdelmelec's victory to "fortune" which he curses as "constant in inconsistency" (4). In this scene we also get more insight into the character of Muly Mahamet's

Son as the embodiment of the "like father like son" proverb. In the previous appearance of Muly Mahamet and his son, his use of language was noted as very similar to his father, and again in this scene there is another, perhaps clearer, hint in the same direction. Trying to calm down his mother, the son explains to her how his father is going to deceive Sebastian:

> He can submit himself and live below,
> Make show of friendship, promise, vow and swear,
> Till by the virtue of his faire pretence,
> Sebastian trusting his integrity,
> He makes himself possessor of such fruits,
> As grow upon such great advantages. (II.iii.58–63)

Peele shows us how the son knows his father's ways and treacherous intentions thoroughly perhaps because this has been his habit in the past and the son has seen his father once and again employ similar methods. The indication is also that, just like chivalry seems to be an inherent feature that Abdelmelec and his heir possess, this other line of the family represents the opposite case: dishonesty passed from predecessor to successor.

The battle itself reveals more of Muly's cheating. In IV.ii we see Sebastian preparing for battle. He urges his captains to go on and chides them for dallying. In order to encourage Sebastian even more, Muly Mahamet spins a lie about Abdelmelec's army being in mutiny and waiting for the Portuguese first blow to desert and join Muly as their "rightful prince" (51). Made enthusiastic by the Moor's words, Sebastian is shown as a rash and inexperienced leader who does not read the facts on the ground or those of history correctly. The people of Morocco were unanimous in opposing Muly at the time of the battle and in fact it was he whom they deserted earlier in one of his battles against Abdelmelec. To put a final seal on Muly's villainy, he is left alone at the end of the scene to soliloquize revealing his real evil intentions like any typical children's comics villain. He shows no concern for any losses on both sides of the battle as long as he gets the crown "Though it be sealed and honoured with blood" (IV.ii.78). Thus, Muly is not only a traitor to his "kin and kind," he also bears no respect to political alliances and common causes. His villainy does not restrict itself to his enemies as his friends also do not matter if they stand between him and his aims.

Peele's confirmation of Muly's treachery does not hide itself in the play, but there is no indication that Peele was showing scenes of "Moorish deception in order to order to warn the Queen against her new allies," as

Matar unconvincingly deduces (Matar *Britain and Barbary* 17). For Peele portrays the Queen's Moorish allies in a complete contrast to Muly's villainy. There is not a single negative indication directed towards Abdelmelec and Seth, nor is there any link that connects their morals to Muly's. Muly Mahamet is unmistakeably shown as the social and political pariah who is in no way representative of his people.

4.4.3. Victims

4.4.3.1. Sebastian

In *The Battle of Alcazar* an effort is made to polish the image of Sebastian, Don António's predecessor, by dissociating him from his partner Muly Mahamet and moving him from the stigmatic category of villainy associated with Muly to the less negative, or rather more sympathetic, category of victims. Critics have often noted this attempt. Yoklavich, for example, noted the gap between what we are requested to think of King Sebastian and his actions in the play. According to him, while the Presenter claims that Sebastian is an "honourable and courageous" king, Sebastian's speech and action never justify this claim (Yoklavich 237). However, Sebastian still gains some sympathy through other means apart from the Presenter's attempts to clear him up.

A look at Sebastian's end in the play is a helpful means towards understanding how this character is intended to be perceived. Sebastian's last words are those of a disillusioned man:

> False hearted Mahamet, now to my cost,
> I see thy treachery, warned to beware
> A face so full of fraud and villainy. (V.i.68–70)

He then exits to die offstage. Although Peele does not show us Sebastian's death, we still expect it from earlier hints in the play (especially in the dumb shows) and we learn of it from Stukeley's dying note: "Now go, and in that bed of honour die / Where brave Sebastian's breathless corse doth lie" (187–188).

We cannot be sure whether Sebastian's offstage death serves to honour him or deny him the privilege of a tragic death which could win more sympathy. What we do know, however, is that he is the only character from the enemy who is honoured by the triumphant Muly Mahamet Seth. While Stukeley is killed by his followers, and the villain Muly Mahamet drowns in a river while fleeing for his life and is then mutilated and flayed,[23] we see that Sebastian is given a state funeral, as it were. Before they leave, the last scene witnessed by the audience would likely be a solemn procession in which Sebastian's body is held by soldiers across the stage. The final moments in the play try to guarantee sympathy for Sebastian and admiration for Seth.

Three main methods are used in order to give Sebastian his victim status: first portraying Sebastian as a deceived person, second finding excuses for his course of action in his young age and recklessness, and third, and most importantly for us, associating him with positive stances towards the English crown.

i. Deceived prince

The most striking example of Peele's interfering in order to clear his Sebastian of some of the original Sebastian's problematic actions is when he skips the information given by his sources about Sebastian luring Muly Mahamet into alliance. As mentioned above, Peele ignored his main source, Polemon, when he talks about Sebastian proposing help to Muly Mahamet twice before the latter accepted reluctantly. In the play, the situation is different as Muly Mahamet first sends ambassadors then visits Sebastian in his palace in order to win his support. In the meeting, both father and son engage in a grandiloquent display of loyalty in order to deceive Sebastian. Although Sebastian welcomes the family with reassuring words promising to "win" for them "a kingdom" (III.iv.9), still Muly Mahamet bursts into a speech to prove his loyalty which was not suspected by Sebastian in the first place. His conscience seems to lead him into proving himself innocent because he is guilty at least in his innermost intentions:

> The hellish prince grim Pluto with his mace
> Ding down my soul to hell, and with this soul
> This son of mine, the honour of my house,
> But I perform religiously to thee. (III.iv.25–28)

A naïve Sebastian falls for these words and the similar encore performed by Muly Mahamet's son. The audience's sense of sympathy towards the deceived Sebastian is heightened at this point by the use of dramatic irony due to their former knowledge of both Muly's villainy, as testified by the Presenter, and the deadly outcome of the Moroccan enterprise as far as Sebastian is concerned.

---

[23] Hence his Arabic nickname Al-Maslukh: the flayed.

Sebastian is the victim of double deception. In addition to Muly, Philip of Spain plays political tricks in order to lure Sebastian into a fatal end. Remarkable in the way Philip's double dealing is portrayed is a method followed by Peele in order to promote both feelings of sympathy for Sebastian and hatred towards Philip. Prediction and fulfilment is the summary of this method. In the induction to Act III, and even before Philip's promise of help the Presenter again takes us through a shortcut of the events and tells us what is going to happen:

> And now doth Spain promise with holy face,
> As favouring the honour of the cause,
> His aid of arms, and levies men apace,
> But nothing less than king Sebastian's good
> He means, yet at Guadalupea.
> He met some say in person with the Portugal,
> And treateth of a marriage with the king,
> But ware ambitious wiles and poisoned eyes,
> There was nor aide of arms nor marriage,
> For on his way without those Spaniards king Sebastian went. (III.Prol.13–22)

As with the case of Muly Mahamet's villainy which was stressed in the first dumb-show, both Philip's promise and reneging are narrated to the audience before they occur. Thus, when the promise is made it is already undermined by the prior knowledge of its breach, resulting in enhanced sympathy with Sebastian and dislike towards Philip through the use of tragic irony.

Based on Peele's sources and emphasised by Peele, Sebastian's character is given a significant and primary component of immaturity leading to fatal blunder. The fact that he is easily deceived, as discussed above, is a testimony to his lack of political shrewdness. His major weakness seems to be taking the verbal for the actual or taking allegations for truth. This is clearly visible in three occasions: believing Muly Mahamet's loyalty, believing Philip's promise of help, and accepting Muly's false allegations of mutiny within Abdelmelec's army to be true. In matters of diplomatic plots and conspiracy, Sebastian is out of his depth. He is presented as a heroic and ambitious king whose youth and religious zeal prompt him to take Muly Mahamet's offer and join him in an ill-prepared war which he loses and dies in. In addition to all this, other juvenile qualities are attributed to him in an attempt to make him seem guiltless. At one point he makes a childish gesture: when offered marriage to the Spanish *Infanta*, he jubilantly says: "Sebastian, clap thy hands for joy" (III.i.43).

ii. Sebastian the anglophile

A subtle but significant hint made by Peele regarding Sebastian's character lies in presenting him as a supporter of the English Queen and the land ruled by her. In his longest speech in the play, Sebastian is giving advice to Stukeley trying to dissuade him from proceeding with his Ireland mission. The purpose of the speech does not strike us as strange because Sebastian did need to convince Stukeley of joining him. However, the long speech digresses from discussing the military hopelessness of such a small expedition against a whole army into a panegyric lavishing praise on Queen Elizabeth in a strikingly hyperbolic manner that makes him look like a servile flatterer.

As D'Amico aptly notes, in this scene "what might have been an occasion for some anti-Islamic rhetoric turns into a glorification of Protestant England as opposed to Catholic Rome" (D'Amico 83). It is very unlikely for King Sebastian to say such words, but Peele is putting into Sebastian's mouth what he wants him to say, even if it seems unfitting for a king to say. Peele's aim might well be to increase public acceptance towards, and sympathy with, Sebastian. But again, why does he want to brighten the image of a dead person? The answer lies in the person of Don António who was at the time either already on his way, or preparing to, claim back the Portuguese throne using English support.

This speech still needs some detailed discussion. At the outset, Sebastian expresses surprise at Stukeley's goal with the small number of men he has. Although Peele gave Stukeley ten times the real number he had, six thousand instead of six hundred (Bradley 151), still Sebastian tells him that:

> Were every ship ten thousand on the seas,
> Manned with the strength of all the Eastern kings,
> Conveying all the monarchs of the world,
> To invade the island where her highness reigns,
> 'Twere all in vain. (II.iv.103–107)

Sebastian is proclaiming Peele's old *topos* of invincible England as he often wrote in his pageants. In a similar use of pageant-like rhetoric, Sebastian then moves on to the person of the Queen mentioning her attributes as well as the divine protection for her and her kingdom: "Both nature, time and fortune, all agree / To bless and serve her royal majesty" (115–116). The speech continues and mentions the geographical invulnerability of the English isle and how from every side nature prepared defences that "do swallow up her foes" and "their ships in pieces split" (118–119). Finally Sebastian suggests to Stukeley that it is against

God Himself to go on in his mission: "Advise thee then proud Stukeley ere thou pass / To wrong the wonder of the highest God" (130–131) and that honour does not lie in this mission but rather in following him to Morocco "If honor be the mark wherat thou aim'st, / Then follow me in holy Christian wars," (134–135).

David Bradley considers this speech to be an "improbable" embellishment to a scene that is "alarmingly short of matter" (156). But I find that Bradley misses an important point here. From the way it is structured and from its resonance with the overall theme of patriotism as well as with previous works by Peele, the praise of Elizabeth looks more like the focal point of the scene than an addition to fill up space.

Peele makes Sebastian speak like a patriotic character from one of his city pageants. His words about divine protection "For heavens and destinies / Attend and wait upon her Majesty" (107–108) sound very similar to those spoken the Moor in the Dixi Pageant "The God of Kings that with his holy hand, / Hath long defended her and her England" (*The Device* 41–42). Just like the words of the Moor in the pageant were written in a manner that makes him seem like a friend to the English, so is Sebastian's speech designed to show his love for the English with the aim of showing that his successor, Don António, is worthy of Queen Elizabeth's support.

Thus, if we imagine Muly to be a magnet of contempt, or the centre of gravity for evil in the play, and Sebastian being dragged by his alliance with him towards a similar position, it can be said that Peele places other gravitational forces to pull Sebastian away from such a position into a favourable one. These forces are sympathy for Sebastian's naïvety and youth as well as a nationalist and royalist redeeming factor which manifested itself in the allegation that Sebastian was actually an anglophile who showed admiration for Queen Elizabeth and her realm in a manner of which only an English patriot is capable.

4.4.3.2. Stukeley

Captain Thomas Stukeley was Peele's stroke of luck. He was already present in his subject matter so that Peele did not have to intervene and add an element of Englishness to the play. But there is a curious legend behind Thomas Stukeley. A renegade and a rebel, Stukeley was, strangely enough, transformed in the public eye into a hero for no obvious reason. In fact, each one of these attributes was enough to represent a despicable villain in an Elizabethan play. The question remains about the role that *The Battle of Alcazar* played in the making of the Stukeley legend. The full title of the play, *The Battell of Alcazar, fought in Barbarie, betweene*

Sebastian king of Portugall, and Abdelmelec king of Morocco. With the death of Captaine Stukeley. As it was sundrie times plaid by the Lord high Admirall his Seruants, is quite indicative of the way Stukeley's name is utilized to achieve popularity using the formula *"With the Death of Captain Thomas Stukeley"* as if it were a "star turn" in the action of the play. The full title does not refer to the death of three kings at the battle, which would have been quite attractive. Rather, Peele, or whoever wrote the title page, chose to mention the death of Captain Thomas Stukeley as the element of the play with paramount advertising importance. The name Stukeley must have been well-known by the time the play was written. The play's intention then was initially to use the name Stukeley for popularity but it also became the first theatrical presentation of the person in what are sometimes called the "Stukeley plays". The other one was the anonymous drama *The Famous History of the life and death of Captain Thomas Stukeley*. Besides these two plays, the storied Stukeley had several appearances in "ballads, tracts, plays, biographies and various prose fictions" (Yoklavich 252).

Because Stukeley represents the English element in the play, it is essential for this study to look at the way *Alcazar* dealt with this problematic character who combined Englishness with disloyalty to the crown, without going against Peele's general line of nationalism. We may not be able to estimate the extent to which *Alcazar* contributed to the Stukeley legend, and strictly speaking it does not fall within the perspective of this study to do so. Nevertheless, the play's presentation of Stukeley is charged with nationalism starting from Stukeley being an Englishman amongst foreigners up to being the only developing character in the play as will be shown below.

i. Traitor and hero

In the eyes of his contemporaries, one positive fact about Stukeley was his adventurous nature which led him on a globetrotting career covering England, Ireland, Spain, Italy, Portugal and Barbary, while negative points about him were his restless search for glory at any cost, lack of loyalty to his homeland and unruliness. Contemporary views on him ranged from the approving to the disapproving, and while a Bishop named Carleton thought of him as one who had "too honorable an end of a dishonorable life," many popular ballads and chapbooks talked of him as a "stout" and "renowned gallant" and a person of "noble valor" (Yoklavich 270, 65).

Confusions also exist in critical appraisals of the character. Samuel Chew argued that Stukeley was not an important character in the play and that the historical figure was ignored by many accounts and narratives

(Chew 525–6). This is a view that this section tries to negate by stressing the importance of Stukeley as an Englishman in a play laden with patriotic elements, as well as the importance of his characterization in theatrical terms as he seems to be the only developing character in a play full of static characters, as will be shown below.

Using Stukeley as an example in his study on *Turks, Moors and Englishmen in the Age of Discovery*, Nabil Matar makes several inaccurate observations regarding the character of Stukeley with the aim of making him fit into a general frame he is trying to establish. Matar argues that Stukeley was "the first English soldier/captain to serve the Muslims and win national acclaim" (Matar *Turks, Moors* 46) and that in the play he is presented as a "warlike Englishman" (IV.i.33) whose "knell" England would "kindly ring" (V.i.176). Thus, he was "the model soldier who never compromised his Englishness, even when serving the Lord Mahamet" (Matar *Turks, Moors* 48). Built on a misreading of the basics of the play, this analysis mistakes Stukeley for a patriotic hero proud of his Englishness and playing the role of a typical English warrior. This is simply not true because the play shows Stukeley clearly distancing himself from national affiliation. Thus, he can hardly be used as an example of a soldier who did not "compromise his Englishness." Moreover, he was not serving the Muslims as such. It is clear in the play that he was serving Portugal in a war against the Muslims despite the presence of Muly Mahamet who the play presents as a traitor to his homeland. Finally, the example given about the ringing of the knell is a clear misquotation as the original context was part of Stukeley's dying speech in which he only wished that his country would forgive him for his disloyalty.

However, Stukeley's "heroism" in the play is not something to be ignored. Between critics totally negating it and critics loading it with that which it does not possess lies an area which caters for a better understanding of Stukeley and the play as a whole, especially as far as views on nationalism are concerned. Taking into consideration the way Stukeley is presented in the play and the methods applied to present a hero in a tragedy, the following is an attempt to bring to light what I see as an important factor in the making of the character of Stukeley.

From the viewpoint of the English political regime, Stukeley was a dangerous and disloyal subject. His pirate activities against English ships were officially proclaimed traitorous as early as 1565 (Tazón 75). *The Battle of Alcazar* makes no effort to hide these well-known tendencies of Stukeley. In II.ii, Peele gives a clear indication of Stukeley's lack of national sentiment. When Diego Lopes expresses disapproval of

Stukeley's expedition as it entails invading land ruled by the Englishmen's own government, Stukeley questions the very roots of national affiliation:

> For why, I make it not so great desert
> To be begot or borne in any place,
> Sith that's a thing of pleasure and of ease,
> That might have been performed elsewhere as well. (II.ii.34–37)

Although these words can function as a valid argument against nationalism as they disestablish its basics, they most likely created a sense of disapproval in an English audience in the time the play was performed when national affiliation was becoming increasingly self-evident. More dangerous in these words is their association with disloyalty to the crown. Because Stukeley is on a mission to invade land ruled by Queen Elizabeth, his disrespect for national affiliation becomes equated with the treasonous action of bringing invaders into one's own country and thus Stukeley's radicalism with regard to nationalism becomes a threat to the English people's own sense of security.

On the other hand, Stukeley's claims to the sympathies of an Elizabethan audience lie basically in his bravery and heroics as well as his unrelenting search for glory. A brave and aspiring person has always been able to seize interest and *Alcazar* does not fail to emphasize this facet in Stukeley. The play describes him as "a man of gallant personage, / Proud in [his] looks, and famous every way" (II.iv.90–91). His "proud" and "warlike" attributes are often associated with his Englishness (Celybin calls him "A warlike Englishman" IV.i.33) and admiration for his character is expressed similarly by his friends and foes. But there is more to *Alcazar*'s Stukeley than the swashbuckler. Sympathy with the countryman is given supporting elements that need some explanation.

Stukeley came from the gentry. Apart from rumours that he was a bastard son of Henry VIII (Bovill 80; Chambers 138), he was son to Sir Hugh Stukeley, sheriff of Devon and a prosperous clothier and knight of the body to King Henry VIII; his mother was Jane Pollard, daughter of Sir Lewis Pollard (Tazón 21). In addition, he won himself a good deal of recognition due to his military prowess. At the time of the play, six thousand soldiers (according to Peele at least) are under his command. Thus, the fate of a large number of people is dependent on this character as well.

In addition, Stukeley expresses a character flaw represented in his lack of commitment to one place, which was behind his wandering the world looking for glory (II.ii.34–37 quoted above). Right before these lines, Stukeley describes his most serious flaw, the one that led most of his life, and finally led to his death. "And I am Stukeley so resolved in all, / To follow rule, honour and empery," (II.ii.28–29). It is fatal ambition, similar to the one that led to the destruction of Doctor Faustus and many a tragic hero. This feature in Stukeley, as presented in the play, is very similar to *hamartia* in the Aristotelian sense of the word.[24] Stukeley's ambition was the drive behind leaving Ireland for Spain, then leaving Spain for Rome, then leading the papal expedition against his own homeland and it eventually led to his untimely death.

Stukeley is thus a man from a noble background, with the lives of a great number of people being affected directly by his life or death. This hero is put through some trying circumstances which expose his personality and he commits a mistake which leads to his demise. Peele's Stukeley then has strong links to characters described as tragic heroes. This view was, I believe, one basis upon which sympathy with Stukeley was built, and which has been so long overlooked by critics and students of *The Battle of Alcazar*. The importance of this observation lies in the fact that aligning Stukeley with such heroes as Faustus and Macbeth allows him the same sympathy they receive despite their villainous qualities.

On a different level, love for the English representative in *Alcazar* is evoked through allusion to a recently popular figure on the English stage, namely Marlowe's Tamburlaine, whose effect on English theatre can hardly be exaggerated. Similarities in theme and character as well as the fact that both plays were played by the Admiral's Men made *Alcazar* one of the major plays considered as offshoots of *Tamburlaine*—what have been called "*Tamburlaine*'s weak sons" (Berek). Critics studying the two plays in comparison note that traces of Tamburlaine's character can be found in two characters in *Alcazar*, Muly Mahamet and Stukeley (Berek 66; Rutter 29). While the former uses Tamburlaine-like overbearing rhetoric which hovers on the brink of the ludicrous, the latter expresses ambition that knows no rest before attaining a crown.

The existence of two characters is important in this regard. Peter Berek is right in observing that "the most important way that sympathy is maintained for the aspiring Stukeley is by contrast with the equally aspiring, but officially vicious Moor" (67). Thus, Peele did not import Tamburlaine's character wholesale into one of his characters. Rather he cleverly splits his attributes into ambition and rhetoric and gives Stukeley and Mahamet what suits his vision of their characters. Thus, sympathy with Stukeley's ambition is not marred by empty bombast and the power

---

[24] "*Hamartia*: the Greek word for error or failure, used by Aristotle in his *Poetics* (4th century BCE) to designate the false step that leads the protagonist in a tragedy to his or her downfall" (Baldick 109–10).

of rhetoric is undermined by Muly's villainous nature and lack of corresponding action. When Stukeley says these lines:

> Deeds, words and thoughts shall all be as a *king*'s,
> My chiefest company shall be with *kings*,
> And my deserts shall counterpoise a *king*'s,
> Why should not I then look to be a *king*? (II.ii.75–78, italics mine)

he is but reproducing Tamburlaine's expressions in:

> Is it not brave to be a *king*, Techelles?
> Usumcasane and Theridamas,
> Is it not passing brave to be a *king*,
> …
> Why, say, Theridamas, wilt thou be a *king*. (*1 Tamburlaine* II.v.51–53, 65)

Tom Rutter also refers to other instances where Stukeley repeats the word "crown" in a way much reminiscent of famous lines uttered by Tamburlaine (Rutter 31).

ii. Stukeley's developing character

From the above examples, it would seem that Peele only reflected contradicting views on Stukeley in his play without intervention. But there seems to be more to the character of Stukeley than this. *The Battle of Alcazar* takes a remarkable approach towards Stukeley between the two extremities presented above. Rather than choosing one stance against the other, or even finding a middle-ground approach, Peele starts with one to arrive at the other. In other words, Stukeley starts as an unrepentant wayward enthusiast and ends as a repentant and sympathy-arousing victim.

Stukeley appears in five scenes in the play and each scene seems to add something new to our understanding of this character. In his first appearance in II.ii, Stukeley shocks his audience by denying the basic principle underlying the concept of national affiliation and love of the homeland. In this scene, upon learning the goal of the expedition, Diego Lopes, Governor of Lisbon, gives a disapproving evaluation of Stukeley's venture. Stukeley intervenes by presenting his point of view on the issue. "As we are Englishmen, so are we men," (27) he says, giving priority to the human trait of ambition and thus to individuality rather than the nationalist sense of belonging.

Stukeley is by and large a personification of ambition, which is not a negative characteristic in itself. However, Stukeley's preference of ambition over, and in opposition to, patriotism is used by Peele to undermine this particular trait, or flaw, in his character. These lines show Stukeley as a restless wanderer, or rather a mercenary, led astray by his overriding ambition and love for rule so much so that he neglects his love for the homeland. Thus, anti-patriotism is portrayed as a sin or a defect in the personality of an otherwise heroic character. Stukeley is made to boast that he carries no special love for England and that he is ready to give his loyalty to any country he chooses. This anti-nationalistic tendency in Stukeley is further stressed in by placing him in direct contrast to archetypal nationalist discourse represented by the Irish Bishop. Upon hearing Stukeley's words, the Bishop intervenes to proclaim a memorable and eloquent piece on patriotism and the way one should love the homeland. The passage, which was famously quoted by Henry David Thoreau in his essay "On the Duty of Civil Disobedience" (Thoreau 243), runs as follows:

> We must affect our country as our parents,
> And if at any time we alienate
> Our love or industry from doing it honour,
> It must respect effects and teach the soul [...]
> Matter of conscience and religion,
> And not desire of rule or benefit. (II.ii.42–47) [25]

Here, the conflict between Stukeley's self-centred quest for glory and the self-denying patriotic ideology becomes clear. Peele shows us that while there is nothing wrong with ambition *per se*, Stukeley's version of it, which has its priorities confused, is a grave danger to national security. In order to make the message more manifest, Peele makes two people criticise Stukeley's attitude: one from Portugal and the other of Stukeley's own companions, both being Catholics. But does Stukeley get the message?

In his retort to the Bishop, Stukeley evades the question and makes a rude joke on his name calling him "The reverent lordly Bishop of Saint Asses" (49). Hercules, an English captain under Stukeley, joins him in ridiculing the patriotic statement of the Bishop and accuses him of fitting his words to the occasion. The dispute is alleviated by Diego Lopes and Stukeley is left alone to soliloquize and fantasize about his ambitions of being "King of Ireland." Stukeley is clearly intent on his unrestrained ambition which, as the speech suggests, has reached disturbing degrees that make him reject any position that is governed by a higher authority: "King of a mole-hill had I rather be / Than the richest subject of a

---

[25] For a discussion of the missing lines, see Edelman p.83 n.45

monarchy" (81–82). Not only is Stukeley obsessed with his ambition, he seems to defy the very notion of being a citizen under any authority. This unruliness is given religious connotations as the person showing it is a known Catholic recusant who betrayed his national affiliation and adopted sectarian difference to achieve personal gains.

In II.iv, Stukeley meets with Sebastian who lectures him on the greatness of Elizabeth and her realm then forces the whole expedition to join his enterprise. The conversation that takes place between Sebastian and leaders of the papal mission is interesting and worth analysis. Upon listening to Sebastian's long speech praising Elizabeth, Stukeley seems confused and he adopts two ways to reply. First, rather scrupulously, he does not comment on Sebastian's panegyric but he resorts to an *argumentum ad verecundiam* (argument from authority) referring his position to a papal order that he cannot violate. Second, he keeps the decision with his fellow members of the expedition:

> Amongst the rest my Lord, I am but one;
> If they agree, Stukeley will be the first
> To die with honour for Sebastian. (II.iv.141–143)

But where does Stukeley's confusion stem from? It is true that ambition led most of his life, but it has also to be remembered that so far for Stukeley ambition has been almost inseparable from his Catholicism and religious difference with Protestantism. Thus, Sebastian's speech which indicated the impossibility of invading Ireland, his offer of "honour" and his attempt to dissuade Stukeley from seeking his "country's overthrow" all seem to put Stukeley at a crossroads: should he follow his dream of following "rule, honour and empery" (II.ii.29) by following Sebastian's footsteps to Barbary and thus betray his Catholicism and the Pope; or should he stick to his "vows" (II.iv.149) despite being now doubtful of their outcome. This is before everything else a question of priorities: self or religion. Hitherto, Stukeley has been able to serve both with no discrepancy but now he has to make a decision.

By referring the question to his colleagues, Stukeley is trying to evade making a tough personal decision. The rest of the mission leaders are clear in their refusal which makes them seem more committed to the cause than Stukeley. The Bishop talks as the voice of Catholic Christian conscience and gives the religious view on the question: "To aid Mahamet, King of Barbary, / 'Tis 'gainst our vows, great King of Portugal" (148–149). Hercules gives the nationalist view on the question: "Our country and our countrymen will condemn / Us worthy of death, if we neglect our vows" (153–154). Finally, Sebastian leaves aside the attempt to convince them and orders them to join him, to which Stukeley retorts in a soliloquy-like manner: "Saint George for England, and Ireland now adieu, / For here Tom Stukeley shapes his course anew" (166–167). In this significant sentence, Stukeley's departure from religion-focused life is clear. His new path will be shown in later episodes.

In II.i, we see a Stukeley who has become an integral part of the Portuguese project using his shrewdness to serve the new course he chose for himself. As Sebastian receives the Spanish ambassadors and takes their promises of help at face value, Stukeley is standing silently aside and he only speaks as the ambassadors and Sebastian exit. Left with Avero, Stukeley addresses an absent Sebastian: "Sit fast Sebastian, and in this work / God and good men labour for Portugal" (48). Interestingly, the second of these two lines shows how Stukeley's priorities stand now: God "labours" for Portugal and not vice versa. He places religion in service of the nation. To Stukeley, Philip, "whom some call the Catholic king" (53), the archetypical defender of religion, has a faith that is not "firm" (54) which he is "disguising with a double face" (50). Unlike a naïve Sebastian, Stukeley knows that Philip's armies "that do multiply in Spain" (56) are headed towards Flanders. Thus, this scene hints at a change that is taking place within Stukeley as he discovers the deceit inherent in Philip's religious facade. Stukeley was witness to Sebastian meeting with the Spanish ambassadors. When Sebastian mentioned the aim of the expedition to the Spanish ambassadors "Say how your mighty master minded is / To propagate the fame of Portugal" (6–7), he was immediately corrected: "To propagate the fame of Portugal / *And* plant religious truth in Africa" (8–9, italics mine). The Spanish ambassadors stress the religious aspect of the war in an attempt both to correct Sebastian's priorities and make him more zealous about the war (D'Amico 82, 83). Thus, by displaying Philip's deceit in front of Stukeley and then showing Stukeley's awareness of this deceit, Peele is probably presenting the start of Stukeley's disillusionment and redemption.

Scene III.iv is another scene that shows us how Stukeley is acting within his new framework. Here, he applauds Muly Mahamet's son as a brave and "princely" boy. Stukeley is of course an authority on such qualities as they have been marking his life perhaps since he was the age of Muly Mahamet's son. In a hint towards secularizing Stukeley, the scene also shows us how Stukeley admires the personal traits of the son regardless of his religious background.

The final scene in which Stukeley dies is of prominent importance as it concludes Stukeley's story and fulfils the promise of the play's title "*with the death of Captain Thomas Stukeley*": not his adventures but his death. It is as if Stukeley is in the play basically in order to die, which gives his dying speech even more importance. As the Portuguese lose the battle, Stukeley is stopped by two of his Italian followers who call him "traitor" and "ambitious Englishman" (V.i.109). The Italians accuse Stukeley of bringing about their demise but he shows remarkable submission to divine will: "he that is the judge of right and wrong / Determines battle as him pleaseth best?" (119–120). With the same submission Stukeley asks for his own death without even resisting the Italians, which is extremely uncharacteristic of the boisterous swashbuckler he is supposed to be. This, I think, is another step in the direction of showing a changing Stukeley into a pensive and self-exploring man who admits his mistakes.

Breathing his last, Stukeley summarizes his life-story in a long soliloquy which is mainly descriptive with little of the contemplation expected in such dramatic moments. But still Peele manages to pass hints that paint a more positive image of Stukeley than hitherto shown. First, we find an indication about a weakness of Stukeley's that brought about the end of him. He says that in Lisbon he was "Dared to the field, that never could endure / to hear god Mars his drum, but he must march" (167–168). Thus, his incurable desire for wars and battles made him join the Portuguese project. The fact that he could not resist a call for war strongly supports the above-mentioned similarity between Stukeley and tragic heroes.

Stukeley's redemption is given the final touches by a remark representing a repenting tone. Stukeley's repentance is especially directed to his homeland which he previously disowned claiming:

> I make it not so great desert
> To be begot or borne in any place,
> Sith that's a thing of pleasure and of ease,
> That might have been performed elsewhere as well. (II.ii.34–37)

Contrary to this, in his final speech Stukeley begs his country to accept him:

> Here breathe thy last and bid thy friends farewell.
> And if thy Country's kindness be so much,
> Then let thy Country kindly ring thy knell. (V.i.174–176)

Peele thus redeems Stukeley who was actually a popular hero before the play was written. While Peele did not approve of the real Stukeley's anti-nationalistic stances, he could not risk disappointing the audience who came to the play to see Stukeley (whose name was on the play's title). Peele shows Stukeley's defect throughout the play and ends his life with a compassionate speech with a redeeming request of forgiveness from his country. Thus, the audience of Peele's play can leave the play still admiring their countryman without having to condone his negative traits as he renounced them in his last words. Another dimension to this presentation is that through this method *Alcazar* avoids the murky waters of presenting on stage a hero who was seen by the government as a traitor. Stukeley was both dangerous and popular. Therefore, Peele could not ignore him nor could he leave his character unedited, as it were, so he had to neutralize Stukeley's rebellious nature somehow. This he did through making him develop from rebellion against nationalism to submission and repentance. These modifications introduced by Peele to Stukeley's character serve the overall patriotic mood of his work and are unlikely to displease the government.

George Peele, thus, plots his characters alongside lines that conform to the general interests of Elizabethan foreign policy. In the same manner that these interests prompted the promotion of Abdelmelec and his successor, they necessitated the demonization of Muly Mahamet for being their enemy. The same rules apply to Sebastian and Philip.

Peele's work in dividing his characters into groups works at another level. Reading the Presenter's first speech, one is alarmed by the high recurrence of negative words associated with certain characters (Muly Mahamet and his father). Looking further into the text reveals further usage of keywords and epithets in association with certain characters for thematic and characterization purposes. A look at the way character names are modified, using certain adjectives and epithets reveals results that support this proposition as the following discussion shows.

4.5. Character epithets

Alcazar's use of certain keywords and epithets is worthy of discussion here. In fact, this is proving to be such an important facet of criticism concerning the play that in a conference about "Humanity and Barbarism in Tudor Literature" in 2006 two papers discussing this very issue in *Alcazar* were presented.[26] Prominent among these words are those pertaining to concepts of race, colour, religion and nationality. In this section, I will try to point out how Peele's use of these keywords fits in

---

[26] *The Fifth International Conference of the Tudor Symposium: Humanity and Barbarism in Tudor Literature* was held in Pázmány Péter Catholic University, Piliscaba in September 2006. The two papers were entitled "Barbarous/Barbarian: The Ambiguity of b/Barbary in Peele's *Battle of Alcazar*" by Francis Guinle, and "Christians and Barbarians in Peele's *Battle of Alcazar*" by Hammood Obaid.

with his pro-government presentation of events and characters. The epithets I study are divided into two groups: racial and religious.

4.5.1. Racial epithets

4.5.1.1. Moor

Because most studies of the play focus on its position in the English literary history as the first play with a Moor in a major role, the word *Moor* is certainly worth some discussion. Although the play presents another major character who is a Moor, Abdelmelec, it is astonishing, as Eldred Jones notes, that it is only Muly Mahamet among all Moors in the play who is called the Moor. Jones tries to justify this by stating that Muly Mahamet had black skin being "born of a Negro mother" (Eldred Jones 43). This claim gains ground from Polemon who gives a detailed physical description of both Abdelmelec and Muly Mahamet with particular stress on Muly's black skin.

Charles Edelman argues that the word *Moor* was not applied to Muly Mahamet only, and that on one occasion Zareo is described as a Moor in stage directions (I.i.OSD) (Edelman *Stukeley Plays* 30). This argument fails to convince because the reference is in a stage direction which is not heard by the audience and might be not Peele's after all. More importantly, Jones talks about the use of the *title* Moor i.e. the use of the word *Moor* to refer to a person. The stage direction reads: "a Moor." The word here is used to indicate Zareo's ethnic origin, in other words the fact that he is Moroccan. Apart from this time, the word *Moor* occurs many times in the text of the play in singular and plural forms referring to Muly Mahamet and Moroccans respectively, but as a title the word *Moor* is used only to refer to Muly Mahamet.[27] As mentioned above in the section on promoting and demoting certain characters to fit a general view that Peele wants to popularize, Muly Mahamet is distanced from the rest of Moroccans by several means. Here he is associated almost exclusively with the title "the Moor" which is used even by other Moors to address him. Any culturally negative preconceptions associated with the term are thus focused on Muly Mahamet rather than the other major Moorish characters, who are Elizabeth's friends.

A helpful observation made by Jonathan Bate regarding the use of the term Moor is that:

---

[27] Nor is there any indication that "the Moor" denotes kingship in the way that "the Dane" does in *Hamlet*. This is because even Muly's enemies call him the Moor and they clearly do not recognize him as a king of Morocco.

The primary usage of the term "Moor" in early modern English was as a religious, not a racial, identification: Moor meant "Mohamedan," that is Muslim. The word was frequently used as a general term for "not one of us," non-Christian. ... The second Elizabethan sense of the word "Moor" was specifically racial and geographical; it referred to a native or inhabitant of Mauretania, a region of North Africa corresponding to parts of present-day Morocco and Algeria. (Bate "Othello and the Other—Turning Turk: The subtleties of Shakespeare's treatment of Islam" 14)

It is of paramount importance that Peele neglects the first meaning of the word and uses it solely for the second meaning as a geographical name. As shown below, Peele does the same with the word Barbarian which also has two meanings. Two outcomes are achieved by this: blurring religious difference and presenting the Moors as a nation (see section 4.2). Other terms need to be investigated through their occurrences in the text. These include epithets of colour (black, dark and Negro), epithets of ethnicity (Barbarian, Portugal) and religious epithets (Christian and Catholic). These are explored below.

4.5.1.2. Black, dark and Negro

In a play like *The Battle of Alcazar*, where critics have been deeply preoccupied with the dialectic of black and white, it is astonishing to find that word searches show that major characters in the play never use the words *black* or *dark*. Still, George Peele seems more inclined to use other words to refer to the idea of darkness in complexion. A search for the word *Negro* indicates that it occurs eight times in the text. Six of these occurrences refer to Muly Mahamet which is a high percentage especially when we consider that the other two cases refer to Muly Mahamet's men as "Negros." A look at the speakers who use the word Negro to refer to Muly Mahamet shows that four out of six occurrences are uttered by the Presenter of the play. If we add the last observation about the use of the word Negro to Jones's note above, it turns out that Muly is the only character called Negro, and the only character called Moor. In fact the expression "Negro Moor" occurs three times in the play, and these are the only times where the word Negro is used as an adjective. Muly Mahamet is thus distanced further from other Moors through the use of specific keywords that collocate with him almost exclusively.

4.5.1.3. Barbarian and barbarous

Two important words in this context are *barbarous* and *Barbarian*. *The OED* shows that the words have a Greek origin βαρβαρος with a sense-development as follows: foreign, non-Hellenic, outlandish, rude, brutal.

The Romans used the word to refer to that which is "not Latin nor Greek," then "pertaining to those outside the Roman empire;" hence "uncivilized, uncultured," and later "non-Christian," whence "Saracen, heathen'; and generally "savage, rude, savagely cruel, inhuman."

Applied to *Alcazar*, my searches show that the words *Barbarian/barbarous* occur eleven times in total (including plurals). Although one might assume otherwise, the two words are used in two different semantic fields. In other words, Peele does not use the word *Barbarian* to mean *barbarous*. Rather, he uses the word *barbarian* five times in his play with one meaning and that is: of or belonging to Barbary, discarding the meaning it shares with *barbarous*. The word *Barbarian* is used in reference to Abdelmelec, Moroccan people (in plural) and a horse. In two occurrences, the word collocates with approving words: "brave Barbarian" (I.Prol.12), and "Barbarian Lord" (I.Prol.12 and IV.ii.24). If we take into consideration the fact that Peele does not utilize the negative meanings of the word, the overall use of the word *Barbarian* in the play tends to be a neutral reference to the place of origin being Barbary.

Opposite to the neutral use of the word *Barbarian*, the use of the word *barbarous* is a different matter. Peele uses the word six times in his play. Although he is using the word according to its original meaning with its negative connotations, his use of the word is not as innocent as it appears. The word *barbarous* seems to form a strong collocation rule with the word *Moor* in *Alcazar*. The two words collocate in four of the six times in which the word *barbarous* occurs. To an average audience or reader of the play, this collocation has a negative effect and with such strong collocation, the words *barbarous* and *Moor* become more like synonyms. Muly Mahamet's distinguishing term, the Moor, is thus tarred with the negative epithet *barbarous* and is burdened with all the culturally disapproving preconceptions associated with it.

4.5.2. Religious epithets

It is a well-known fact that the word *Muslim* does not appear in English before 1615 (*OED*) and words like *Mohammedan* and *Mahometan* were used before this date. But Peele does not use any of these words to refer to the Moors. Thus, religious difference is blurred in an attempt to familiarize the religious otherness of these Moors with whom Elizabeth is making friends. But is this the same with all words of religious nature? In fact, the case is different and looking into these words reveals some very interesting findings.

The search for the word *Christian* returns fourteen results. In four of these occurrences, the word *Christian* is used as a noun to refer to a person who professes Christianity. In the remaining ten, the word is used as an adjective. Moreover, the words that collocate with it are mostly of approving meaning like "wholesome Christian laws" (III.iv.47) to "brave Sebastian our Christian king" (III.iii.15). The phrase "holy Christian war" occurs two times. The characters who use the word *Christian* are mainly Sebastian and the Presenter, who understandably use the word with positive connotations. More interesting, though, is the Moroccans' use of the word, four times in total, which is never accompanied by disapproving or negative word. Abdelmelec, for examples, sympathetically refers to Sebastian as "a careless Christian prince" (III.iii.16), and in the final scene, Muly Mahamet Seth orders the soldiers to "tread a solemn march" for "this Christian king" (V.i.258, 256). The Moors' positive use of the word *Christian* is indicative of their inherent respect for their honourable adversaries, the Portuguese. At the same time, it gives a positive message to Londoners about their government's new allies.

The word *Catholic*, however, receives a significantly different treatment. Peele adopts a subtle way of using the word to underline the fault lines between the different parties of the play as he saw them. Rather than adopting the word *Catholic* as a comprehensive term to refer to all European parties taking part in the battle, who were all Catholic, Peele restricts the use of the word to Spain and the Papal expedition. More precisely, out of the seven occurrences of the word, it is used only once to refer to Stukeley's men (importantly before they join the Portuguese) and the remaining six times refer to Philip of Spain himself as the "Catholic king" not to the Spanish in general. A strange stylistic method is adopted by Peele when using the title "Catholic king." In three of its six uses, it is accompanied by expressions that undermine Philip and his relationship to the title. The three occurrences are:

Stukeley	Philip whom *some call* the Catholic king,
	I fear me much thy faith will not be firm
	(III.i.52–53, italics mine)
Abdelmelec	*He that entitled* is the Catholic king,
	Would not assist a careless Christian prince
	(III.ii.15–16, italics mine)
Stukeley	There had I welcome and right royal pay
	Of Phillip, whom *some call* the Catholic King
	(V.i.144–145, italics mine)

This can be seen as a sneer directed against Philip and his title "the Most Catholic King." On the other hand, the Portuguese are saved from collocating with the word *Catholic*. In an attempt to find a common denominator with Don António's people, the Portuguese are called Christians and not Catholics.

The study of Peele's use of adjectives, epithets and other keywords reveals an underlying, and perhaps unconscious, conviction in the need to use language that serves government views and stances. Peele's language shows how England's new allies, the Moors, are brought closer, her enemies are attacked, and Don António's cause is supported. This presence of propaganda on such a level can be seen as the result of a deeply-held belief in this patriotic agenda which reflected itself on several levels in the play.

5. Conclusion

The Battle of Alcazar is no doubt a landmark in English renaissance drama as far as Muslims are concerned. Before *Alcazar*, many images and pieces of information existed in the English cultural repertoire, the majority of which were negative and unflattering. Not only does Peele give the English drama its first Moor in a major role but he also gives a positively portrayed Moor. This fact has bothered critics for some time as the introduction to this chapter has shown. Critics tried to fathom the way the play interacted with the expectations of an early modern audience and whether it challenged these expectations, reinforced or even toyed with them superficially. Although some decent attempts have been made in this regard, still the major point, in my view was not tackled rigorously enough. Topical allusions in the play were not merely a reference to recent events but were rather essential instigators for writing and actual building blocks for the text.

Hence, this chapter on *The Battler of Alcazar* has tried to establish that George Peele's product was influenced so much by topical and contemporary factors that approaching it as a "representation" of Moors or Muslims becomes moot. Little of the Muslim Other is left in Peele's play because the writing was prompted by special political, cultural and topical purposes. As a result, the playwright showed the interests of his government in the constructed form of a story happening elsewhere.

In a sonnet concluding his long poem *Polyhymnia*, George Peele wrote:

> *Blest be the heartes that wish my soveraigne well,*
> *Curst be the soules that thinke her any wrong.* (15–6, italics in original)

These two lines sum up quite a good deal of Peele's stance in many of his works including *Alcazar*. The discussion of Peele's recurring themes showed that praising Queen Elizabeth, her government and policies was the norm in his other works. Peele's pen was more often than not put in the service of government propaganda in works that ranged between the elevated court-performed *Arraignment of Paris*, and the populist street-performed pageants.

The government's general views towards foreign relations were often more pragmatic than principled. Viewing herself at the time as a Protestant nation that did not have to answer to the Holy See, England pursued her political goals with less religious scruples than before. Thus, Elizabeth established relations with the Sublime Porte and the Barbary states to spite Rome who issued papal bulls against that. English merchants traded with the Muslims in a similar manner, while English privateers did not respect pope-endorsed Catholic control of maritime trade and colonization.

Two events of the late 1580s brought these ideas to the forefront and to public awareness. First was the Spanish Armada that increased English feelings of nationhood (Birch 135). The second event that followed shortly was the spectacular visit of the Moorish ambassadors to London, which raised many questions for the public as to the nature and customs of these new friends of the government.

Peele's play was an answer to such sentiments, recognizing the unbridgeable gap that was created by the Reformation between state and pope-led church. Peele picked up a historical incident that was somehow behind the recent Armada, and presented to his audience Moors and Portuguese among its characters. Peele remoulded his material hastily in a form that befits government policies, answers some public questions on Moors, and wins support for the government-endorsed claimant to the Portuguese throne, Don António.

Peele's "representation" of Moors in his play is seen from this angle in this chapter, an outcome of topical political factors, and a construction of them at the same time. This construction is seen as part of a greater picture depicted by the play. Thus, looking at the image of Moors in *Alcazar* in isolation of the whole will result in an incomplete comprehension and false assumptions of which many a critic has been guilty.

Throughout this chapter, we have seen how George Peele composes his play along the lines of government propaganda: supporting the government's causes, promoting its friends and demoting its enemies. Peele's writing of the *Alcazar* displays a scrupulous, though hasty, literary mind at work. Thematic concerns of the play are weaved into several webs and parallels. Friends of the crown are made heroes and enemies are made villains. Peele pays special attention to Sebastian and Stukeley whom he depicts as victims of inexperience and ambition respectively. On a deeper level, Peele's choice of words is also meticulous as he carefully associates and collocates positive and negative epithets with the characters and motifs he wants to promote or demote, hence the title of this chapter.

The next chapter, however, reveals a completely different method followed by the author. In William Percy's *Mahomet and his Heaven*, topical issues are portrayed and the government is criticised in clandestine ways through using Muslim characters and settings.

CHAPTER TWO

REFLECTING THE SELF
IN WILLIAM PERCY'S
MAHOMET AND HIS HEAVEN

Rather some Malady she is, crept new
Furth Pandoraes Bottle, into the world.

1. Introduction

This chapter studies William Percy's *Mahomet and his Heaven* in its cultural, religious and political context. Along the lines of my argument in this work, this study shows how the play's themes, characters and even vocabulary relate to both external factors, present in contemporary England, and personal ideology of the author himself. In the case of William Percy, by external factors I refer to factors featuring in the politics of his country and the fortunes of his family and his Roman Catholic sect; and by personal ideology, I refer to the experiences and beliefs apparent in the life of the author.

The study reveals that in three major areas where the "representation" of Islam could be looked for by critics, topical factors play a key role in determining the shape of what we read in the play. Firstly, in the case of the Muslim magus, Geber, we find reflections of the contemporary tensions surrounding new sciences and their relation to magic, in addition to attempts to brush up the image of Percy's brother, "the Wizard Earl." Secondly, Muslim women in the play, especially Epimenide, suffer from contemporary misogynistic views as well as the heated debate on gynaecocracy. In this sense, Epimenide is more an allegory for Queen Elizabeth than a Muslim woman. Finally, topical references to Christian unity, the advent of King James and the Turkish threat are all strongly present in Percy's appendix-like episode on Muslim reconciliation. The Sunni-Shia schism is used to portray a way forward for the Catholic-Protestant antagonism. Little of Islam thus remains to be seen amid this jungle of topically-relevant material in Percy's *Mahomet and his Heaven*.

However, before moving to the detailed discussion, two introductory parts need to be furnished in order to gain a better understanding of the play. First, being the obscure work it is, it is necessary to give a short summary of the events and character names of the play; and second, as done with *Alcazar*,[1] a brief look at the sources will help us see how much of the content comes from genuine Islamic sources and how much comes from elsewhere. The aim is to see the play's relationship with existing knowledge about Islam and how much of a representation or a construction of Islam it is.

---

[1] Ch1, section 3.3

1.1. Précis

Mahomet and his Heaven, or *Arabia Sitiens* (thirsty Arabia) as one of the alternate titles goes, tells the story of the drought inflicted on Arabia by heaven-dwelling Mahomet due to the spread of sin amongst its people. Enraged by the situation on earth, Mahomet decides to destroy Arabia within twenty-two days. The angels try to dissuade him and he agrees to send two of them to earth in order to investigate the levels of sin there. The two angels, Haroth and Maroth, descend and wander in Arabia disguised as a poet and a musician. They discover that the situation is far worse than they imagined and as they prepare to return to heaven, they meet the Empress of Arabia, the beautiful Epimenide. They fall in love with her at first sight and they beg her to allow them to become her followers and she agrees. As time goes by and as they become desperate for her, they reveal their real identity to her. She asks for a proof which is the prayer they use to ascend to heaven. Upon learning the prayer, she suddenly appears in heaven to a shocked Mahomet and angels. After the two angels follow her, the three are punished by being cast into the moon. A subplot involves Belpheghor, porter of heaven, sending two spirits, Pyr and Whisk, to earth to search for the ultimate example of knavery. The two spirits kidnap a Chiause (Lawyer) and a Dervis (Friar) and take them back to heaven. The Dervis abused his authority over his Meschit (Mosque) and monopolized water supplies in the drought to amass money while the Chiause cuckolded him with his wife Tib. Another subplot involves two "pastors of the desert" seeking Epimenide's love. She asks them to prove their love by stealing a signet and purse from an old Magician, Geber. They do but she does not fulfil her promise. Towards the end of the play, a separate episode includes an encounter between Mahomet and Haly (Ali) which ends in reconciliation and peace.

The question that arises from reading this play is how much of the content comes from genuine Islamic sources and how much comes from elsewhere. Answering tis question shows that very little of the play's content is Islamic and even less is Quranic, a fact that gives credence to the argument of this work that what we see in the play is a construction of contemporary material rather than a representation of information about Islam.

1.2. The play's Islamic content

In the Prologue to the play, the Weather-Woman makes the following claim:

From highest Turret of sheene Empyrye,
Where blaze the gates of burning Porphirye,
A Text out of the Alcoran wee bring you. (Prol. 1–3)

However, there is actually very little in the play that can be traced to
Islamic sources available to Percy at the time. The names of the two angels
Harut and Marut occur only once in the Muslim holy book. In verse 102 of
the second chapter of the Quran, "Al-Baqarah," the names occur as
follows:

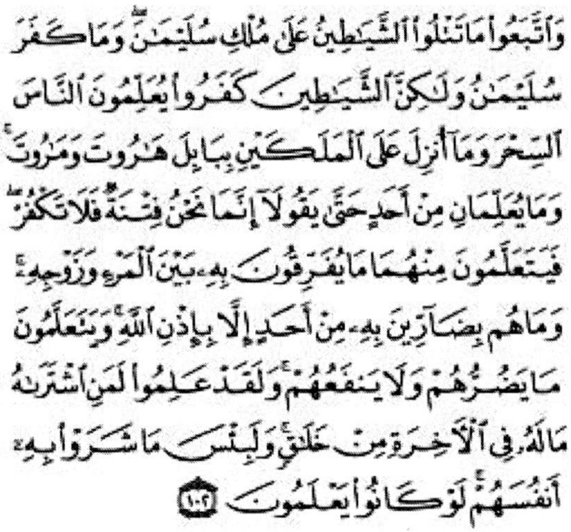

وَٱتَّبَعُوا مَا تَتْلُوا۟ ٱلشَّيَٰطِينُ عَلَىٰ مُلْكِ سُلَيْمَٰنَ ۖ وَمَا كَفَرَ
سُلَيْمَٰنُ وَلَٰكِنَّ ٱلشَّيَٰطِينَ كَفَرُوا۟ يُعَلِّمُونَ ٱلنَّاسَ
ٱلسِّحْرَ وَمَا أُنزِلَ عَلَى ٱلْمَلَكَيْنِ بِبَابِلَ هَٰرُوتَ وَمَٰرُوتَ ۚ
وَمَا يُعَلِّمَانِ مِنْ أَحَدٍ حَتَّىٰ يَقُولَا إِنَّمَا نَحْنُ فِتْنَةٌ فَلَا تَكْفُرْ ۖ
فَيَتَعَلَّمُونَ مِنْهُمَا مَا يُفَرِّقُونَ بِهِۦ بَيْنَ ٱلْمَرْءِ وَزَوْجِهِۦ ۚ
وَمَا هُم بِضَآرِّينَ بِهِۦ مِنْ أَحَدٍ إِلَّا بِإِذْنِ ٱللَّهِ ۚ وَيَتَعَلَّمُونَ
مَا يَضُرُّهُمْ وَلَا يَنفَعُهُمْ ۚ وَلَقَدْ عَلِمُوا۟ لَمَنِ ٱشْتَرَىٰهُ
مَا لَهُۥ فِى ٱلْءَاخِرَةِ مِنْ خَلَٰقٍ ۚ وَلَبِئْسَ مَا شَرَوْا۟ بِهِۦٓ
أَنفُسَهُمْ ۚ لَوْ كَانُوا۟ يَعْلَمُونَ ۝

Fig. 2-1. Quran, Verse 2:102

They followed what the evil ones gave out (falsely) against the power of
Solomon: the blasphemers were, not Solomon, but the evil ones, teaching
men Magic, and such things as came down at Babylon to the angels Harut
and Marut. But neither of these taught anyone (Such things) without
saying: "We are only for trial; so do not blaspheme." They learned from
them the means to sow discord between man and wife. But they could not
thus harm anyone except by Allah's permission. And they learned what
harmed them, not what profited them. And they knew that the buyers of
(magic) would have no share in the happiness of the Hereafter. And vile
was the price for which they did sell their souls, if they but knew! (2:102)

The verse refers to a group from the People of the Book[2] who practised magic. It redeems Solomon from the rumours that he blasphemed and practised magic himself. Harut and Marut are blamed for teaching people magic, but still they would not teach anyone before warning them that magic is blasphemous. Depending on the above verse, the only piece of information we can end up with is that there are two angels named Harut and Marut, and that they taught people the magic arts. This is all the information found in the Quran about Harut and Marut. Dimmock finds a possible source for the story in a work by Riccoldo da Montecroce (*Mahomet* 20). Riccoldo gives more details on the story including how the two angels were sent down to Earth; how they were fascinated by a woman; how they taught her the prayer to ascend to Heaven; and her metamorphosis into the morning star (Venus).

As will be shown below, three of the play's most salient themes are not borrowed from the sources but Percy's own invention. This finding supports the argument of this chapter by confirming that Percy was writing very consciously about the three themes discussed below because they were topical and contemporary rather than Islamic and exotic.

1.3. The Structure of the chapter

The chapter starts with a necessary background to the history of the house of Percy with a special focus on their relationship with the English monarchy. As a member of the nobility, Percy is supposed to give students of his life more information than, say, Peele who was a commoner. Unfortunately, this is not the case and William Percy proves to be highly "enigmatic" as Mark Nicholls describes him ("Enigmatic" 469). Most of what we know of him comes from his involvement in the activities of his brother the Ninth Earl of Northumberland or from notes and dedications by his Oxford friends. In fact, apart from the vital period of literary activity in his life, 1601–1603, there is a feeling that he led a solitary life. He spent the last forty years or so of his life in Oxford. When the Earl's heir was sick and it was feared he might die, a letter mentioned William as follows "Will. Percy . . . lives obscurely in Oxford, and drinks nothing but ale" (qtd. in Hillebrand 399).[3] This self-imposed social seclusion seems to have only begun after the plummet in his family's name and fortunes

---

[2] "The People of the Book" is the term the Quran uses to refer to followers of Christianity and Judaism.

[3] Brenan mentions, without naming an authority, that this was the result of an unrequited love experience (Brenan 207).

because of the Earl's imprisonment on charges of links to the Gunpowder Plot conspirators. Therefore, in this section the life of William will be traced along the lines of his brother's activities and his possible involvement in them. After all, what matters most to this study is William Percy's life up until 1603, when he wrote *The Faery Pastorall*, which was possibly played before James I.

As noted above, three main areas receive discussion in this chapter. After the biographical section on the Percys, which notes the mystical side of Henry Percy's life, a special part is dedicated to study the link between William Percy's magus, Geber, and the Wizard Earl. The central idea of this section is the positive image of the magus in the play, and the argument is that Percy wanted to redeem his brother from negative concepts associated with magic. The Earl's nickname is questioned in an attempt to probe its relevance and aptness as an epithet describing his life and interests. The contemporary meanings of "magic" are also discussed with a special focus on the confusion between science and magic. This confusion is also relevant to the concept of the hermetic tradition and its role in Renaissance Europe and contemporary views on science and knowledge, especially the philosophy of humanism and the return of the golden age through the practice of magic. Defending magic was the topic of many contemporary works, and the section "The Earl's circle" notes how member of this group were engaged in similar arguments, which in a way justifies the assumption that William Percy could be trying to make a similar statement. Geber also bears remarkable points of resemblance to Marlowe's creation in *Doctor Faustus*. Similarities and differences are studied in a special section that shows what contemporary ideas Percy adopted, modified or discarded. Finally comes a textual study of the play and its treatment of the magus.

The second major area in which topical issues and Percy's background feature prominently is his treatment of female characters, especially Epimenide. Two questions that pose before us as we read the play are (i) how much did Percy know about Muslim women and (ii) how was this reflected into his play. As a special section tries to establish, Percy's women share very little, if anything, with contemporary conceptions, and even imaginings, about Muslim women. The remaining parts try to demonstrate how the heroine of the play shares a lot of ground with Queen Elizabeth, then move on to link the characterization of Epimenide with contemporary views on women and female rule, or gynaecocracy. A short section sheds light on minor female characters in the play. The aim of the part on women is to show how little of the Muslim woman is present in *Mahomet and his Heaven* and how much of contemporary debates on women in general is present. The outcome strongly suggests that women in the play are treated more in terms of satire and allegory than anything else.

The reconciliatory episode at the end of the play receives the last dedicated section in this study. The background to the parallelism used by Percy to allegorize his call for peace is explored first with the aim of pinpointing Percy's unique use of the Muslim schism for a peaceful purpose. It is necessary, then, to show how Percy's peaceful overture comes within a contemporary ambience which prevailed near the end of Elizabeth's reign especially among English Catholics. The trend saw coexistence as the only viable way forward especially with the advent of James VI of Scotland. The latter's background in ecumenical projects is explored to support the idea that the new monarch was, at least at the time, sincere in his promises of tolerance made to Northumberland in private correspondence. James was a true proponent of conciliar Christian unity and a true hater of the Turk, two themes which are conspicuous in this episode of *Mahomet*. In a shocking final revelation, Percy reveals his Mahomet, who has so far been portrayed in a favourable manner, as the antichrist. This example of anagnorisis makes a strong statement as to who the real enemy of Christendom should be, thus stressing the message of unity adopted by Percy in this final episode.

The chapter conclusion reiterates the findings of the sections preceding it stressing their importance in advancing the argument of this work. Percy's work may claim to be a story from the Quran and critics may rummage it in search of the "representation" of Islam, but the case is nothing more than topical concerns given Islamic cover, or England in Islamic clothing as stated elsewhere.

2. The Percys and the crown

William Percy belongs to a noble family that played major roles in English history throughout medieval and early modern times. Although their power has especially been manifest in the north of England, the Earls of Northumberland were also influential in London, though this influence waned and almost disappeared toward the end of the sixteenth and start of the seventeenth centuries. In addition to the life of the writer of the play himself, most relevant to our study here are the lives and activities of the Eighth and Ninth Earls, William Percy's father and brother respectively, especially their relationship with the Queen and their position as far as the Catholic-Protestant question is concerned. Because William Percy led a life that was relatively in the shadows for an Elizabethan noble, I will be trying to gain better knowledge of the circumstance of his life and works from the lives of his father and brother.

This part tries to map, as far as possible, the complex relationship between the House of Percy and the English monarchy during this period, William Percy's life until 1603, against the political and religious background. The aim is to get a better understanding of the way the circumstances surrounding William Percy's production of *Mahomet and his Heaven* affected his general views on religion and politics and how they were reflected in this work. The Catholic tendencies of the Percys are important to highlight here because they were denied, and critics and historians almost agree that this was more political disguise than Protestant belief (Flynn 85).

2.1. The Eighth Earl

Under the reign of Elizabeth I, Henry Percy Eighth Earl of Northumberland (c.1532–1585) died while imprisoned in the Tower in 1585, an incident that had great repercussions on the lives of his sons, Lord Henry and William in particular. Before his arrest and death, Northumberland's relationship with the court had been a fluctuating relationship mainly because of doubts on behalf of the Privy Council towards his attachment to the old faith. For example, while still sheriff of Northumberland (before his accession), Henry made a move that endeared him to authorities. When his brother Thomas Percy Seventh Earl of Northumberland led an uprising of the Catholic northern earls, known as the Northern Rebellion of 1569–1570 (Fletcher and MacCulloch 168), Henry Percy remained loyal to Elizabeth during this tumultuous time and won her favour (Levin "ODNB"). He became the Queen's servant and he conformed to Anglicanism with apparent enthusiasm but the privy councillors, Cecil and Sadler, never trusted him, as they saw his compliance as mere politics (Flynn 85).

Even during the rebellion, he was suspected of not favouring "her majesties proceedings in the cause of religion" (Flynn 88). This tendency materialized shortly after that, in 1571, when Henry Percy was involved in a plot to free the Catholic Mary Stuart from her prison in Tutbury, for which he was arrested on suspicion of treason (Flynn 91). Upon begging for mercy, he was released (Levin "ODNB"). Then, in another reversal of fortune, he received inexplicable attention from the Queen. Flynn quotes a contemporary source that noted this attention:

> In all exercises of recreation used by her Maiestie the Earl was alwayes called to be one, and whensoever her Maistie shewed her selfe abroade in

publique, she gave to him the honour of the best and highest services about her person, more often then to all the noble men of her Court. (Flynn 93)

However, other reports indicate that later, the Queen hated Northumberland and considered him as the greatest threat to her kingdom (Flynn 96 & 213 n.44). This inconstancy in dealing with the father was perhaps one source for William Percy's views on Elizabeth as a fickle person.[4] Elizabeth was perhaps aware that Northumberland kept on playing the dangerous Catholic card and he associated himself with a group of Catholic sympathizers in Court who considered Mary Stuart for succession and supported the marriage of Elizabeth to François de Valois, Duke of Anjou. Both of these issues carried strong Catholic connotations (Flynn 93-94; Levin "ODNB").

Meanwhile, on the family side of his life, the Eighth Earl was keen on his sons' education and he sent three or four of them, Henry and William for sure, to Paris to learn French, but still doubts were cast that he sent them to learn Catholicism (Flynn 95). They were under the custody of Charles Paget, a Catholic conspirator who was involved in many plots, including assassination of the Queen and invasion of England (Holmes "ODNB"). Upon learning this, Northumberland's enemies at court raised an outcry against him and the Queen herself "urged their return to England" (Hillebrand 392). Thus, despite the objections of his Catholic advisors, the Earl agreed to have his younger sons return to England, while his heir Henry most probably continued his studies in Paris (Brenan 36-37; Hillebrand 392). William and his brothers thus became political pawns in the religious game of their time too early in their lives.

2.2. Henry and William in France

It was in France that young Henry's early interest in sciences and the occult started. After an early interest in trivial pursuits, Lord Henry dedicated his time to history, alchemy and astrology (Brenan 35). He even bought himself a "speculative glass" or a crystal globe used for reading the future (De Fonblanque 187). This pursuit of strange and interesting knowledge became a trademark for Henry and dominated his future reputation, almost overshadowing his political and military career. But Henry's presence in France was not innocent after all and there were rumours that the Eighth Earl used his communications with his sons to get in touch with people on the continent (Flynn 95). Henry was himself

---

[4] See section 5 below.

involved in political intrigue and his letters show that he was in touch with agents in the French Court and was meeting with Anjou, Elizabeth's Catholic suitor (Flynn 96). This tendency of getting in touch with a prospective royal of the realm comes to surface more importantly later in Henry's life when he enters into correspondence with James VI of Scotland before his succession.[5] It also indicates an early political awareness on behalf of the man who is often thought of as a reclusive wizard.

The Eighth Earl's position with the government became worse as a result of covering up a secret visit by Charles Paget to England in September 1583 which was thought to be a preparation for an invasion. Convinced of Northumberland's involvement in the issue, the government placed him under house arrest in December 1583, then sent him to the Tower in January 1584 as "Sir Francis Walsingham was convinced that he was a Catholic" (Levin "ODNB"). Gerald Brenan argues that it was Northumberland's enemies in court who pushed forward his prosecution "with a persistent malevolence" (22). Brenan also presents a number of pieces of evidence to prove the Earl's innocence with regard to this particular plot. Northumberland "tacitly" admitted reverting to the old faith and he did not conceal support for the imprisoned Mary, but he categorically denied any part in a treasonous plot. Rather, he was so sure of his innocence that he demanded a full investigation and refused all offers of compromise, something that "speak[s] volumes in his favour" (Brenan 22-23). The government never prosecuted him for treason and they "did not even dare to accord him the poor privilege of a secret inquiry" (Brenan 23).

2.3. Father's death

Events took a dramatic turn in June 1585, when the Earl was found shot in his cell and the government announced that it was suicide. The event provoked considerable political and public attention. An anonymous contemporary pamphlet, *A True and Summarie Report of the Declaration of some part of the earle of Northumberland's treasons*, was published containing a lot of current comments on the issue (Burns 12). Brenan mentions no less than four theories about the Earl's death each claiming to be telling the truth. These theories came from these sources: the "puritan government" who adopted a treason and suicide theory; "moderate Protestants" who accepted suicide but refused treason; "persons of note"

---

[5] See section 6.3 below.

like Ralegh accused Northumberland's personal foe Hatton of murder; and finally "the Catholic and Marian faction" accused the Queen herself of perpetrating the crime (Brenan 24). In their defence, the government noted that it was in their interest to let the law take its course and convict Northumberland of treason and thus be able to obtain attainder of his property, the counterargument questioned the ability of a prisoner in the tower to obtain a pistol (Burns 17). There is no definite source on the number of bullets which were found in his body (which was buried hurriedly the next day) but some claimed that three shots were found and this rules out suicide (Holmes "Paget, Charles (c.1546–1612)"). Thus, the question was never satisfactorily resolved.

After the Earl's death, young William was sent to France to deliver the news to the new Earl his brother. He also gave Henry an account "of the inquest and of the many highly suspicious circumstances connected with the death of his unhappy parent" (Brenan 36). From the point of view of the Earl's sons, the question was not as puzzling as others saw it. Historians and critics agree that the sons of the Eighth Earl were sure of foul play in their father's death (Brenan 36; De Fonblanque 183; Hillebrand 392). In fact, Henry is reported to have been so angered by the "murder" that he got involved in a plan to invade England. De Fonblanque reports a "recorded reference" to the event of the father's death in a correspondence between Henry and Sir George Carew. The latter wrote: "the matter we last spoke of touched me so nearly that upon weighing the Effects, and with the view *to satisfy my present Discontent*, no way is so convenient as the first Resolution." In reply, Henry Percy wrote in June 1587: "You need not fear that my Mind will alter; my Resolutions once determined are not so quickly revoked" (qtd. in De Fonblanque 183-4, italics in original). The present discontent, De Fonblanque argues, is a reference to the death of the father.

A letter by spy Thomas Rogers to Walsingham, sent in August 1585, stated that the Earl and his brother William were implicated with the "Duc de Guise" in the preparation of a great naval and military expedition against England, with the dual object of placing Mary Stuart upon the throne and avenging the supposed murder in the Tower (Brenan 37). The young Earl's allegiance to the crown's religion is also reported to have suffered a major blow as a result of the incident. According to Brenan, "a rumour spread abroad, and was duly conveyed to England, that he had embraced the Catholic Church, and forsworn all allegiance to Elizabeth" (Brenan 36). Matthew Dimmock dismisses this as lacking truth (*Mahomet* 13) but Edward Barrington De Fonblanque makes an important point: "however little truth there may have been in such rumours, there is no doubt that for some years after his accession apprehensions were very generally entertained as to the sympathies of the young earl with the party in whose cause his father and uncle had died" (De Fonblanque 183). Henry Percy's discontent was not a temporary feeling generated by the loss of a dear person. Five years after the death of the Eighth Earl, Burghley's foreign spies wrote: "The present Earl of Northumberland, *who is in discontent about his father's death*, may be seduced to the See of Rome" (qtd. in De Fonblanque 184, italics in original).

2.4. Back in England

Whatever sentiments he might have had against those in power, the Percy heir asked permission to return to England and was granted it early in 1586. He resided in the family residence in Blackfriars and set up his famous library and started his political career (Brenan 39). The first serious test for his patriotism and loyalty came two years later with the attack of the Spanish Armada. Nicholls casts doubt on the Earl's participation in the war effort claiming that the only evidence is from a 1688 work by William Camden, but there is more evidence that confirms this. Apart from De Fonblanque's assertion that Henry "generously supported the war effort against the Armada" (193-94), the Calendar of State Papers mentions Northumberland's name as "master of the horse," his name being listed only third among names of leaders (*Calendar of State Papers, Domestic, Elizabeth, 1598-1601* 282). It was customary for nobles to take part in financing state wars, but when a Percy, often mistrusted for Catholic inclinations, takes a major role in defending the Protestant nation against Catholic Spain, this indicates either a high level of political shrewdness or a true belief in the superiority of national security over religious difference. Some might think that Percy was obliged to take part in order to clear himself from suspicion, but this does not justify the "generosity" and the personal involvement in action which he displayed in this matter. Our playwright William is thought to have also taken up arms personally and fought against the Armada. This suggestion is made by critics who read the vivid description he makes of events in the Armada in his play *Cuck-queanes and Cuckolds Errants* (Burns 19; Fenn 6).

This move must have had a very positive effect on the government's view towards Northumberland, and indeed a change in the relationship between the two parties, the Percys and government, seemed to have been initiated by this action. Henry Percy played on the Queen's eagerness to add to her coffers and he kept on frequently presenting her with costly gifts. As a result he started to regain the favour his father once enjoyed. In 1591 he was restored to the governorship of the strategic Tynemouth Castle and in April 1593 he was installed a knight of the Garter "with due pomp and ceremony" (Brenan 46). None other than our friend, George Peele, "seeking a patron," wrote a series of poems entitled *The Honour of the Garter* in which he praised Northumberland thus:

> Young Northumberland,
> Mounted on Fortune's wheel by Virtue's aim,
> Become thy badge, as it becometh thee:
> That Europes eyes thy worthinesse may see. (377–380)

Henry Percy, a man who knew his literature as much as his sciences, rewarded Peele with the respectable sum of £3 (Brenan 47) for what proved to be "the noblest of [Peele's] court poems" (Horne 173). The poem presents significant points for discussion and will be returned to below.[6]

Favour at court brought up a sensitive subject for Northumberland. His Catholic friends and allies suggested to him that he should offer his hand in marriage to Lady Arabella (Arbella) Stuart, who was second in line to the throne after James VI of Scotland. A contemporary pamphlet listed 12 eligible claimants to the crown starting from James VI of Scotland and Lady Arabella to Percy himself in eighth place (De Fonblanque 203).[7] Such an "illustrious union" would have had considerable consequences on the question of royal succession. Elizabeth was surely against any Catholic inclinations in an heir and both Henry and Arabella were not free from them. Therefore, and perhaps due to other reasons, the Queen is reported to have looked unfavourably on the idea of this marriage (Brenan 49). Brenan notes that this suggestion was harmful to Northumberland and might have been actually broached by his adversaries because of the Queen's sensitivity towards the issue of succession. Thus, the suggested marriage remained merely an idea opposed by the Queen. Shortly after, "Arabella Stuart was placed under close restraint, while the Queen hastened to procure for Northumberland a wife less liable to involve him

---

[6] See section 4.2 below.

[7] Brenan mentions an interesting allegation made by Northumberland's more ardent supporters who claimed that Edmund Earl of Lancaster was actually the elder, not younger, brother of Edward I which meant that both the Tudors and the Stuarts had no right to rule and after ruling out the Spanish and Portuguese royals and the outlawed Earl of Westmoreland, Henry Percy became the "*de jure*" sovereign of England (Brenan 49).

in dangerous designs" (Brenan 49). Northumberland was married in 1594 to Lady Dorothy Perrott, widow of Sir Thomas Perrott, and sister of Robert Devereux, the famous Earl of Essex.

Links with the Earl of Essex had other, more perilous, dimensions for the Percys. The charismatic young man had many admirers in England at the time including three of Northumberland's brothers, Charles, Josceline and Richard, who served under Essex in his Ireland campaign in 1599. Essex failed in Ireland and his failure was seen as a result of many factors most of which related to him personally, like his unwise military decisions and his insubordination. In addition to this, he had enemies at court, like Burghley, who worked against him. As a result, he fell from royal favour and was constrained to his house. After more political complications, Essex decided to take up arms and he entered London with 300 armed followers on February 8th 1601 (Hammer "ODNB"). Part of the plan was to gain public support from Londoners whom he thought favoured him. Charles and Josceline, who had joined Essex, were among those who hired actors in London to play Shakespeare's *Richard II* in a bid to raise the public to support Essex's half-baked plan (Fenn 9-10). The weak king in *Richard II* was meant to become identifiable with Elizabeth and thus Essex would be seen as Bolingbroke who will save England from a weak monarchy (Clegg 60–61). The incident was a chance for the Ninth Earl to shine. He supported the Queen vigorously and was a major figure in her faction (Fenn 9-10). Upon their arrest, the two Percys were meant for the scaffold like Essex their leader. But their brother's wise stance and the intercession he and others made, including Raleigh, led to their release in May of that same year with a lenient payment of £500 (Brenan 67).

2.5. Northumberland and James VI

Northumberland's status in court at this stage must have been better than ever and with Elizabeth looking nearer to her death, he had to play a role in the issue of succession. De Fonblanque describes him as patriotic and "a true lover of his country," who "could not contemplate without dismay the prospect of a disputed succession, or the throne falling vacant" (225). As eyes began to look towards Scotland for the next monarch, Henry Percy had a disapproving attitude towards James VI of Scotland as a candidate. There are records of him falling out with his wife, who favoured James, over this issue (De Fonblanque 224). However, the Earl did not have a static opinion in this regard for he started to look into the person of the new candidate more thoroughly by opening a line of correspondence with him. The prevalent theme of the correspondence was

Northumberland's emphasis on religious tolerance and James's confirmation of his openness to Christian unity. In this view, William Percy's play, written around the time the letters were being exchanged, with a stress on unity and integration between different sects, cannot be properly understood without placing it into a perspective of contemporary religion and politics.

Northumberland changed his view towards James VI and this change could be traced to the place of his early education, France. The mainly Catholic European neighbour had a new king, Henry IV, in 1589. After his ascension, Henry enacted a proposal for religious reform in the kingdom named the Edict of Nantes on 30 April 1598. Himself an ex-Huguenot who converted to Catholicism only to secure the throne, Henry IV gave the Protestant Huguenots full civil rights including admission into public office and into colleges and universities (Alcock 6). Considered one of the earliest examples of secularism and religious tolerance, the Edict of Nantes was very likely to inspire a person like the Earl of Northumberland to think of similar steps in his homeland. The epistolography between the Earl and James VI supports this view and sheds light on an important side of Percy's religio-political principles which were based on openness, promoting tolerance and total disregard for needless adulation and flattery.

Northumberland's main objection to James's accession was his fear of religious intolerance. De Fonblanque notes how the Earl himself listed the reasons that made the English become apprehensive about the issue. In addition to fear of intolerance, he mentions fears "that his Council should be too largely composed of his own countrymen" as well as "national prejudice against the Scots" (251). Thus, the Earl decided to be open about his reservations and discuss them with the heir apparent but he was wise enough to distance himself from Catholicism. In a letter from James's secretary sent to Cecil, Northumberland is described as follows:

> He says not that he is a Catholick himself, but that sundry of his retinue and dependants hath oares in their boat; and that they are not able to resolve in any course into the whiche he shall not be made acquainted. (qtd. in Brenan 84-85)

This declaration in the Earl's letters to James was not a political move to avoid trouble. Gerald Brenan argues that the Earl was genuinely not a "Romanist" and that historians who mistook him for one were in error because they assumed that from his defence of Catholics and calls for tolerance (Brenan 78).

Upon Percy's first offers of unconditional support if "toleration for the Catholics" was part of the King's new policy, James "replied in a conciliatory manner and promised abundant favour to all, Catholic or Protestant, who embraced his cause" (Brenan 79). James made further promises of fairer treatment for the Catholics in his letters, and Percy and English Catholics had many reasons to believe him including his mother's devotion and suffering for Catholicism and his desire to have better relations with Catholic Spain (De Fonblanque 250-51). In a hint that reveals the influence of the developments in France on the Earl's views, he wrote in a letter to James that "It were a pity to lose a good Kingdom for not tolerating a mass in a corner" (qtd. in Brenan 81). Northumberland wanted James to take example from his French counterpart, who proclaimed upon converting to Catholicism: *Paris vaut bien une messe* (Paris is well worth a Mass) (N. Davies 506). On the very day of Elizabeth's death, James sent a letter to Northumberland stating:

> As for the Catholics, I will neither persecute any that will be quiet and give but an outward obedience to the law, neither will I spare to advance any of them that will by good service worthily deserve it. (qtd. in Lockyer 269)

On 25 July 1603, James was crowned king of England and the Jacobean era started. Although generally speaking James kept his promises of toleration, the Percys in particular did not prosper under his reign. Henry Percy, who became a privy councillor for James, soon fell out of favour because of his cousin's involvement in the Gunpowder Plot (1605). Northumberland was imprisoned in the tower between 1606 and 1621 which was a harsh sentence by all measure as he had no relation to the plot except that Thomas Percy was previously used by Northumberland as a messenger in his correspondence with James VI (Nicholls "ODNB").

2.6. William Percy

Our playwright was always somewhere around these important events in the history of his family and his country. Although he does not appear in the official records, there is circumstantial evidence that he was involved in a lot of his family's political affairs (Kincaid 14). Percy's year of birth is not certain. Reavley Gair sets it at 1574, Dodds argues for 1573, and Dimmock adopts Nicholls' date of 1570 (Gair; Dimmock *Mahomet* 13; Dodds "A Forrest Tragaedye" 246). Whichever the actual year is, William could not have been more than 15 years old when he had to deliver the news of his father's death to Henry in France. Thus, our playwright was immaturely dragged into a complicated and sinister web of Catholic-Protestant intrigue which involved the death of his father. It is hard to overemphasize the importance of this traumatic incident on the psychology of our playwright especially at such a young age. As mentioned above, rumours were spread about the two brothers' preparation for revenge and war, but this cannot be verified and William soon returned to England with his brother.

Next we hear of William Percy is his matriculation from Gloucester Hall, Oxford in June 1589. Gloucester Hall was described as a "hotbed of popery" (Hillebrand 393). Percy studied under Dr John Case, "the great tutor for Roman Catholic scholars" (Gair) but he never graduated from Oxford for reasons unknown. Kincaid argues that although it is possible that Percy was not studious enough,[8] there is the possibility that this action required the swearing of an oath accepting the Queen as supreme head of church, and Percy did not want to take such an oath (Kincaid 24). Nevertheless, Percy lived between Oxford and London most of his life and he was known to have a circle of literati including Barnabe Barnes (1571–1609) who dedicated two of his works to "M. William Percy, Esquier, his deerest friend" (Hillebrand 394). Between 1593 and 1596, William seems to have had some financial and personal troubles as he was imprisoned for debt one time. He was also imprisoned shortly on suspicions of murder due to a duel he fought in 1596 (Burns 25–6). Dimmock links Percy's stays in London to the fortunes of his family and his brother with whom he seems to have shared a very close relationship (*Mahomet* 15). One of the Earl's few literary works is a dissertation "On Love and Learning" (1604) which, G. R. Batho argues, is dedicated to his brother William (Batho 249). Between 1596 and 1601, the year *Mahomet and his Heaven* was written, Percy spent most of his time in Oxford (Burns 26).

To conclude, certain issues stand out from Percy's life and are related to our play. First, we can sense Percy's distress at a young age at the death of his father which, very possibly, left a deep impact on his feelings towards the government and perhaps the Queen, who is ridiculed through his character Epimenide. Second, we note his Catholic affiliations even outside his family affairs, as in the places where he studied and the people who taught him. Adopting and promoting a Catholic view is another issue that will come up in the discussion of 'schism and unity' below. Finally, the good terms Percy held with his brother the Earl are vital in understanding the character of Geber who has been mistaken by Dimmock as a comic representation of the Earl (Dimmock *Mahomet* 40).

This summary of William Percy's life shows that it was mostly a shadowy and inactive one. However, as Hillebrand argues, something

---

[8] Kincaid notes that "Percy's failure to graduate is not unusual: University records show that in 1589—the year of Percy's matriculation—of 264 students who had matriculated, 156 did not graduate" (24).

must have happened between 1601 and 1603 as William Percy suddenly became interested in play writing and wrote five plays. This prolific period of activity is the subject of the next section on Percy's works.

3. Percy's other works

Against the complicated background of politics and religion discussed above comes the moment of our play. For William Percy wrote five of his six plays in the short period of time around James I's coronation 1601–1603. This sudden literary activity, which was never repeated again in Percy's life, calls some attention, and as Harold Hillebrand notes "there must be a cause" (397). Historians and critics studying Percy's life and works cast doubt over his involvement in his family's political life after he went to Oxford (see for example Brenan 207–8), but what seems most probable is that, though William was not personally involved in the events, his penchant for literature and the arts was utilised during this remarkable period. Robert Denzel Fenn points out the important notion that "if [William] took any … part in the political machinations of his family, he did so with his pen" (Fenn 1). Hillebrand hypothesizes that the five plays written in this period were all written to be used in entertainments given by his brother the Earl in an attempt to secure support for James's accession (Hillebrand 398). Fenn proposes a subtle link between Percy's plays and Shakespeare's *Richard II*: "perhaps the Earl's imagination was sparked by his younger brothers' treasonous use of dramatic performance during the Essex rebellion" (10). Thus, though not a certainty, the best standing explanation of Percy's writing of his plays is the activity in the house of Percy at the start of the new century, mainly caused by James's prospects and Essex's fall.[9]

In this part, I attempt to shed some light on the presence of political motifs in Percy's other works with a special focus on the Essex rebellion and King James's advent to England. Of course, these aspects will be given a full discussion in our play *Mahomet and his Heaven*. The aim is to give more evidence to the conclusions reached in the discussion of *Mahomet* about Percy's topically-sensitive approach to playwriting especially in the case of current affairs of his family. This section thus supports the idea that Percy was keen on satisfying the audience for whom he wrote his plays and that it may well have been the case that he got instructions from his brother on the composition of these plays. In the following discussion, I focus on two of Percy's plays in which topical

---

[9] See section 6.2.

issues present in *Mahomet and his Heaven* are particularly salient. I also review some critical opinions on the other plays by Percy and the presence of relevant material in them.

3.1. *The Aphrodysiall* or *Sea Feast*, 1602

This is one of two plays by Percy which have never been published in books or edited in dissertations.[10] As the title suggests, the play is set in the sea. It includes a main plot with three subplots which are loosely intertwined. The main plot is about a feast (called Aphrodysial) which is held by King Oceanus once every year in honour of Cytheræa. In this visit by Cytheræa to the court of Oceanus, she is given the chance to rule for a day after which she returns the crown to Oceanus and ascends back to heaven (Dodds "Aphrodysial 1" 237). Another theme is the story of a "Balene" or Leviathan that perplexes a group of fishermen by its speech and prophesying and turns out to be a boy inside the whale. Two characters, Arion and Talus, are enamoured of Thetis (Tethys more accurately) who sets them a quest to recover her lost bracelet. The classical lovers Hero and Leander are also present in the underwater plot as Oceanus tries to win Hero from Leander. Another subplot is possibly taken from Shakespeare's *The Merry Wives of Windsor* (Dodds "Aphrodysial 1" 237). It involves Vulcan sending two love letters to Humida and Arida and the two letters getting mixed up.

The play seems to have been written for a specific occasion, hence quite a few themes and scenes bear resemblances to contemporary events and persons. Madeline Dodds links the play's composition date with the christening of the Ninth Earl's first son. Algernon Percy was christened on 13th or 14th October 1602 (Drake; Dodds "Aphrodysial 1" 237). Dodds quotes a letter by John Chamberlain in which he mentions the christening noting the fact that "the Queen by the Lady Marquise [of Northampton] her deputie, being godmother, and the Lord Treasurer [Lord Buckhurst] and Lord Admirall [the Earl of Nottingham] godfathers" (qtd. in Dodds "Aphrodysial 1" 237). The play courts the favour of two attendants by inserting references to their positions and occupations. It also includes hints about the Wizard Earl's interests in the supernatural.

As the discussion of *Mahomet and his Heaven* below will show, Percy did not have a positive opinion towards Queen Elizabeth. His views are based on misogynist ideas against gynaecocracy. In sixteenth century England, women's rule was at best viewed as a digression from the norm

---

[10] The other one is *Necromantes* or *the Two Supposed Heads*, 1632.

of male authority, which meant that the reigns of Mary and Elizabeth were considered temporary periods after which the rule must return to the ideal ruler: a king. In *The Aphrodysiall*, the character of Cytheræa is used as an allegory for female rule and its transitory nature. In Act V scene iii, a nymph "invests Cytheræa empress of the seas and crowns her with the crown of blue and white seaweed" (Dodds "Aphrodysial 2" 260). The patronising tone of the words addressed to Cytheræa upon her crowning is indicative of patriarchal attitudes towards gynaecocracy:[11]

> Nymph.   Lady, you about to receive the crown,
> If good you do, may it, with Cressies, bloome
> But if you do rule your people Amisse
> Turn may his sedges to Adders that hisse,
> God keepe you fro [sic] Ruth, God keepe you fro kere
> So for the while live you our water Queene
> Whiles with this song I do conclude my theame.   (W. Percy)[12]

These lines indicate how a woman's rule, basically temporary as the plot suggests, is bound by expectations of performance. The female ruler is also suspected of being prone to mistakes, hence "ruth" in the sense of remorse in this context. After a short reign, Cytheræa resigns the throne and leaves the stage in a touching final speech:

> Cyth.   Much good doe it you, noble Lords, I wish.
>   Now my discharge, this day longs to me but
>   Now I do see, I have performed each
>   According to the equity of each
>   Hard were the cases, and many were the smiles,
>   The Tumults rang, so were the Accidents,
>   Mighty the wonder and perplexity,
>   But now I find my knowledge at an end
>   And to owners must resign my Roome,
>   As in rightfull equitie it is sweete
>   Therefore, loe, Lordes, you all, with Love I greete
>   Withall resign the kingdome where tis meete.
>   The Direction:
> Here she rose with the rest, The Imperiall ghirland taken from her and
> hurled up the crue [crew]
> Cyth. Is my ship come; I think it be late
> Thet. Madame. I come, to give you humble thanks

---

[11] See Fig. 2-2
[12] Unpublished manuscript, The Archives of the Duke of Northumberland at Alnwick Castle: DNP: MS 509

> For the speciall favour you have done mee.
> Cyth. Pardon mee, Lady, if vigrous I have been,
>> A Judge may never discharge well his dewty,
>> Unless, of Affection, he do despoyse [dispose] him,
>> More, where Cythereas Breast hath beene ever
>> Ope to Lenitye, the case required her
>> To invest the marble heart of Jonu,
>> But now I must to heaven, the day grows old,
>> Besyde, frome hence, it is a good way up.
>> My noble Lords, I bid you all farewell,
>> The bountious Gods reward your merits well.

In the year 1602, when the play was written, Elizabeth's legacy was on the mind of everyone who had the slightest interest in politics. The sixty-nine year old Queen was already sick and she "aged visibly after the Essex rebellion and his subsequent execution" [Levin *Reign* 21]. Despite the message of male superiority and support of androcracy over gynaecocracy, Percy still tries to put his audience in a pensive and appreciative mood towards Elizabeth's reign. This is especially important as James's succession by this time was almost certain and because the Earl of Northumberland was already in contact with the conciliatory James who promised a new start without disrespecting his predecessor. Thus, lines like "Hard were the cases, and many were the smiles" are meant to cast an affectionate look toward a past that is about to leave, and at the same time look forward to a new start. Some of Queen Elizabeth's attributes are praised in this excerpt like her "Breast" being "ever Ope to Lenitye" despite having to be "vigrous" at times.

Another salient theme in the play is the maritime motif designed to meet the interests of the Lord Admiral. Not only did Percy set his play at sea, but he also made a collage of diverse classical characters and figures related to sea or water. Thus, he brought Oceanus (Greek god of the ocean), Proteus (his son, another sea deity), Glauce, Humida and Arida (three nymphs of the sea) as well as a number of fishermen and the classical lovers Hero and Leander who drowned in the sea (see respective entries in Dixon-Kennedy).

Another person whose interests become motifs in the play is the Earl himself. As is expounded below, Northumberland was nicknamed the Wizard Earl due to his general love for knowledge, languages, sciences and the supernatural. The play presents a weird character named the Balene, or Leviathan. The fishermen are puzzled by the whale's actions. Not only does this whale speak, but it does so in several tongues "he roareth Latin, Hebrewe, Greake, Caldee, Italian, French, Spanish, German, Dutch, Welsh to boote" (qtd. in Dodds "Aphrodysial 2" 239). The men complain to Proteus that he also frightens them by "prophesying the future and telling their fortunes" (Dodds "Aphrodysial 2" 239).

> Rud Will tell you what the money is in thy purse, Proteus
> Prot. A bad propertie by my Faith (Percy, *Aphrodysial*)

As mentioned in the biographical section above, the Earl possessed a crystal ball which he used to read the future "with the ease of a Nostradamus" (Brenan 35). One of the languages listed by the fishermen is "Caldee" which was interestingly associated with magic. Sir Walter Raleigh associated the Chaldean with magic in his *History of the World*: "amongst the *Babylonians* they [magi] were differenced by the name of *Chaldaeans*" (Raleigh 201).

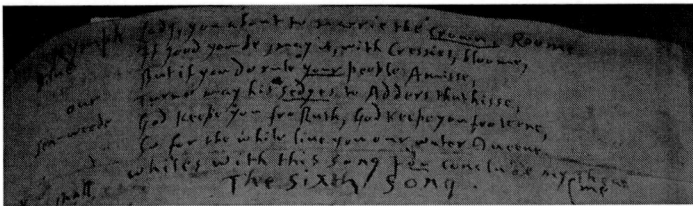

Fig. 2-2. Cytheræa's coronation, Alnwick MS509

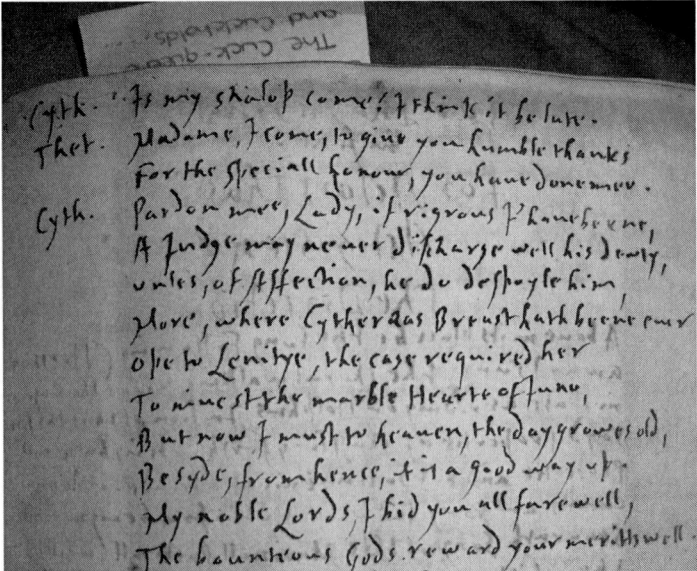

Fig. 2-3. Cytheræa's abdication, Alnwick MS509

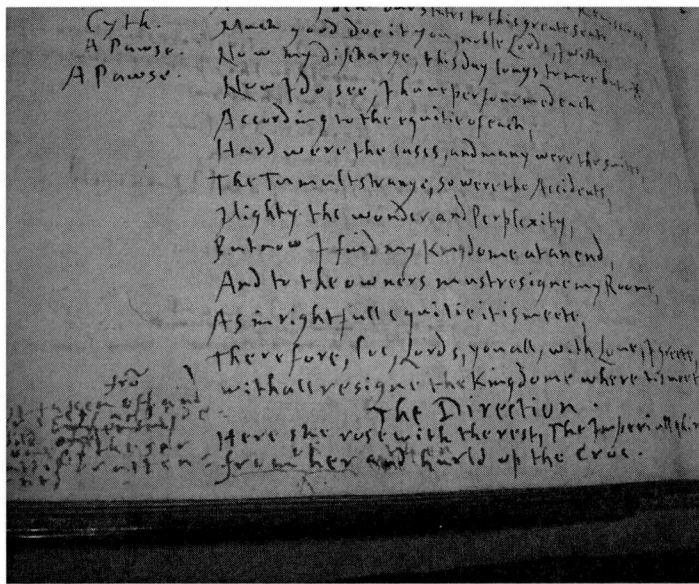

Fig. 2-4. Cytheræa's abdication continued, Alnwick MS509

3.2. *The Faery Pastorall* or *the Forest of Elves*, 1603

A critical edition of *The Faery Pastorall* was completed by Robert Denzel Fenn in 1997 as a doctoral thesis in the University of British Columbia. The play takes place in a forest and the participants are classic deities and hunters. Dodds wittily notes that the play is not a proper "pastoral" but a "venatoral," if such a word existed ("William Percy and James I" 13). The main plot line of the play involves Oberon king of the fairies deposing Hypsiphyle princess of elves from her position as keeper of Elvida forest due to negligence. As she protests, Orion agrees to enter a hunting contest with her, the loser of which shall yield to the other. In the end, the couple get married. Other subplots run along the play in which a number of comic characters contribute to the action.

Madeline Dodds argues convincingly that the words "Your Maiesty," used in the prologue, address James I who was on a visit to Henry Percy's Syon House on 8 June 1603 ("William Percy and James I" 13). In his critical edition of the play, Fenn agrees with Dodds and adds supporting thematic elements that suggest the presence of King James in the audience, or at least suggest Percy having his presence in mind as he wrote for a performance of the play is, again, not a certainty (Fenn 29-36). The themes and motifs in *The Faery Pastorall* relating to *Mahomet and his Heaven* include praising androcracy over gynaecocracy, misogyny as well as the proposed relationship between peers of the realm and the new king.

The play's opening scene displays how the princess of the elves is asked to leave office as gamekeeper and, as in the restoration scene in *Aphrodysiall* discussed above, female rule is described as incompetent and a deviation from the norm. Dodds saw in the scene "a cautious compliment to James on succeeding Elizabeth" ("William Percy and James I" 14). In another article, Dodds also notes the general theme in the play that "a country should be ruled by a man and not by a woman" (Dodds "The Financial Affairs" 99).

At the beginning of the hunting contest, Hypsiphyle takes off her imperial garland and "*hurld [it] vp to Front of the Fane or Chapell*" (I.i.117SD) as a symbol of anarchy prevailing in the forest. Thus, Orion's crowning at the end is also presented as a solution to a problem of a vacant throne which was the case with James's advent from Scotland to rescue England from the death of an heirless queen's. Fenn notes that during the contest subjects sought their own desires, played tricks and caused many wrongs but "After [Orion] is crowned, the various wrongs are righted, and order is restored in the forest" (Fenn 33). In another hint towards masculine superiority, Percy inserts a scene in which a character named Sylvius is presented as a symbol for male fertility and power, being a good lover and hunter. Sylvius is the one who later crowns Orion, and the scene is intended to portray him as a perfect male character fit to crown Orion (Fenn 34).

King James, the first monarch with a traditional family to rule England for almost a century, is further praised by another inserted scene.[13] Totally unrelated to the main plot, the scene includes Oberon king of the fairies, Chloris his wife and the blind prophet Tiresias. The three discuss constancy in love between the sexes and they conclude that men and women are either equal in their love or not in love at all. Dodds and Fenn note in this scene a compliment to the royal couple and a celebration of married life (Fenn 34; Dodds "William Percy and James I" 14).

Another important theme, pertinent to the Earl's correspondence with James VI of Scotland, is the relationship between the peers of the realm and the monarch. As Fenn notes, upon Orion's instalment, the corrections he makes and the discipline he imposes are not "overly harsh" (34). Fenn further notes that Sylvius's words upon crowning Orion emphasize the

---

[13] Percy uses inserted scenes quite often. The primary examples are the Haly episode and Geber's soliloquy in *Mahomet and his Heaven*.

importance of a restrained authority, and that "the fairy lords and ladies are left to proceed with their conclusion without royal interference" (36). Fenn links this to the views of English noblemen who wanted less government interference in their affairs. However, based on the Earl's correspondence with the king, these hints can as well be linked to toleration for the Catholics which was a main request by the Earl from James.

These two plays by Percy, as has been shown, abound with topical allusions and contemporary concerns. In them, Percy shows a degree of alertness to the political and religious atmosphere of his times, especially from the point of view of his family interests. Such tendencies do exist in Percy's other plays and in *Mahomet and his Heaven*, similar alertness shows itself in several themes and characters as will be shown below.

3.3. Other plays

Critics studying Percy's other plays also noted similar methods in them. For example in *The Cuckqueanes and Cuckolds Errants* or *the Bearing down the Inn*, (1601), Percy deploys two characters from Oxford who could be identified with some of his friends. He also includes a vivid description of the war against the Armada which could be personal experience as he is believed to have participated in the war himself (Kincaid 43; Dodds "Fitzjeffrey" 421).

A Forrest Tragœdye in Vacunium or *Cupid's Sacrifice* (1602) includes a topical reference to French politics through an incident in the play in which a character eats a poisoned "citron" and dies. Dodds links the story to a very similar rumour on the death of Henry IV of France's mistress Gabrielle d'Estrées (Dodds "A Forrest Tragaedye" 253). Percy's last play, written almost thirty years after his period of literary activity, is entitled *Necromantes* or *the Two Supposed Heads* (1632). In this play, Percy returns to the magic motif which he uses so potently in *Mahomet and his Heaven*. The play includes three magicians (or to be precise a magician, a necromancer and a witch) in different plots.[14]

It is therefore reasonable to assume at this stage that allegory for current affairs, references to characters from his life and the use of his plays to serve special purposes are issues that permeate Percy's plays in general. From this conclusion I move on to the discussion of the play, *Mahomet and his Heaven*, itself. I start first with the motif which is most relevant to the biographical sketch given above, and that is the interest in

---

[14] See Hillebrand for summary.

magic and the occult in the play and the resemblances between Geber and the Wizard Earl.

4. Geber and the wizard earl

William Percy's presentation of the magus in his play raises vital questions about to the character of the Wizard Earl, the position of occult tradition and the public view of scientists and magicians in late Elizabethan England. This part tries to highlight relevant contemporary debates on these issues and tries to bring the play into full context as far as they are concerned. The following discussion tries to explore the validity of the Earl's nickname as a "wizard" and his possible indignation at it. Then it moves to show the importance of magic and the hermetic tradition in the general scientific milieu of the time. The discussion then explores the presence of men of science in the Earl's circle in whose interest it was to defend magic against allegations of demonology and witchcraft. The aim is to show that the redemptive representation of the magus in the play does not come by coincidence, but is rather born out of a hot contemporary debate concerning the role of magic and hermetic tradition in the early modern scientific world. The play presents a rather positive image of the magus, especially as opposed to Epimenide. In a manner that simultaneously promotes the magus and denounces the female ruler, the wizard Geber is credited with using his magical powers in saving Arabia from several plights caused by Epimenide's whimsicality. Despite his few appearances in the play, Geber strikes us as a positive image of the magus in an era that did not value dissident forms of knowledge.

The character of Geber is based on a famous Arab scientist named Jabir ibn Hayyan (c.721– c.815 AD). John Erick Holmyard, a historian of chemistry, examined the historical identity of Jabir, clarified his high standing and noted his contribution to the development of chemistry as an experimental science. Holmyard concluded that Jabir's significance in the history of chemistry is equal to that of Boyle, Priestley and Lavoisier (Holmyard "Jabir"). There was another Jabir, however, in Medieval and Renaissance imagination. This Jabir, or Geber in the Latinized form, wrote many works in Latin which were attributed to the Arab chemist. "The Geber problem," the question of the real author of the Latin works on alchemy, was first discussed in the nineteenth century by the French chemist Marcellin Berthelot (1827–1907). The discrepancy between the two Gebers is very pertinent to the current study as it epitomizes the confusion, discussed below, between science, alchemy and magic. The hitherto-unsettled debate proposes that the author of the Latin works might be an unnamed[15] thirteenth-century Spaniard who wrote books on alchemy (Holmes and Levere 45). The distinction between the historical figure of Jabir ibn Hayyan and the pseudo-Geber can be made on grounds of the interests of their *opera*. Jabir is claimed to have composed over "six hundred books and three hundred leaves on a variety of subjects" including "alchemy, astrology, medicine, instruments of war, mechanics . . . language, philosophy, logic, mathematics, sermons, occultism, cosmology, music, charms, poetry, etc." (Glick et al. 279). The Latin author, however, seems to have been mainly interested in metallurgy and transforming base metals into gold (Holmyard *Makers Of Chemistry* 60–61). William Percy, most likely unwittingly, got involved in the confusion over the character and scientific significance of Geber/Jabir. The Earl of Northumberland was similar to the Arab scientist in more ways than the obvious link of alchemy with magic. Like Jabir, Henry Percy was a polymath and a true intellectual of his times. His scientific interests, as will be shown in the discussion of his *Advice to his Son*, spanned various fields of knowledge but, again like Jabir, his reputation as a wizard overshadowed all the other facets to his personality making him known as the Wizard Earl just like Jabir ibn Hayyan became known as Geber.

4.1. Questioning the nickname

Three years after his death, Henry Percy was described by Alexander Read (or Reid) as "the favourer of all good learning, and Mecænas of learned men" (qtd. in Batho 246). The remark would come as no surprise to students of the life of Henry Percy who always had a penchant for philosophy and different branches of knowledge. While still a student in France, he dedicated much of his time mingling with men of science and philosophy. Pursuits of a metaphysical nature seem to have caught his interest. But their impact on the general conception of this member of the aristocracy, and his nickname the Wizard Earl, was perhaps greater than they really occupied of his time. In other words, although he was a "favourer of all good learning," this facet of his interests seems to have overshadowed his other pursuits which did not occupy less interest on his behalf. Thus, minor facts like his purchase of a crystal ball with which he "cast his friends' horoscopes" and that he "laboured hopefully to transmute the baser metals into gold" (Brenan 35) became material for

---

[15] Holmes and Levere attribute one of the fake books to a Paul of Taranto (45).

both rumour and news about Percy more than, say, his knowledge and study of mathematics, medicine, or classical philosophy.

For young Lord Percy was an Elizabethan intellectual with good and diverse learning as well as knowledge of the world. Although in his early life his interests were as he described them in his *Advice to his Son* "Then were my felicities (because I knew not better) hawks, hounds, horses, dice, cards, apparel, mistresses" (81), Percy seems to have become an avid reader and scholar as many sources confirm (Batho 246; Brenan 35-36; Shirley). I think that it is in his *Advice*, which shows the devoted father's care for his son's upbringing and education, that the Earl's polymathic nature is most evident.

In the *Advice*, the Earl gives his son a summary of different fields of knowledge and gives his verdict on them in a way that shows detailed familiarity with them. As far as languages are concerned, the Earl believed that "the attaining to the Latin is most of use" while "the Greek [is] but loss of time" (67). Moving to sciences, Percy describes them briefly with some personal judgment. "Arithmetic in his height containeth," he writes, "rules of operation calculatory, both absolute and algebraic" (67-68) while geometry "teacheth of figures" and "extendeth itself to all purposes" and in it "is comprehended a great part of our knowledge" (68). "Universal Grammar" teaches "the best ways to signify the concepts of our minds to others" it possesses the "grounds of all occultations, ciphering, deciphering, etc" (68–69). Logic, "the Doctrine of Motion," and optics are briefly described as well. Percy does talk about branches of knowledge closer to alchemy and his attitude towards them sounds remarkably scholarly. For example, he explains metaphysics as it "containeth in it the division of *Ens*"[16] but then he undermines it by saying that the knowledge of it is still "very slenderly delivered and uncertain" (69). Astronomy, "the study of celestial bodies," is described as "not arbitrary and fantastical" as it is "consonant to all former course of philosophy" (69). In his summary of "The Doctrine of Generation and Corruption" the Earl touches very briefly upon the significant topic of alchemy. The application of this doctrine:

> satisfieth the mind in the generation and corruption, as also for the qualities of all substances actually existent . . . which part of philosophy the practice of Alchemy does much further, and in itself is incredibly enlarged, being a mere mechanical broiling trade without this philosophical project. (70)

---

[16] *Ens*: An entity regarded apart from any predicate but that of mere existence (*OED*)

From this brief comment, there seems to be a slightly derogatory note of alchemy as a "mechanical" meaning "artisanal" as opposed to theoretical (I. B. Cohen 337). The Earl's note on the importance of the philosophical background for the elevation of alchemy above deceitful practices is reminiscent of Pico della Mirandola's *Oration on the Dignity of Man*, where he compares *magia* (philosophical magic), which he praises, with *goetia* (witchcraft), which he denounces (qtd. in McAdam 53). Thus, the *Advice* shows how the Earl's scientific interests were wide ranging and covered most areas of knowledge of his time and that his interest in alchemy was but one of these areas. The Earl's possible predilection for it should not have overshadowed the fact that he was an all-round intellectual.

Another important subtlety to note here is the contemporary confusion in nomenclature over the term *magic*. In Renaissance England and because of the novel nature of sciences, popular belief often ascribed to magic many things that fell outside the realms of traditional knowledge. J. Peter Zetterberg, for example, dedicates an essay to explaining the nature of this confusion. In "The Mistaking of "the Mathematicks" for Magic in Tudor and Stuart England," Zetterberg gives plenty of early modern examples of how the public reacted to new inventions. Interestingly his examples relate strongly to the Earl of Northumberland, as they were incidents that occurred to members of his circle. In his trip to Virginia, Thomas Harriot, a friend of Northumberland,[17] showed the Indians many novelties including "a perspective glasse" and "spring clocks" (Zetterberg 83). The Indians were overwhelmed by what Harriot called "Mathematicall instruments," in reference to both the glass and the clocks. The term thus seems to be confusing even to men in the know. Another interesting incident involves John Dee, the "English Nostradamus" with whom the Earl was often associated (Brenan 60). Zetterberg notes that Dee's reputation as a "conjurer" did not stem from his undeniable metaphysical activities, but rather from an early episode in his life when he used a mechanical device for a Cambridge production of Aristophanes' *Pax*. In this production, Dee devised a flying scarabæus which made people think some sort of demonic help was involved in it (Zetterberg 83-84). Dee in one of his works expressed deep anger over allegations made in John Foxe's *Actes and Monuments* of him being a conjurer. He enquired why "any honest student, or a modest Christian philosopher, [is] to be, for . . . feats, mathematically and mechanically wrought, counted and called a conjuror? . . . shall that man be condemned as a companion of Hellhounds

---

[17] Harriot "received at [Percy's] hands a yearly pension of £120" (Brenan 97)

and a caller and conjuror of wicked damned spirits?" (qtd. in Forshaw 403).

4.2. Renaissance humanism and the hermetic tradition

George Peele's poem in praise of Northumberland, *The Honour of the Garter*, quoted above, has some extremely apt and relevant lines to this topic. In praise of Northumberland, Peele writes that the newly knighted earl:

> (Leaving our schoolesmen's vulgar troden pathes)
> And following the auncient reverend steps
> Of Trismegistus and Pythagoras,
> Through uncouth waies and unaccessible,
> Doost passe into the spacious pleasant fields
> Of divine science and Philosophie (12–17)

In these six lines, Peele put his finger on important facets of the Earl's scholarly lifestyle and interests. They show how he sought unconventional branches of knowledge and that his aim was to combine science and philosophy in a divine concoction. The mentioning of Hermes Trismegistus is of particular importance as it demonstrates contemporary views on the Earl's relationship to the Hermetic tradition. But what is the Hermetic tradition?

The tradition is named after Hermes Trismegistus, or "thrice great Hermes," who was a semi-mythical figure of vague ancient Egyptian, Greek and Latin origins. Identified also as the god Mercurius, Hermes became the centre of a large body of literature "concerned with astrology and the occult sciences, with the secret virtues of plants and stones and the sympathetic magic based on knowledge of such virtues, with the making of talismans for drawing down the powers of the stars" (Yates *Bruno* 2). In Elizabethan England, Hermes was thought of as a real person who authored books and writings in ancient Egypt (Yates *Bruno* 6). Now since Renaissance literati generally held a belief, stemming from the concept of the Golden Age, that the older the knowledge the purer it was (Yates *Bruno* 5), and because the Egyptian civilisation was the oldest known at the time, Hermetic philosophy and gnosis became associated with better knowledge of the esoteric and in effect magic and the occult. For a better understanding of the Hermetic tradition in the Renaissance, a few points need to be made.

Central to European Renaissance was the philosophy of humanism. Difficulties will be faced by whoever attempts to find a consensus in relation to defining this school of thought. Critics like Mike Pincombe and Tony Davies, for example, recognize major difficulties in adopting a singular definition of the term (See for example T. Davies 2-3; Pincombe *Elizabethan Humanism* ix; Keßler 181-82). However, for the purposes of this study, non-specialized in humanism as it is, I will be using the definition suggested by John Mebane adding some modifications to it later. For Mebane, humanism in the Renaissance refers to "the historical movement which promoted a new understanding of the Greek and Roman classics, and which reasserted the importance of literature, moral philosophy, and rhetoric as essential subjects in the education of competent citizens and political leaders" (8). Worth noting here is the fact that the philosophy takes its name from the central position it allocates to the human being in the universe. According to this doctrine, God gave humankind the potential to achieve perfection and control over nature and it is every person's duty to use their talents to the full in order to achieve this goal (Hunt 17).

Because the Golden Age was thought of as the time when humanity was in perfect harmony with nature and with the divine, some humanists sought the lore of that age through seeking hidden knowledge and the occult. As Mebane puts it:

> the *archetypus mundi* had been fragmented but enlightened and virtuous individuals who have become aware of their divine origins can help to reassemble it...the world would become perfect when humanity regained the knowledge and power it had lost through original sin (84).

Further to this belief, Frances Yates proposes the idea that the Renaissance magus was a direct predecessor of the modern natural scientist because according to the *Corpus hermeticum* "the magus could regain the ability to rule over nature that the first man had lost with the Fall" (Szőnyi 9).

In *Mahomet and his Heaven*, a binary opposition stands out between the heavenly bliss of Mahomet and his companions on the one hand, and the worldly distresses of Arabia. Interestingly, Geber is the only figure in Arabia that is capable of sending

> [a] Thousand Drom'daryes loade with charmd drinks,
> For a releife for her [Epimenide], and for her Deserts,
> In tyme of so mortiferous a drough [sic], (I.iii.46–8).

Thus, magic and hermetic knowledge are presented as the solution to earthly suffering and the magus is the only character who escapes divine punishment.

However, Hermetists had to struggle against the popular beliefs and negative associations with which the concept of the occult was associated. Mordechai Feingold asserts that "until the middle of the seventeenth century the occult tradition was essentially an intellectual tradition" and that "most of its practitioners were university-educated men." He also notes that figures such as John Dee "strove to legitimize occult studies, make them distinguishable from magic, atheism and popery, and convince a skeptical audience of their truth and superiority" (Feingold 89).

But what was the relationship between the philosophy of humanism and occult tradition as far as contribution to scientific revolutions is concerned? Frances Yates argues in her book *Giordano Bruno* that "Renaissance magic" played an important role "in bringing about fundamental changes in the human outlook" (Yates *Bruno* 155). For Yates, humanism alone was essentially a conservative force, but it was the Hermetic, or Hermetic-Cabalist as she later preferred to call it (*Occult* 1-2), that was the motivating force behind reform movements in sixteenth-century England (Mebane 2). Nor were the Hermetists absent from the political scene. Prominent Hermetic-Cabalist philosopher, Giordano Bruno, played an important part in Elizabethan politics during his short but prolific stay in England and he wrote of "proffered friendship from France to England in the face of the menace from the Catholic reaction" in his book *Lo Spaccio de la Bestia Trionfante* (Yates *Bruno* 287). Another facet of Bruno's activity in England relates to his attempt to fight religious bigotry as he saw himself as "a missionary of conciliation" (Yates *Bruno* 254). In fact, the Hermetic tradition importantly featured in the discourse of moderate Catholics and Protestants who called for Christian union and toleration (Yates *Bruno* 286), which is reminiscent of the Earl's own discourse in his correspondence with King James.

Thus, we find that in Elizabethan England the concepts of science and magic overlapped to such a great extent that the sobriquet "Wizard Earl" did not necessarily refer to black magic and could have had a wide ranging frame of reference indicating involvement in various branches of knowledge some of which were considered questionable only because of their novelty. In between science and magic there were "figures like John Dee" who are difficult to categorize as scientists or magicians (Mebane 3). The most problematic field of knowledge, to which the Earl was related, was occult philosophy and the Hermetic tradition. This tradition itself is not as sinister as it was deemed to be. Many philosophers and intellectuals were well versed in it and essayed its redemption from the social stigma attached to it.

4.3. The Earl's circle

The Earl of Northumberland must have been very aware, to say the least, of these anxieties. He could have been part of the effort to redeem the occult himself. Northumberland's circle of intellectual friends included "some of the greatest intellects in England . . . [like] Thomas Hariot, John Dee, Walter Warner, and Nathaniel Torporly 'the Atlantes of the mathematical world'" (French 171). The Earl's relationship with some of these names was strong indeed. I have already noted the pension and patronage provided by Northumberland for Thomas Harriot. Dr Dee was also to describe Percy later as his "brother wizard" (Brenan 167).

It is interesting to find that many of the people who were involved in defending this art were, in one way or another, acquaintances of the Earl or part of his circle. But the most enthusiastic defence dedicated to magic from the Earl's circle comes from Sir Walter Raleigh who dedicated a chapter in his *History of the World* for the defence of *magia* and the description of its ancient history. In Chapter XI of his first Book, Raleigh writes:

> NOw for Magicke it selfe; which Arte (saith MIRANDVLA) *pauci intelligunt, multi reprehendunt; Few vnderstand, and many reprehend. Et sicut Canes ignotos semper allatrant; As Dogs barke at those they know not:* so they condemne and hate the things they vnderstand not. (Raleigh 201)

Raleigh then sets off to demystify magic. The first obstacle he tries to remove is the connection between magic and the work of the devil. Accused of being an atheist by his enemies (see Nicholls and Williams), Raleigh tries to establish a link between magic and the worship of God saying that the first of the three types of magic, which comes from the Persian word "magus," is related to being "altogether conuersant in things diuine" (201). He cites the Bible's three magi as examples and Plato's definition of the word to support his argument. The second kind of magic is "Astrology, which had respect to sowing and planting, and all kindes of agriculture and husbandrie: which was a knowledge of the motions and influences of the Starres into those lower Elements" (202), but this does not seem to be a point of argument in the book. The third type is perhaps the most important one for Raleigh as he deals with it in more detail than the other two. He writes that this type "contayneth the whole Philosophie of nature not the brabblings of the Aristotelians" (202). The latter remark reminds us of the idea expressed in the Earl of Northumberland's advice to his son about alchemy when he stressed the importance of the philosophical side to alchemy without which it becomes "mere mechanical broiling" (70). But while the Earl was being more academic about his description of alchemy, Raleigh seems more esoteric as he believed this branch of magic reaches into hidden truths of nature, what he called "*Virtutes in centro centri latentes*; Vertues hidden in the center of the center" (202). Raleigh expands his defence of magic in another section where he focuses on claims of devilish interference in the art of magic. He refutes this argument by admitting such interference in magic and in other fields of knowledge as well. Thus, "if we condemne naturall *Magicke*," argues Raleigh, "then may wee by the same rule condemne the Physician, and the Art of healing . . . but the abuse of the thing takes not away the Art" (205).

This argument can be seen as a response of contemporary uncertainty towards the new advances in science and philosophy. Of particular interest is Raleigh's reference to King James's book, *Daemonologie* (1597). King James had written this short book to attack both contemporary extremes concerning the question of magic and witchcraft: complete denial of its existence and influence on the one hand, and defence of the practice on the other (3). Raleigh quotes the King on the religious origins of the word magus and, in a way, his argument that the abuse of magic does not render it illegitimate can be seen as a response to the popular belief expressed in *Daemonologie* that magic is the work of the devil.

Hence, Hermetic philosophers and proponents of new science and untraditional knowledge, like Northumberland and his circle, were deeply involved in an effort to clean up their image in the first place and prove the validity of "magic" as a field of scholarship that can help improve the human experience. William Percy's *Mahomet* comments on these issues most notably through the character of Geber who is a fictionalized defence of the benign magic in whose defence Raleigh wrote and for whose redemption other intellectuals, including members of the Earl's circle, extended many efforts.

However, one major obstacle that hindered these efforts was the public attachment to negative images of the magus. Perhaps the most enduring representation of magic on the English stage was in *Doctor Faustus*. Marlowe's masterpiece was hugely popular throughout the 1590s and there are indications that it never really lost its appeal until the closing of the theatres by the Puritans in 1642 (Jump 43). The play's importance in this study stems from various factors that relate it strongly to *Mahomet and his Heaven* especially its presentation of the magus. The links between *Faustus* and *Mahomet* are many and it would be reasonable to assume that William Percy had this important work of stagecraft in mind as he wrote his play. This suggestion gains ground also from the fact that Christopher Marlowe was actually included by some historians as a member in the Earl's circle of intellectuals (French 171).

4.4. Geber vs. Faustus

This part will try to demonstrate how William Percy's familiarity with the magical exploits of Marlowe's Faustus manifested itself in his play through the character Geber and how Percy's preoccupation with brushing up the image of wizardry led him to counterbalance the negativities of *Faustus* with a positive image. Thus, similarities in topic between *Mahomet* and *Faustus* do not necessarily entail similarity in presentation. While Percy agrees with Marlowe on the wizard's status, he departs from *Faustus* in other respects including the role of magic and the onstage presentation of the wizard's career. As will be shown below, conformity and difference are tools by which Percy tries to correct and improve the image of the magus in his play.

4.4.1. The wizard's status

As the audience finds him in his study at the beginning of *Doctor Faustus*, the eponymous hero gives a survey of contemporary fields of knowledge, similar in principle to Northumberland's survey in his *Advice to his Son*. But while the Earl tries to be scholarly and sensible as much as he can, Faustus's survey is targeted, biased and laden with value judgments. Faustus praises analytics as "sweet" only to discover that he has attained its utmost point: "to dispute well" (I.i.9). Moving to medicine, whose end is "our body's health" (17), Faustus finds a major shortcoming in its limited nature and its inability to perform miracles. The physician can never "make men to live eternally" or raise the dead to life (24, 25). Looking at law, Faustus sees it as a "paltry" profession that only "fits a mercenary drudge" (30, 34). In these three cases, Faustus has been reading selectively from his books, but his flawed and selective reading reaches an absurd nadir when he reads two verses from St. Jerome's Latin Bible. Combining two half verses: "the reward of sin is death" and "If we say that we have no sin, / We deceive ourselves, and there's no truth in us" (40, 42–43) (Gill 29), Faustus expresses despair in theology and religion in general. Magic is the final destination for which Faustus seems to have started the whole journey of evaluation. Its lack of boundaries and infinite possibilities, in his view, are the most important characteristics he has been seeking. In each of the other fields of knowledge, Faustus has been seeking the "end" or the highest achievement possible. While all of them were by default definable and had a specific goal, magic in its shapeless and volatile nature seals the deal for Faustus. Thus, his boundless ambition led him to the "study" that could make "a sound magician . . . a mighty god" and enable him "to gain a deity" (62, 63). Faustus later gives full vent to his dreams by listing what he will ask the spirits to do:

> I'll have them wall all Germany with brass,
> And make swift Rhine circle fair Wittenberg;
> . . . .
> I'll levy soldiers with the coin they bring,
> And chase the Prince of Parma from our land,
> And reign sole king of all our provinces.
> Yea, stranger engines for the brunt of war,
> Than was the fiery keel at Antwerp's bridge,
> I'll make my servile spirits to invent. (I.i.88–89, 92–97)

As Mebane notes, this view of the role of the magician may well have stemmed from the Hermetic philosophy where the magus "attains a godlike status through the reflection of the entire cosmos within the magician's own soul: the mind becomes all things, and in doing so, it becomes one with God" (123). The idea of the philosopher's elevation above ordinary human experience and ability to comprehend its nature from a divine point of view is deeply rooted in Hermetic literature. In a summary of the *Corpus Hermeticum*, Frances Yates quotes the following words supposedly directed to Hermes from "The Mind," or the divine source of knowledge:

> Believe that nothing is impossible for you, think yourself immortal and capable of understanding all, all arts, all sciences, the nature of every living being. Mount higher than the highest height; descend lower than the lowest depth. (*Bruno* 32)

In Percy's *Mahomet*, Geber is a minor character and we have less space to look into his reasoning and worldview. However, the status he is accorded and the description of his abilities, both by him and by others, give an impression very close to the one Faustus dreams of obtaining especially in his early flights of fancy. Apart from Geber's main monologue in which he describes how he used his magic to save Arabia once and again, characters in the play speak how, amid the overwhelming drought, Geber has been able to send to Epimenide a "Thousand Drom'daryes loade with charmd drinks, / For a releife for her, and for her Deserts" (I.iii.46–47).

There is, however, some ambiguity surrounding the position of the character of Geber especially his demonic incantations. In Act III scene vii, when Tubal snatches his signet, Geber calls upon his familiars:

Raüm, Haiphas, Foculor, Brifrons, Num,
Gamagin, Zagun, Urias, Valuc,
Smolkin, Furcas, Murmur, Caim, Vapalour,
Come along, helpe your Master, I adjure.   (III.vii.3–6)

It is possible to assume when reading this scene that it would cast a doubtless negative shadow on the character of Geber as a black magician. I think such an argument would be valid in the case of any play acted on a popular stage. But the case is different with *Mahomet*, with its special writing circumstances and lack of evidence for performance. Critics who have speculated a possible performance have indicated it to be a university performance (see Dodds "A Dreame" 189). Thus, the intellectual debates and anxieties surrounding human beings' relation to the forces of nature, especially Hermetic philosophy, must be taken into consideration more seriously than a populist play. That William Percy was aware of this particular strain of philosophy is a view adopted by Dimmock, using Hilary Gatti's reading in the Ninth Earl's Library lists (Dimmock *Mahomet* 43-44; Gatti). Reading the above excerpt needs to be done in light of Hermetic belief that a human being should "know the genus of daemons as if one were by nature related to them" (Ficino, qtd. in Mebane 123).

Geber is kept at a distance from the plights of Arabia due to his knowledge of the occult. He does not suffer from the drought and is able to save others from it. William Percy thus seems to adopt the points of view expressed in Hermetic Literature, as reflected in Marlowe's *Dr Faustus*, which teaches that the magus occupies a high social and natural position because of his knowledge of the occult which enables him "to gain a deity" or become one with God. The magus's relationship with demons and the lower world is but one side to his omniscient soul which acquaints itself with realms of nature in order to control them.

4.4.2. The role of magic

Faustus's obsession with playing a key role in the world at large is further expressed in Act I, scene iii. Faustus says that he wants to:

make a bridge through the moving air
To pass the ocean with a band of men;

I'll join the hills that bind the Afric shore,
And make that land continent to Spain,
And both contributory to my crown.
The emperor shall not live but by my leave,
Nor any potentate of Germany. (106–112)

While this may be seen as a continuation of the motif set out in the opening soliloquy, a notable and valid comment has often been made regarding the use of magical superpowers in *Faustus*. As John Mebane puts it, "One aspect of *Dr. Faustus* which appears thoroughly traditional is its apparent denial of the possibility of benevolent magic" (121). This is because all these promises and fantasies of miraculous achievements using occult knowledge virtually come to nothing more than some tricks and sleight of hand. In fact, distinctions between magic and witchcraft have been applied to *Faustus* by several critics who saw his downfall as a comment on the futility of magic and a stress on the morality-based aspect of the play (Matthews; G. Roberts "Necromantic Books").

A significant comment on the uses of magic is the very first act Mephistopheles performs for Faustus after the pact is written and signed is the following:

Enter [again] with devils, giving crowns and rich apparel to Faustus;
they dance, and then depart

Faustus	Speak Mephastophilis, what means this show?
Mephastophilis	Nothing Faustus, but to delight thy mind withal, And to show thee what magic can perform. (83–85)

Ironically enough, this is all magic can do for Faustus: "nothing" but a show to delight his mind with no real-life achievements. Even the knowledge promised in return for his soul becomes a series of elusive answers. For example, when he asks Mephistopheles about the universe, Faustus notices that the demon's answers could have been provided by Wagner: "these slender trifles Wagner can decide!" (I.v.225). However, his scrutiny is only skin-deep for when Mephistopheles evades the question again and tell him that the stars move "*Per inaequalem motum respectu totius,*" through an irregular motion so far as the whole is concerned (Gill 58), Faustus says that he is satisfied with the answer which adds nothing to his human knowledge. Thus, Marlowe's representation of magical power and occult knowledge is remarkably reductive and disparaging.

Percy's take on wizardry is a different type altogether. From the few appearances he has, Geber seems to have achieved some real super-human feats using his knowledge of magic. From what we see, Geber is also in charge of his demons whom he summons as he wishes to serve his purposes. The large number of his familiars, quoted above, is further testimony to this view. While Geber can summon no less than 14 demons by name, Faustus is basically in touch only with Mephistopheles and, according to the latter, Faustus did not summon him but he came of his own volition. William Percy's presentation of the magician can thus be seen as a positive image where the negative aspects of magic are blurred and its positive applications in real life are highlighted. Percy departs from Marlowe on this point as Marlowe's view does not serve to promote the position of the wizard-figure.

4.4.3. The wizard's career

One notable shortcoming of the representation of the magus in Marlowe's *Faustus* is the downwards direction of his career. For while we are impressed by the magnitude of his dreams, sampled above, and the magnanimity of his attitude towards helping humanity, we gradually begin to see him transform from a sublime magician into a "witch." The distinction between the two is not simply gender-based as Ian McAdam explains. "According to popular conception," he writes, "witches and magicians" could be distinguished on the grounds that "the latter succeeded in being master and commanders of devils and spirits, while the former foolishly subordinated themselves to, and served, the devils or spirits" (McAdam 53; See also Dijkhuizen 8-9 n.3). Orthodox magic/witchcraft opponents discarded this distinction as baseless. King James I in his book *Daemonologie* refuses to acknowledge such a distinction by stating that:

> It is not by anie power that they can haue over him [the Devil], but *ex pacto* allanerlie [only]: whereby he oblices [obliges] himself in some trifles to them, that he may on the other part obteine the fruition of their body & soule, which is the onlie thing he huntes for. (9)

The Devil, according to King James I, will only do trifles for them until he obtains their souls. As a result, any magician or witch with any superhuman powers must have damned themselves first by signing the deal with Satan.

Marlowe, however, adopts a different outlook. A look at the wizard's progress shows that Faustus's signature of the pact for selling his soul is the point that marks the line in the sand distinguishing the move towards his downfall. Gareth Roberts has noted how "high magic," pertaining to control over nature, happens only in the early stages in the play: in the early soliloquies, preparations of the conjecture and only shortly after it. But as soon as Faustus signs the pact "magic recedes in the play" ("Marlowe" 66). Not only that, but Marlowe's hero receives many warnings on his way to damnation. The congealing of his blood, the blood inscription reading *homo fuge*, and Mephistopheles' evasiveness are the main example that denoted this downfall. As Jump notes, Faustus was too infatuated with magic to infer that "the power he was acquiring so presumptuously fell far short of the 'omnipotence' of which he had dreamed" (Jump 29).

William Percy presents his magus in a light different to both approaches by King James and Marlowe. He does not show or indicate a soul hand-over by Geber to his devils and at the same time he shows how Geber has power over them. The play adopts a static approach towards this control over demons. In other words, Geber does not become at any stage a minion to his familiars. On the contrary, an almost contrary effect is achieved through another method.

Before we ever see Geber, he is mentioned by name in two scenes. In I.iii, when the Queen's two desperate admirers, Caleb and Tubal, discuss their passions, the latter expresses disappointment:

> Trust mee, Pastor Caleb, since Geber first,
> Th'inchanting Astrologer of our Deserts,
> Began his suite to her, I never hoped
> For love or favour at her hands. (I.iii.18–21)

This is the first time we hear of Geber and he is described as an "inchanting Astrologer" who has been seeking Epimenide's favour. The implication is that he has higher chances of winning the Queen's favour than the two Pastors as his presence on the list of the Queen's admirers makes Tubal despair of ever getting a chance with her. The word "inchanting," however, is likely to cast an unfavourable shadow on the character of Geber as it implies links with the occult.

In the second time we hear of Geber in I.iv, Epimenide is describing him to her suitors, Caleb and Tubal, as:

> You know Geber, th'incaunter [sic] of these Deserts
> Now prosecutes my Love with goodly Things,
> He that sent mee these the Bottle-backs all,
> That Foolosopher, that Figure-Setter.   (I.iv.100–103)

Again, it is notable, the word "incaunter" or enchanter is used to refer to the magus. His ridicule further by Epimenide's trademark tongue-lashing as a "Foolosopher" is associated with his figure setting. Epimenide's commonness or vulgarity is expressed here in her lack of respect for philosophy as an important branch of knowledge. These two episodes can thus be seen as Percy's presentation of what is expected to be the layman's view towards magicians and philosophers. The audience will expect an ordinary wizard figure who is bent on "enchanting" and "figure-setting." However, an anti-climax comes when we actually meet Geber in the scene where he describes his exploits for saving Arabia (III.iii). Thus, Percy's depiction of the magus can be seen as contrary to Marlowe's Faustus. While he is offstage, he is ridiculed and disrespected, but as soon as he appears, he commands respect through his philanthropic nature and benevolent use of magic.

4.5. William Percy's Geber

Popular negative views of the magus as exemplified by *Faustus*, as well as the confusion over the naming of magic and distinguishing it from empirical sciences give us a better understanding of the cultural background against which William Percy was writing and perhaps trying to correct. The Earl's notes to his son that the empirical side of alchemy has its basis in philosophy is indicative of the importance of benevolent magic. William Percy tries to redeem magic and his brother through the redemption of the magus in his play. As will be shown below, Percy gives the wizardly Geber a redeeming presentation that can be seen as a response to criticism and attack against his brother for being a favourer of the occult.

In I.iii, Tubal expresses frustration in his love for Epimenide. What adds to the difficulty, he says, is that:

> She's growne, of late, so proud, so humorous
> That easier it is (as I can gather
> By every circumstance) to wrest the club
> From Hercules' fist, then one good looke from her. (I.iii.22–25)

This idea of Epimenide's recent change into a proud and whimsical person is later elaborated on by Geber in III.iii. In this scene, Geber is unhappy with Epimenide and he starts casting astrological incantations on her while counting the seven deadly sins that dominated Epimenide and recalling how he saved her from them. Geber's incantation mentions all seven deadly sins: envy followed by wrath, slothfulness, covetousness, lechery, gluttony and pride.

The question that immediately arises is what Percy wanted to achieve by inserting this rather wordy episode into his play. The scene can be understood as an attempt by Percy to add an Islamic touch to the general atmosphere of the play. As will be shown below, one of the play's main sources is John Lyly's *The Woman in the Moon*. Here, the original story of a woman being influenced by classical gods represented by planets is modified to become that of a woman influenced by the Seven Deadly Sins. This modification is an obvious move from the mythological world of *The Woman in the Moon* to a world of religious connotations. Percy wanted to indicate his heroine's fluctuating personality and preferred a religious replacement to the classical deities. The only problem is that the replacement he used, the Seven Deadly Sins, is by and large a Christian concept that shares little common ground with Islam.[18]

Another point about this scene is that it presents Geber in a light totally different to the way others describe him. In general, Geber is presented as a magician and enchanter, largely negative attributes. Epimenide also describes him as "That Foolosopher, that Figure-Setter" (I.iv.103). However, reading this passage by Geber, by far his longest contribution in the play, one feels that this man saved Arabia from disaster after disaster caused by Epimenide's whimsicality. As each one of the seven sins took control of the Empress of the Desert, some form of harm would eventually smite the people she is ruling but Geber explains how he used his magic to save his country and people. Thus, upon meeting Geber, we know more about this magus and his exploits. We have enough reason to believe his stories about Epimenide's whimsicality due to her actions throughout the play. Epimenide's triviality and vulgarity thus testify to Geber's

---

[18] It is interesting though that one *hadīth* of the Prophet Muhammad does warn against seven grave sins. It translates like this: "Avoid the seven noxious things [...] associating anything (in worship and obedience) with Allah; magic (equivalent to witchcraft and sorcery in English); killing one whom Allah has declared inviolate without a just case, consuming the property of an orphan, devouring usury, turning back when the army advances, and slandering chaste women who are believers but indiscreet." Apart from the fact that the sins are not exactly the same as the Christian ones, the Islamic view of these sins seems to be a bit different. This list by the Prophet is not seen as an exhaustive all-inclusive list of major sins. Many other sins are warned against in other places in the Quran and Hadīth. Some scholars even collected them in a list that contained as much as seventy major sins or *Kaba'ir* (See adh-Dhahabi for more).

accusations against her as a bad ruler, and by extension her disparaging comments about him become baseless accusations.

The soliloquy is also interesting in that it is not connected to any other action or speech in the play. It looks like a stand-alone insertion into a story that runs smoothly without it. Therefore, looking for a reason behind this addition into the story is a necessity for a better understanding of the play. A first thought might be that William Percy is giving the character of Geber a new dimension in an attempt to make him more lifelike. A character that is shown to perform the humane actions described in the scene is a much finer work of art than a one-sided villainous sorcerer. However, a deeper look at the play shows that Geber is by no means a major character and his presence in the play is perhaps negligible as far as action and story are concerned. In other words, he himself is an insertion. So why should Percy venture to make Geber a rounded character while he does not seem to be doing this with other, more significant, characters? Epimenide, for example, is tediously monotonous in her mood and attitude towards all other characters. In addition, Geber has very few lines to speak, almost ninety lines in total, of which sixty-one lines are in this soliloquy alone, Thus, two thirds of his role in the play lies here. This observation makes questioning this scene even more valid as Geber seems to be inserted into this play essentially to say the words in this scene.

Dimmock sees the way Percy portrays astrology and alchemy as a "comic comment upon his brother's interests, designed to ridicule the self-obsessed, introspective and hysterical alchemist/astrologer as ineffectual" (*Mahomet* 40). This assertion seems to ignore the content of Geber's main speech in the play and it depends mainly on the idea that Geber is an alchemist and that alchemy did not have a positive reception at the time in addition to the short comic scenes in the subplot where Geber's purse and signet are stolen by comic characters. What is significant, in my view, is the message delivered in Geber's words. Moreover, Dimmock himself has the following to say about William Percy's relationship with his brother: "If we accept that it is to William the Earl addresses his personal and affectionate essay, 'On love and learning' (1604?), then their relationship may at times have been very close indeed, since the addressee is 'nearer to me then any'" (Dimmock *Mahomet* 15). This observation reduces any likelihood of Percy using Geber to ridicule his brother's lifestyle.

If we look at things in the play from a secular point of view, or putting aside the fact that what Percy presents on stage was seen as a representation of an evil faith or superstition, then it becomes clear that there is an attempt to clean up Geber, a blasphemer, as opposed to other, apparently religious characters. This view is supported by comments that

William Percy "shared his brother's relaxed religious beliefs" (Nicholls "As Happy a Fortune" 301). Seen under this light, the situation in Arabia would be like this: the afflicted country is ruled by a woman who appears to be religious; she goes to a temple and prays for an end to the drought. This woman, we are told later, has been imperilling the country with every disaster possible as a result of her whimsicality. On the other hand, we have a possibly demonic figure, an alchemist, who is predictably seen by the public as irreligious and untrustworthy. However, later we learn that had it not been for the magic of this person, the people of Arabia would have perished a long time ago because of the temperamental nature of their Empress. In other words, there is enough evidence to make us think that Percy is suggesting that an irreligious alchemist is better than a religious Empress if the former does good to the society while the latter only jeopardizes it. These implications of the inferiority of one's religion in relation to the welfare of society are given further discussion in the part of Schism and Unity.

This observation of Percy's pragmatic and secular approach towards life and state instantly brings to mind the associations that the words Empress or Queen would bring to an Elizabethan audience i.e. reference to Queen Elizabeth. Dimmock alludes to this idea through pointing out Elizabeth's association with the Moon. He adds that the character description of Epimenide as imperially crowned would have suggested parallels with Elizabeth (*Mahomet* 50). The first observation is especially true because of the associations already present in the source play, *The Woman in the Moon*, between Pandora and Elizabeth. Dimmock adds that "Epimenide's association with both Venus and the Moon in the source material (and her punishment at the end of this play), further suggests such a connection" (*Mahomet* 50). In her introduction to *The Woman in the Moon*, Leah Scragg points out such a connection: "the name of the central figure invites identification with the monarch, in that 'Pandora' is among the names used by court poets with reference to the Queen" (Lyly 26; see also Pincombe *Eros* 175-6). However, Scragg recognizes that this identification is problematic because of Lyly's expectations of royal favour which would have been harmed because of Pandora's negative attributes (Scragg 26). Lyly's hidden intentions are not the purpose of this study but still Percy's hidden intentions certainly imply complexities that need further discussion. Hence we move to the following section on Percy's female characters especially the link between Epimenide and Queen Elizabeth.

5. Percy's Women

This part of the study aims at discussing the way William Percy presented his female protagonist, Epimenide. The main question being discussed here is the extent to which topical factors played a role in portraying this character. These factors are sub-headed into two main areas. First comes contemporary views on Muslim women in late sixteenth century England. The aim is to establish what Percy might have known about Muslim women and how much of this knowledge is employed in the play. Second, there is the vital question of Epimenide's relationship to Queen Elizabeth I. This part first establishes Percy's indebtedness to John Lyly's play, *The Woman in the Moon*, with its clear references to the Queen, then tries to show Percy's use of this material and how the classical tale is reflected in *Mahomet*.

The history of the Percy family's relationship with the crown, discussed above, comes in to play a part in understanding what views Percy might have held towards his liege. Moreover, in this part a study of contemporary misogynist views is used to illuminate Percy's creation. This is especially important in view of accusations of misogyny levelled at Percy himself. Finally, based on these arguments, conclusions can be made regarding the "Islamicness" of the representation of Muslim women in *Mahomet and his Heaven*. This argument will enable us to see how little of a Muslim tale Percy presents and how contemporary and English it actually is, and as I said in the introduction this idea is quite central to the development of my argument.

5.1. Muslim women in English imagination

Elizabethan England knew very little about Muslims in general, and even less about Muslim women. Many recent studies have dedicated considerable effort to examine the extent of this knowledge. These studies tried to gather their information from travel literature, Christian polemics and history books available in Elizabethan England. However, the question that arises at this point is whether or not William Percy read such accounts and polemics or at least held a commonplace conception about women in the Islamic faith. With the lack of information we have about him, the best we can make is an educated guess at what a man of his position, an intellectual and a man of letters, could have known in the period in which he lived. Given the conclusion reached in this section that the Muslim women in *Mahomet* display few or no Muslim characteristics (according to contemporary views), there are two possibilities that will arise out of this situation. Either Percy held these views, or at least knew of them, and decided to disregard them; or he was not aware of them and thus his presentation was merely born out of his own milieu. It is important for this study that in both cases the topicality of the play is not affected. In other words, in both cases the creation is topical and not based on Islamic sources.

A survey of the studies on early modern views on English women shows that the little information available about Muslim women were focused around three major, remarkably orientalist, areas: their place in the social order, their chastity and modesty, and their religious habits.

5.1.1. Obedient women

Elizabethan society was ostensibly not an equitable place for women and their rights. Worse even was the Ottoman society, as reported by English travellers to the Levant. These travellers noted how "Turk" women were given a certain position in society which, they saw, was less favourable than that enjoyed by English women. In 1615, George Sandys noted the dedicated family life Muslim women led focusing on their adherence to a mostly indoor lifestyle:

> All that is required at their hands is to content their husbands, to nurse their owne children, and to liue peaceably together: which they do (and which is strange) with no great iealousie, or enuy. No male accompanies them aboue twelue yeares old, except they be Eunuchs: and so strictly are they guarded, as seldome seene to looke out at their doors. (qtd. in Matar "Muslim Women" 54)

As Sandys notes the way women lived their lives, he is astonished by the lack of envy and jealousy among them, which can be seen as an indication of his admiration for their good manners.

Sandys' observation was not new to English travel literature for in 1609 William Biddulph, who wrote in detail about his Levant pilgrimage, used his description of Muslim women's life in order to preach obedience to his female fellow citizens. English women should be "more dutifull and faithfull to their husbands" and appreciate their freedom in comparison to Muslim women who were treated like "slaves" (qtd. in Matar "Muslim Women" 52). Bernadette Andrea saw in Biddulph an example of the "conflation of patriarchalism and orientalism" when he writes to his English audience:

Heere wives may learn to love their husbands, when they shal read in what slavery women live in other Countries, and in what awe and subjection to their husbands, and what libertie and freedome they themselves enjoy. (qtd. in Andrea 277)

Biddulph used his misinformed view on the Muslim society in order to preach a local message of male superiority and female subordination.[19]

Nabil Matar refers also to Massinger's play *The Renegado* in which "an English slave is made to reflect before the North African Muslim Queen about the differences between the status of women in England/Christendom and in the domain of Islam" (Matar "Muslim Women" 51). Matar quotes the Queen saying that Christian women have more freedom and that Moorish women are not allowed to go out except "the publique Bannias [bagnios], or the Mosques/ And euen then vaylde, and garded" (Matar "Muslim Women" 51). Unlike Biddulph's didactic discourse on female obedience, Massinger's reference to Muslim women's home-confinement appears in a piece of literature and is more of an observation than a moral lesson. Regardless of the purpose, Muslim women's obedience manifested in their indoor lifestyle was one of the more significant points about them that triggered documentation and comment from English authors.

Percy's version of the Muslim woman is different to these views. Epimenide and the other women in the play are far from the second-rate members of society which they were portrayed in travel literature. In fact, looking at Epimenide, her maids and Tib, we can see them as the reverse of this image. They are not subjugated by men but rather treat men on equal terms. They are not restricted to their homes and they are allowed to visit places other than the mosque.

5.1.2. Chaste women

Notable in writings on Muslim societies and descriptions of Muslim women is the recurrent indication of their modesty and chastity. Similar to the way women's suppression was used to address home issues, the apparent reason Muslim women's manners were praised was the call for English women to learn from their Turkish counterparts. This is most evident in Alexander Ross's writing of the modest conversation between Turkish women and men, criticising English manners. For Ross, Turks are "more modest in their conversation generally than we; Men and Women

---

[19] For more on these misinformed accounts see, for example, Andrea "Islam, Women, and Western Responses" 274.

converse not together promiscuously, as among us" (qtd. in Matar "Muslim Women" 51).

One sign of this chastity in women was the veil, which was, remarkably, not a point of interest in Christian polemic against Islam (Dimmock *Mahomet* 223). However, a marked interest in the veil seems to come into existence from travel narratives. Robert Schwoebel quotes a German traveller, Arnold von Harff, who around the start of the sixteenth century "described the dress of Turkish women he saw in the streets. They wore veils which obscured their faces, and both maidens and older women wore breeches down to their knees, made of leather, linen, or silk" (Schwoebel 196). Dimmock notes an early English travel book that contained illustrations of Muslim women's dress. This was Nicolas de Nicolay's *The Nauigations, peregrinations and voyages, made into Turkie* (London 1585) (*Mahomet* 223). Samuel Purchas also points out in his book that "The [Arabian] women couer their faces, contented to see with one eie, rather than to *prostitute* the whole face" (qtd. in Dimmock *Mahomet* 223, italics mine). The use of such a strong word as "prostitute" by Purchas also indicates an approving tone towards veiling the face as opposed to a perceived promiscuity in revealing it. Sandys also praised Turkish women who never exposed their "beauties unto any, but unto their fathers and husbands" (Matar "Muslim Women" 52).

Again, Percy's Muslim society seems completely out of touch with this image as portrayed in travel literature. Apart from the free mixing between men and women, including inside a mosque, two of the four women in the play, Epimenide and Tib, have questionable moral behaviour. Tib is an adulteress who betrays her husband with the Muslim Friar of all people and shows little care for the loss of her husband in bizarre circumstances. Epimenide is the *femme fatale* of the play who, although not actually involved in a sexual affair, does not mind promising her love to multiple partners, even two at a time. Percy's Arabia clearly lives the promiscuity attacked by Ross and ascribed to English society.

5.1.3. Religious women

The religious side of the life of a Muslim woman also features in travel writing in a manner that reflects personal prejudices of the author. For example, Gerald MacLean quotes Thomas Dallam who when first met with Muslim women in Algiers had the following to say:

> The Turkishe, and Morishe, weomen, do goo all wayes in the streetes with there facis covered, and the common reporte goethe thare that they beleve, or thinke that the weomen have no soules. And I doe thinke, that it weare

well for them if they had none, for they never goo to churche, or other prayers, as the men dothe. (qtd. in MacLean 15-16)

Apart from the groundless nature of this assumption of women being seen as soulless in Islam (See Jawad 1, 11), it reflects actual Christian theological debates taking place back home on which Dallam clearly takes sides.

Muslim women were ignorantly denied another advantage by another writer. Linda McJannet studies what appears to be "the first descriptive and historical account of the Turks published in England in the sixteenth century ... Richard Grafton's *The order of the greate Turckes Courte* (London, 1542), a translation of Antoine Geuffroy's *L'État de la cour du gran Turc* (Envers, 1542?)" (McJannet 35). In this account, we learn that Muslims believe that women cannot enter Paradise but "shall tarry at the gate with the Christians which have well kept their law" (39).

Muslim marital laws also interested travellers and writers on Islam. Most important was the topic of polygamy (polygyny to be accurate). The issue was unanimously agreed upon among Christian polemics attacking Islam and was referred to throughout the Middle Ages (Daniel 158–63). It is important to note this here, as Percy seems to indicate the opposite in his play. In one incident, two men are jointly promised consummating their love with Epimenide, which could be a misunderstanding of polygamy to mean polyandry.

The important issue of the *harem* is also significantly absent from Percy's Arabia. Bernard Lewis noted how western travellers stereotyped the Muslim man as lascivious and licentious with excessive sexual prowess. However, the women were always portrayed to be secluded in the *saray* or harem (Lewis 82, 83). In another reflection of personal prejudices, as Nabil Matar noted, English travellers knew of the harem, and how women were brutally forced into it. They did not criticize it, but were rather fascinated by it (Matar "Muslim Women" 58). This concept of the harem is absent from *Mahomet* as the women are leading a relatively normal life and are not secluded away from society.

In view of the other issues, Percy's women are not what the above writers reported Muslim women to be. They obviously have the souls that allow them to go to the "meschit" and perform prayers.[20] In addition, they surely have the souls that will enable them to enter Paradise as they indeed do during the process of the play. True one of the three female intruders on

---

[20] Dimmock detects the word 'meschit' for mosque in several sources which could have been used by Percy. Most important is Purchas's *Pilgrimage* (see Dimmock *Mahomet* 193).

Heaven is cast out, but the remaining two are rewarded for their virtue and remain in Heaven to live happily ever after with their husbands.

Percy's women seem to share very little with Muslim women as far as the knowledge of the day went. Epimenide, Percy's heroine who has more claims to stick in an audience's memory than any other female character in the play, is quite different to these contemporary perspectives on Muslim women. She is not obedient to any man, including Mahomet himself who receives the worst treatment from her. She does not strike us as chaste as she keeps entangling men and seeking their infatuation. Nor does she seem to be religious for her practice of prayer in one scene is immediately offset by an amorous encounter. If these women are not Muslim then what are they exactly? The following argument tries to show how much they share with contemporary English views on English women especially Queen Elizabeth.

5.2. Epimenide and Elizabeth

Queen Elizabeth I was often associated with certain classical and mythological figures in literary works written by her admirers. An interesting and succinct list of these figures appeared in Thomas Dekker's play *Old Fortunatus* (1599). Frances Yates quotes the following excerpt from the play:

> Some call her Pandora: some Gloriana: some Cynthia: some Belphoebe: some Astraea: all by several names to express several loves: Yet all those names make but one celestial body, as all those loves meet to create but one soul. I am of her own country, and we adore her by the name of Eliza. (qtd. in Yates "Queen Elizabeth as Astraea" 27)

It is of great importance to this work that Epimenide's counterparts in Percy's two major sources (Pandora in Lyly and the seductress in the supposedly Islamic myth) both bear strong links to the figure of Queen Elizabeth I. In the source used by Percy for the Islamic tale, Riccoldo de Montecroce mentions that when the woman who seduced the angels ascended to Heaven, God made her into the morning star:

> Deus autem uidens haec, & justitiam quam habebat audiens, fecit eam Luciferum, ut esset haec in coelo inter astra ita pulchra, sicut & in terra suit inter mulieres.

Dimmock translates this as follows:

However, God seeing her and hearing the justice she had, made her the morning star, so that she was just as beautiful in the heavens as she also was among women on earth. (*Mahomet* 20)

The morning star is of course another name for planet Venus. The goddess Venus, Dimmock notes, must have suggested the reigning queen to an Elizabethan audience (Dimmock *Mahomet* 50; see also Hackett 107-8). However, Elizabeth was more often associated with goddesses Diana and Cynthia than with Venus-Virgo (King "Queen Elizabeth" 30). Percy makes the important change to his sources by having Epimenide cast into the moon instead of the morning star, thus adding more stress to the identification of Epimenide with Elizabeth.

Lyly's *The Woman in the Moon* has good claims to being a source for *Mahomet and his Heaven* (Dimmock *Mahomet* 22; Dodds "A Dreame" 185). In this play, which was written for the court and performed before the Queen (Lyly 49), the central character Pandora bears a good deal of resemblance to the Queen. Apart from the well-known fact that Elizabeth was often likened to the "all-endowed" Pandora in praise for her perfection, Lyly made Pandora more like Elizabeth by having her waited upon by two handmaids (Lyly 26). Finally, the association of Pandora with the Goddess Luna is a clear reference to the Queen who was often nicknamed Cynthia, an epithet for the Greek Goddess of the moon.

It is true that Lyly's political allegories in his play have been long debated. Some critics found them far from flattering to the Queen while others doubted that Lyly, a court poet and royal favourite, would have written a satire of the Queen in a play that was presented before her. Regardless of the answer to this debate, our play is free from the factors that cast doubt on the intended satire against the Queen. Percy was never a courtier nor was his play performed before a royal audience, if performed at all. Furthermore, as discussed above, his and his family's view towards the Queen were unfavourable to say the least.

It seems reasonable thus to assume that Percy had in mind a satire of Elizabeth when he created his female protagonist. This assumption is further supported by the fact that Percy's earliest manuscript of the play (Alnwick 508) refers to Epimenide as "Empresse" while the two later ones (Alnwick 509 and Huntington 4) both use "Marquesse" instead. Dimmock rightly notes that this change might well have been made because "Percy felt the potential parallels irrelevant after Elizabeth's death in 1603" (Dimmock *Mahomet* 50). Madeline Dodds has also noted the links between Epimenide, or the Weather Woman, and Elizabeth. The Prologue is a topical comment on the Essex rebellion which ends by lines intended "to congratulate the Queen on the suppression of the rebellion" ("A

Dreame" 190-1). Further, the stage direction *"Here she brandished her glaive [sword] over hed twise over"* (Prol.29), is seen by Dodds as an allusion to a recent incident, narrated by Sir John Harington, in which the Queen did something similar ("A Dreame" 191).

Given the connections between Epimenide and Elizabeth, what new dimensions can be seen in Percy's presentation of women in *Mahomet and his Heaven*? And where does his less than flattering view towards the female sex come from? In answering these questions, and taking into consideration that his women are, as established above, far from Islamic, it becomes necessary to look for the contemporary views on Queen Elizabeth as a woman and a ruler. Percy's depiction of Epimenide, as I show below, shares a lot of ground with the general tendencies of Elizabeth's critics who had objections to Elizabeth as a woman on the throne in the first place. Their attacks included stereotypical accusations of women in general being fickle and shrewish. They also attacked Gloriana personally for being immoral and promiscuous. These themes are discussed in detail below.

5.2.1. The Queen's gender

Queen Elizabeth's position as a female head of state in an overtly patriarchal society was a major cause for concern and criticism for opponents of gynaecocracy in general and Elizabeth herself in particular. As Louis Montrose aptly notes: "as the female ruler of what was, at least in theory, a patriarchal society, Elizabeth incarnated a contradiction at the very center of the Elizabethan sex/gender system" (Montrose "Shaping Fantasies" 77). Elizabeth herself was aware of the delicacy of her position and adopted a male-like approach to state affairs in order to assuage her critics. Her famous words at Tilbury as she was preparing the troops to defend England against the Armada are indicative of this self-awareness: "I know I have the body of a weak and feeble woman, but I have the heart and stomach of a king," a statement which "neatly encapsulates the struggles and contradictions for a woman in a position of power" (Levin *The Heart and Stomach* 1). The dialectic of women and power in Elizabethan England was a complex and multifaceted issue which is beyond the limits of this study, however, with regard to our play study two major issues can be highlighted regarding gynaecocracy: the first is outright condemnation and the second is the attack on female weakness and fickleness. Furthermore, misogynist views on female shrewishness also play a role in the play as expounded below.

5.2.1.1. The gynaecocracy debate

Elizabeth Tudor was the second queen to ascend the English throne. Before Mary I, England was never ruled by a female monarch. Thus, after two consecutive queens and towards the end of Elizabeth's reign, the public mood became even more apprehensive towards gynaecocracy than it had started. Steven Mullaney quotes the French Ambassador as saying in 1597 that despite their love for the ageing Queen, "the English would never again submit to the rule of a woman" (Mullaney "Mourning and Misogyny" 139). When the Queen died, Mullaney adds, "the streets of London were lit by festive bonfires and punctuated by cries of 'We have a king!'" ("Mourning and Misogyny" 139). This joy for having a king does not stem much from hatred of Elizabeth herself, for the English generally loved Elizabeth, but rather from misogynistic views towards gynaecocracy and the insecurity the country feels under a queen for fear of an ill-advised foreign marriage for example. Elizabeth was able to assuage this insecurity by adopting the title and position of a Virgin Queen thus protecting England's sovereignty through giving up an important part of her femininity. But her position as Virgin Queen did not save Elizabeth from becoming an emblem for yet another misogynist concept: that she was a good Queen only because she was an exceptional woman, a woman unlike any other. This last concept manifested itself clearly in one of the most ferocious debates of the second half of the sixteenth century: the debate over gynaecocracy sparked by John Knox's *The First trumpet Blast Against This Monstrous regiment of Women* (1558).

During the last years of Mary I's reign, around 800 Protestants fled persecution to the Continent. Obviously, they were unhappy about the state of the country and saw gender as an important factor in the disintegration of what they wanted to see in England (Palazzolo 106). Knox's work was directed at Mary Tudor primarily but it also hinted at the "monstrous regiment" (unnatural government) of two other Marys: Mary Stuart and her mother Marie of Guise (Jansen 13). Knox wrote to argue that gynaecocracy was "repugnant to nature, contumely to God, a thing most contrarious to his ruled will and approved ordinance, and finally it is the subversion of good order, of all equity and justice" (Knox 9). Unfortunately for the Protestant Knox, his work was published in 1558 shortly before the tables were turned and Elizabeth Tudor became queen (Palazzolo 108). The work was very influential and controversial. Many treatises and pamphlets were written to counter its argument. The replies, though discrediting Knox's argument, indirectly stressed the misogynistic views to which he gave vent by arguing that although women in general were unfit to rule, special cases must be admitted. Knox's importance stems from the fact that, although written and published before Elizabeth's reign, its repercussions sparked the gynaecocracy debate. Knox's "criticism of female rulers," "combative tone" and his timing of publication made his work "not only noteworthy but notorious" (Lee 243). In a sense, the large amount of works that joined the gynaecocracy debate throughout Elizabeth's reign can be seen as echoes to Knox's "blast."

One of the major responses to Knox was John Aylmer's *An Harborowe for Faithfull and Trewe Subjectes against the late blown Blast* (1559). Palazzolo notes that in the course of his response to Knox, Aylmer admits that "God allowed many women to be the Devil's instrument," but he asserts that God "could also make a special woman His own" (109). For Aylmer, women were unworthy of rule but exceptions can be made, and the woman who rises above her inferior female nature could become monarch.

Knox, who seems to have felt the inappropriateness of his views after Elizabeth's ascension, tried to express support for the new Queen in a letter to William Cecil dated 10 April 1559. However, he still made the same assertion of his views on gynaecocracy even when he wanted to praise Elizabeth. He noted:

> the miraculous work of God's comforting His afflicted by an *infirm vessel* I do reverence, and the power of His most potent hand, exalting whom best pleaseth His wisdom, . . . I will obey, albeit that nature and God's most perfect ordinance repugne to [are contrary to] such regiment. (qtd. in Jansen 44, italics mine)

Knox further writes that he is only able to accept Elizabeth's "regiment" as a "miraculous work" by God who granted her a position which is denied by "both nature and God's law" (Jansen 44). Even Protestant reformer John Calvin was involved in the debate. He was reported to have said to Knox in a private conversation that his view on gynaecocracy was that it was "a deviation from the original and proper order of nature, it was to be ranked, no less than slavery, among the punishments consequent upon the fall of man" (Jansen 40). Again, in trying to mend his relationship with an upset Elizabeth, he wrote to William Cecil confirming the statement but at the same time admitting the "peculiar" nature of Elizabeth's case. Calvin was convinced, he wrote, that "there were occasionally women so endowed, that the singular good qualities which shone forth in them, made it evident that they were raised up by divine authority" (Berry 66).

The debate was also remarkable for the perpetuation of negative stereotypes of women which was shared by both sides of the debate. In his denunciation of womankind, Knox listed some of their vices quoted from St. Chrysostom, archbishop of Constantinople. The list is reminiscent of the seven deadly sins in *Mahomet and his Heaven* which can be signs of the failure of gynaecocracy as seen by Percy. Knox's list included weak-will, imprudence, softness, in addition to sins they share with men like vainglory and quickness to anger, which were worse in women as they lacked men's redeeming virtues (Palazzolo 107). Aylmer, in trying to answer Knox, makes the list even more exhaustive and stereotypical. He writes that women can be:

> fond, foolish, wanton, flibbertigibbets [chatterers or gossips], tattlers, triflers, wavering, witless, without counsel, feeble, careless, rash, proud, dainty [delicate], nice [foolish], talebearers, eavesdroppers, tumult-raisers, evil-tongued, worse-minded, and in every wise doltified with the dregs of the devil's dunghill. (qtd. in Jansen 38)

The same contradiction of women's fallibility and Elizabeth's uniqueness among her sex recurs in preachers' discourse regarding their queen as discussed by Margaret Christian. In her article, Christian sheds light on the tense relationship between Elizabeth and her preachers and how they maintained a view that, as a woman, she was ultimately subordinate to them by nature (561). While her position as Queen was not above criticism, her gender was attacked and blamed for issues like military indecisiveness and she was portrayed as a "helpless victim who depended on God for success" (Christian 564).

One would expect to see the heated debate which baptised Elizabeth's reign by fire, and the unfavourable views on gynaecocracy to wane with time, and they did (Cf. Jansen 35–62). However, the craze gained momentum again towards the end of her reign (Palazzolo 104). The reason could be a complicated set of factors like, for example, Protestant fears of the return of popery (McLaren 743). However, it is relevant to note here one side of patriarchal thought that could have led to a resurgence of anti-gynaecocracy. It was hard for these intellectuals and preachers to see women as capable of rule over men let alone countries. Thus, the condescending exception that was made for the case of Elizabeth was a double-edged sword. While it allowed for an interpretation that gave her right to rule, it still maintained an inferior state for women. Thus, if the queen whom they commended falls short of any expectation imagined by the patriarchal society she is ruling, she will immediately lose that commendation and return to her original position as an "infirm vessel." A suitable example of the expectations from female rule has been noted above in the way Cytheræa was crowned in Percy's *The Aphrodysiall*.

Percy's Epimenide is portrayed as a woman who is by nature unfit to rule. Reasons pertaining to her frailty as a woman will be discussed below. However, Epimenide's gender plays another salient role the way Arabia is run. Percy presents Epimenide as unfit to rule her country simply because she is a woman. The objectification of the Empress of the Deserts as a sexual object, wanted and desired by all her male subjects, deprives her of her human and intellectual side. She is simply a woman to be fantasized about, regardless of her being on the throne. Percy's view thus seems to endorse the basic principles of anti-gynaecocracy current in his time. The misogynistic excuses found by Aylmer and Knox for Elizabeth are not present in the play because Epimenide does not rise above the imagined position of her sex but rather affirms it by her sexuality. She is not a Virgin Queen but rather a promiscuous empress. Moreover, we do not see her as a reigning monarch throughout the play. Thus, the "body politic" is conspicuously absent from Percy's view of this woman ruler and when we connect this view with Epimenide's close relationship to Elizabethan iconography and cult mythology, new dimensions can be found in Epimenide that emphasize the topicality of the play.

5.2.1.2. Female fickleness

"Of women kynde suche indeed is the loue" wrote Sir Walter Raleigh in one of his poems, whose subject is generally presumed to be the Queen, complaining about his beloved's mutability. The Queen's inconsistency, viewed as a female trait, was a source of concern for Elizabethan courtiers and politicians who had "a tendency to regard her [the Queen] dismissively as a "typically" unpredictable, wilful and irrational woman" (Hackett 181). In 1597, the Earl of Essex told the French Ambassador that "they laboured under two things at this court, delay and inconstancy, which proceeded chiefly from the sex of the Queen" (qtd. in Eggert 97). Blaming changes in policy on the Queen's sex is a clear reflection of contemporary misogyny as it was Burghley who was "partially if not primarily responsible" for them (Eggert 46). Eggert quotes J. E Neale reporting an interesting story that was widely spread about the Queen's change of mind. This is the story of a carter who "on being informed for the third time that the Queen had altered her plans and did not intend to move on that day, slapped his thigh and said, 'Now I see that the Queen is a woman as well as my wife'" (Neale 351 qtd. in Eggert 46).

All these comments and observations were doubly ironic when combined with Elizabeth's adopted Latin motto *semper eadem* (always the same) which had, as Leah Marcus notes, "an oxymoronic feminine twist, in that her use of *eadem* instead of the usual masculine *idem* associates the feminine gender with steadfastness rather than the more stereotyped flightiness and changeability" (Marcus "Dramatic Experiments" 147).

Of all women's "vices" and stereotypes current in his time, Percy seems to have been interested in female inconsistency and weakness above all. This interest can clearly be seen in his depiction of Epimenide but before discussing this in detail, it is necessary to look at this theme in his source, Lyly's *The Woman in the Moon*.

Elizabeth's description as Cynthia, the Moon goddess, was one of the most persistent among her mythological associations. Lyly chooses the classical goddess Luna as protector of his Pandora and the moon as her final abode. The moon's changeable shape and its presidency over the ebb and flow of the sea associated it naturally with inconsistency and mutability (see Hackett 182-3).

In her penultimate speech, Nature describes women as:

> mutable in all their loves,
> Fantastical, childish and foolish in their desires,
> . . . .
> And stark mad when they cannot have their will (V.i.329–332)

Leah Scragg comments that this passage combines in it "both sixteenth-century constructions of the nature of women and the misogynistic tenor of the myth regarding the origins of the woes of the human race" (Lyly 20). She further notes that although Pandora's box is not referred to in the play, the heroine herself is the box of woes in that "it is her unstable personality that brings strife and sorrow to the world of the play" (20).

It is worth noting that while the idea of female fickleness being responsible for strife requires critical analysis, like Scragg's, to be brought to light, Percy makes it absolutely clear that Epimenide is responsible for her country's woes. In another unfavourable change, the mutability of Percy's heroine is sex-based and not caused by external factors like gods' interference. The concept of the seven deadly sins committed by Epimenide places a stress on personal choice and weakness towards temptation and denies the heroine the redeeming excuse of external influence.

Percy's intention on inverting all the perfections of Pandora to imperfections in his play is given clear expression in the final scenes of the play. Commenting on the great confusion Epimenide causes in Paradise, Adriel says that "Rather some Malady she is, crept new / Furth Pandoraes Bottle, into the world" (IV.v.14–5).

Other scenes in *Mahomet and his Heaven* show criticism of stereotypical female characteristics which were criticised by misogynists and anti-gynaecocracy campaigners. The negative female characteristics ascribed to Epimenide include weakness, inability to rule men, being a fantasy-inducing sexual object and frivolity. One scene where these attributes are more salient is III.iv where Epimenide is approached by the two disguised angels Haroth and Maroth. This scene, identified by Dodds as the one of main scenes adapted by Percy from Lyly's *Woman in the Moon*, is hard to follow due to plenty of incomplete sentences, obscure references and vague stage direction. However, the light-hearted nature of the scene can be easily made out. Earlier in the play, Tubal and Caleb proposed to Epimenide and she took their proposals seriously and defined certain demands for the fulfilments of their desires. Here, the scene looks more like one of the comic subplot scenes popular in renaissance drama. Epimenide does not take the new suitors seriously. The pleading words of the disguised angels do not mean anything to her and sometimes she does not even listen to what they are saying as she gets deep into a game of words with her handmaids.

Epimenide starts the scene by asking Haroth and Maroth what they want in a quasi-sacrilegious question that combines the Lord's name with "Divells mattens"[21] (III.iv.1). When Haroth and Maroth make their proposals for love, the dialogue is diverted by Epimenide and her two handmaids to a side talk of puns and sexual innuendos. For example, when Nabatha urges the Empress to "graunt them their Loves," (III.iv.9) Epimenide accuses her of having an affair with Haroth and Maroth: "Y'have had the first cutt at the brown loafe?" "Nor a Toast of the white one" (III.iv.11–12) replies Nabatha indicating that her mistress's chastity is related to her own.[22] The scene continues on the same level of dialogue with apparent triviality and incoherence. This can be seen as a sign of Percy's mediocrity as a playwright, but the rest of the play is plain enough to understand unlike this scene. The inconsistency, I believe, is related to Epimenide's commonness, in that her speech is similar to that of clowns and fools. As far as the heroine's characterization is concerned, the scene

---

[21] *Mattens*: morning prayers, matins (Dimmock *Mahomet* 213 n. 1)

[22] The brown and white loaves in this dialogue may refer to the mistress and her maids respectively, and having a slice of one of them means staining their chastity. In *Titus Andronicus*, as Chiron and Demetrius are preparing for the rape of Lavinia, Demetrius says: "and easy it is / Of a cut loaf to steal a shive" (II, i, 86-7). The loaf is used to refer symbolically for a woman's chastity and Demetrius is hinting that it is difficult to tell the chastity of a married woman as it is difficult to know if a shive was taken from an already cut loaf.

emphasizes the fact that Epimenide is essentially a flawed human being and this and similar scenes are but a manifestation of this basic personality trait. This is in complete contrast to the all-endowed Pandora who is essentially perfect but she undergoes trying circumstances that make her err. Thus, Percy's allegory of Elizabeth is that of a typical woman from the point of view of an Elizabethan misogynist: flawed by her nature.

Another important difference between the two scenes (*Mahomet* III.iv and *The Woman* I.i) is that, in *The Woman*, Pandora is presented as melancholic, sorrowful and tongue-tied. Despite her haughty and indifferent attitude towards the shepherds, Pandora still wins our affection because of these characteristics. She is presented as the victim of a magical spell under which she has no choice but to be the way she is. Thus, when she runs away screaming "Will you not suffer me to take my rest?" (I.i.226), she leaves an audience who will most likely sympathize with her as her departure means that she can no longer tolerate her own sorrowful mood, let alone intrusion on her privacy.

The case is different when we come to Epimenide. She attacks and humiliates the two angels in a manner that also takes away a good part of her dignity. In other words, her own stature as an empress is much debased through her use of language and her relationship with her handmaids. As far as language is concerned, she speaks in an unpoetic and homely language that does not fit royalty and this is further stressed through contrast with the poetic language used by Haroth and Maroth. The following is but an example:

> Maroth   Our boanes, you see, be full and sappie, As
>   Be the kiddes that bound from Hill to hill
>   In Aprill. Why should you then, kind Partridge,
>   Compare us to your Fathers rotten boanes?
> Epimenide Have you never heard of a gilted scull?
> Maroth   Never, deare Madame.
> Epimenide Then I will tell you.
>   Scythians made drinking cups of deadmens sculls.
>   (III.iv.77–84)

The contrast between the refinement of the angels' speech and the dullness of Epimenide runs throughout the scene and marks the queen as unfit to rule even on the level of her vocabulary.

At one point, Nabatha makes the following remarks to Epimenide about the two suitors, who are angels dressed up as a poet and a musician: "they be Poets, and Poets speake / Ever by Metaphores" (III.iv.54). This observation is quite vital in understanding the composition of this scene. Throughout the dialogue, there seems to be a lack of communication between the two parties involved. While men speak in metaphors as Nabatha notes, women, especially Epimenide, take metaphors literally and play with words producing a bawdy farce. This type of play on words is typical of clowns and fools in Renaissance drama. Epimenide's actions also stress the same point as she does some comic stunts on stage as well. Near the end of the scene, as her ridicule of Haroth and Maroth reaches its height, she claims that they stink and she and her handmaids close their noses and leave the scene running away. As a result, Epimenide is not only degraded from the dignity of an empress, she is also presented in a manner similar to a kitchen-maid in her words and actions. Interestingly, calling Elizabeth a "pisskitchen," which according to *The Routledge Dictionary of Historical Slang* means "kitchen-maid" (Partridge), was an actual libel recorded by Cressy as uttered by Sir John Perrot, Elizabeth's lord deputy in Ireland (Cressy 75).

Another point that degrades the figure of Epimenide in this scene is her relationship with her maidservants. The way the three characters interact is far from a typical monarch-servant relationship. In a scene which shows Epimenide's lack of dignity or respect to others as well as her inability to concentrate on what is being said, Nabatha and Shebe, though they take part in her verbal games, plead on behalf of the suitors asking Epimenide to accept their plea. Compassion with others is one positive attribute the maids have and the empress obviously lacks. Moreover, they sometimes mock her as a person and even as a state figure. When Epimenide gives Shebe a "flirt" (a blow) and screams at her, the following dialogue occurs:

Nabatha	You would have made Bag-pipe, Madame, you give
	So sound a Blowe.
Shebe	Wanting a cup of Ale
	To make her looke fatt.
Epimenide	Best grace may be in
	Empresse of our state, know you not that? Ha.
Nabatha	Your Empresses state lyeth in your choppings.
Epimenide	Then the choppins beene Pillars to the state.
Shebe	Trewe, deare Madame. (III.iv.20–26)

This dialogue, in which Epimenide at one point says that her choppins, or shoes, are the pillars to the state, is a debasement of the position of empress and a presentation of Epimenide as a person who does not appreciate her own position in the political and social hierarchy. John Aylmer's list of women's vices is of help here. He mentions that women can be "flibbertigibbets [chatterers or gossips], tattlers, triflers, wavering, witless" (qtd. in Jansen 38), characteristics which are apparent in this scene. Percy's presentation thus emanates from contemporary misogynist views on women especially women in power and his Epimenide is a manifestation of women's triviality and lack of wit.

5.2.1.3. The Shrew Queen

Epimenide's last episode in the play is by far the most striking of her actions. Having learned the secret prayer to ascend to Heaven, the shrewish Empress arrives in the Mahometan bliss and wreaks havoc in the place. She insults everyone present, attacks Mahomet physically more than once and rudely asks him to "Make cleane [her] shooe" (V.iii.25). Her insolence reaches an apogee when she asks him to kiss her "cul" (V.iv.6), or buttocks. Throughout her career onstage, Epimenide has covered prominent contemporary misogynist stereotypes (interestingly listed by Aylmer above) like: inconstancy, wantonness, wavering, carelessness and pride. Percy leaves to the end one of the more salient contemporary conceptions about women: that of being shrews or scolds.

Interestingly, one possible source for this episode in *Mahomet and his Heaven* is a ballad entitled "The Wanton Wife of Bath," an anonymous work published in 1600. The ballad uses the character from Chaucer's *Tales* and narrates an imagined scene where the wife has died "And then her soul at Heaven's gate / Did knocke most mightily" (7–8). A series of biblical personages ask her to leave because she is a sinner. The list includes Adam, David, Solomon, Mary Magdalene, Paul and Peter among others. But the wife abuses each of them in turn reminding them of their own sins. Finally, Jesus comes and accepts her into his paradise.

Mahomet and his Heaven bears clear links to the ballad in Epimenide's Heaven scenes. Both present a shrewish woman who insults and attacks everyone who confronts her. However, unlike Epimenide who is punished at the end, the wife is pardoned and accepted into Jesus' paradise. Percy's linkage of his heroine with such shrewish behaviour was a dangerous topic and if authorities had come across it, he would have been in trouble. Ernest Kuhl noted in 1929 that the Ballad was censored as "disorderly" and the two men who published it were heavily fined (Kuhl 177). Kuhl tries to find the reasons behind such a tough decision towards an apparently innocent work like this ballad. The Essex rebellion is Kuhl's central point. He argues that the ballad offended those in power because of its "emphasis on mercy and forgiveness" (183) in a time when Essex was on trial and had already sought forgiveness from the Queen. Of the exact reason behind the ban, we cannot be sure. But we can be sure that whatever reason it could have been, Percy's use of the theme in his play, is far more "disorderly" as it links the shrewish hell-raiser of Heaven to

Queen Elizabeth. This episode has not been identified as a source for *Mahomet and his Heaven* before[23] and his incorporation of the ballad into his play gives Epimenide, and consequently Elizabeth, yet another stereotypical female attribute in being a violent woman and a scold.

In a patriarchal society like Elizabethan England, women who rebelled against their position in society were seen as a threat to the social order. Thus, ascribing the quality of fiery mood to Elizabeth only adds to the criticism of her right to the throne. After all, as Jacqueline Eales notes, women who defied the social hierarchy "were potentially a source of disorder and sexual licence" (Eales 22). Religious discourse supported this view, and the Wife of Bath's inability to enter paradise at the beginning runs along the lines of a later religious work. In *A bride-bush: or, a direction for married persons*, William Whately wrote that a woman's "chiefest ornament" as "lowliness of mind" and submission to her husband. Moreover, Eales notes that Whately "warned that a woman who believed herself to be her husband's equal or his superior could not attain a state of grace, or spiritual salvation" (24). Thus, a woman's entry to Paradise was linked to her obedience to male relatives and her rejection of shrewishness.

The heaven scenes in acts IV and V in *Mahomet and his Heaven* have an overall concern with highlighting the issue of female aggressiveness and lawlessness. For example, astonished by Epimenide's entry to Heaven, the angels assume she must be "Doubtles some witch" (IV.v.10). Witches were on the extreme end of social exclusion and were emblematic of women's disorderly nature and affiliation with the devil. The whole episode is presented as a case in point for proving female tendency towards shrewish behaviour. Thus, having suppressed Epimenide's heavenly mutiny, Mahomet and his angels comment on her behaviour concluding that:

> For now wee may learn, taught by proofe of Nature,
> No Beasts so headstrong as the woman creature (IV.vii.16–7).

Considering Epimenide's misbehaviour, Mahomet asks his archangels what punishment they should administer to her. Interestingly, the two suggestions, as Dimmock correctly notes, are related to contemporary views on proper chastisement for scolds. Gabriel suggests that:

---

[23] In an informal chat, Matthew Dimmock did mention coming across a source for the play after the publication of the critical edition. He said it was related to Epimenide but did not specify the title.

she be sett up unto chin in water,
And if that in one year coole not her chollar,
Then to duck her ore eares for good and all. (V.x.12–14)

Dimmock notes that this punishment "corresponds to a contemporary tract that insists 'scolds ought to be ducked over head and ears in the water in a ducking stool'" (Dimmock *Mahomet* 235 n.12). The mentioning of choler in relation to Epimenide's hot temper is another reference to contemporary understanding of bodily fluids and their influence on temper as choler was believed to be responsible for hot-tempered anger (See Paster 13). Adriel suggests that "she bleede seven ounces at the Tong" (V.x.15). Again, Dimmock points out that this could be a reference to the "scold's bridle" (*Mahomet* 236 n. 15) which was a form of punishment for scolds. It consisted of an iron muzzle or cage for the head with an iron curb-plate projecting into the mouth and pressing down on top of the tongue. The curb-plate was "often spiked" and thus caused bleeding of the tongue (*Mahomet* 236 n. 15).

Moreover, the topic of ill-tempered women is given fuller vent in a semi-comic manner in the form of a song. Based on the popular proverb "better be a shrew than a sheep" or "better marry a shrew than a sheep," the song is sung as an argument between two parties about which of the two types of womankind is preferable. Thus, the Lawyer and Pyr sing: "Better a shrowe than a sheepe be" to which the Fryar and Whisk reply "Better sheepe be then shrowe, say wee" (IV.ix.111–2). Belpheghor, who plays the arbiter of the debate, repeats the refrain "By the foregoing Premisie / Whither the better is, Troe wee" (117–8) and at the end of the song he sums up its misogynistic mood by concluding that "By the foregoing Premisie / Neither good Barrill I agree" (133–4). In other words, he does not prefer either of the two evils of female mood.

5.2.2. The Queen's immorality

As is the case with many rulers and members of royalty, Elizabeth Tudor's personal life was subject to close scrutiny and experienced many scandals. Thus, her detractors found plenty of material to criticise her. Her position as a female ruler was central to many of these attacks on her which stopped at nothing to show her as unworthy of the throne. The scandals around her life started from her younger years and continued into her reign as queen. Her critics even extended their attacks to her parentage and right to the throne. As will be shown below, all this accumulated in a body of criticism that worked against the position Elizabeth and her government were trying to portray for her: that of a Virgin Queen. This

part will also try to establish that William Percy's presentation of
Epimenide stems from, or at least supports, the position taken by
Elizabeth's critics against her personal conduct and thus undermining her
position as a Virgin Queen, and, as the discussion will show her very royal
position as well.

As a young princess, Elizabeth lived at the household of her father's
widow, Katherine Parr, in Chelsea and Hanworth in Middlesex. During
this stay she came in touch with "the handsome, dashing, but fatally
reckless Sir Thomas Seymour" who had already been in trouble for
Katerine Parr's hasty marriage to him after Henry Tudor's death (James).
Even before Katherine's death in September 1548, Seymour was rumoured
to have started taking liberties with the young princess and later he was
considering her as an attractive marriage possibility (Cavanagh 10). At his
trial for treason, he was accused of plans to kidnap the young king,
Edward VI's, and Elizabeth with the aim of marrying the princess and
installing himself as governor of the king's person (Bernard). The trial
heard from witnesses the extent to which Seymour took liberties with the
royal heir while she dwelt with him. Elizabeth's governess, Katherine
Ashley, testified that:

> He wold come many mornyngs into the said Lady *Elizabeth*'s chamber,
> before she were redy, and sometyme before she did rise. And if she were
> up, he would bid her good morrow an ax how she did, and strike her upon
> the bak or on the Buttockes familiarly . . . And if she were in hir Bed he
> wold put open the Curteyns, . . . and make as though he would come at hir:
> And she wold go further in the Bed, so that he could not come at hir. And
> one mornyng he strave to have kissed hir in hir bed: and this Examinate
> was there, and bad hym go away for shame. (qtd. in Cavanagh 12 italics in
> original).

Katherine Parr was also suspicious of her husband's behaviour. Thus,
"One tyme," according to Ashley, "the [dowager] Quene, suspecting the
often accesse of the Admirall to the Lady Elizabeth's Grace, cam sodenly
upon them, wher they were all alone, (he having her in his Armes)" (qtd.
in Bernard). These stories were further confirmed by many servants who
gave witness in the case (Cavanagh 13). Critics studying the incident noted
Elizabeth's awareness of the gravity of Seymour's moves. However, G.
W. Bernard still pointed out that when she became aware of Seymour's
intentions to marry her and "though aware of the political sensitivities,"
Elizabeth was "far from reluctant" (Bernard). Regardless of the actual
extent to which these "familiarities" went, the rumours that accompanied
Elizabeth's teenage years may well have set the tone for her critics to see
in her a woman far from chastity and virginity.

Elizabeth's Catholic enemies tried to extend the accusations of immorality to reach Elizabeth's mother, Anne Boleyn, and thus criticise the grounds on which she became an heir to throne in the first place. J. E. Phillips notes that in one of the Catholic accounts of the execution of Mary Stuart, claims were made that undermined not only Elizabeth's right to the throne but more sinister issues pertaining to her parentage. A supporter of Mary, Adam Blackwood, wrote *Martyre de la Royne d'Escosse* (the martyrdom of the Queen of Scotland), in which he asserted that Elizabeth was a bastard and a usurper who had no right to claim the throne. Not only was Henry's marriage to Anne illegitimate, claimed Blackwood, but it was incestuous as well for Anne was in fact Henry's daughter due to a previous sexual affair he had had with her mother, Lady Elizabeth Howard. Elizabeth being born six months after his marriage, Henry was suspicious that she not was his daughter as "Anne had slept with many men [including] her brother George" (Phillips 174).

On the throne, Elizabeth faced rumours about her personal conduct that were no less rampant. In a chapter dedicated to slanders against Elizabeth, Carole Levin notes that arrests due to "lewd words" against the Queen were not rare during her reign and that "the records of the Privy Council are filled with examples of people charged with the crime of slandering the queen" (*The Heart and Stomach* 69). These rumours were made by both the public and people in position. Levin's examples of people convicted of slander included normal citizens, clergy as well as members of the upper class. Even abroad, the humorous Henry IV of France was famously quoted as saying that "There were three things inscrutable to intelligence," the third of which was "Whether Queen Elizabeth was a maid or no" (Baker 84).

One of the most remarkable themes for the rumours was Elizabeth's illegitimate children (Cressy 69). These rumours, Adam Fox notes, were popular as they appealed to two different sectors of the society "opponents of the crown and its religion" as well as "supporters who hoped vainly for an heir to the throne" (Fox 362). The latter section justifies what Levin noted about the increased intensity of the rumours in the last two decades of Elizabeth's reign. The number of alleged children reached as many as five in some cases (Levin *The Heart and Stomach* 88, 90). Rumours of alleged children were perhaps just a reflection of the gossip that accompanied the Queen's amorous adventures back in her youthful days (and childbearing age as well). While the Seymour incident was perhaps more of an improper advance by a rash man towards Elizabeth, the later rumours about her love affairs involved her personally as a culpable sinner in addition to the social condemnation for a woman's sexual adventures inherent in a patriarchal society like Elizabethan England.

Elizabeth's partner in those rumours of love was more often than not Robert Dudley, Earl of Leicester (Cressy 69). Apart from the fact that most stories related to alleged children by Elizabeth name him as the father, it was a fact that he was very close to her and she was seen everywhere with him during the first five years of her reign (Levin *The Heart and Stomach* 71). This closeness sparked the expected deluge of gossip which started from home and reached interested parties abroad. In April 1559, the Spanish Ambassador, wrote to King Philip that "during the last few days Lord Robert has come so much into favour that he does whatever he likes with affairs and it is even said that her Majesty visits him in his chamber day and night" (Hume 31). Levin finds the rumours to be not completely baseless as she narrates the incident when Elizabeth feared for her life due to severe smallpox and instructed that Dudley be made protector of the realm. The suspicious detail, Levin notes, was that Elizabeth also ordered that Dudley's servant be given a large salary, an instruction "which does suggest there were aspects of her relationship with Dudley that she did not want exposed" (Levin *The Heart and Stomach* 74).

Elizabeth's haters among her people capitalized on these rumours to achieve a political effect. The claims that the queen was not chaste were not simply slanderous statements stemming from malcontent. In Elizabethan England, Elizabeth's chastity was an essential part to her political stature and right to rule. The complex relationship between the Queen's personal conduct and her chastity on the one hand and her political position on the other was embodied through two intertwining concepts: the assumption of the position "the Virgin Queen" and the political theory of the king's "two bodies."

The Queen's virginity was one of her most salient attributes since the 1580s. The term "Virgin Queen" understandably gained more importance with the Queen moving closer to old age and losing hope of begetting an heir to the throne which meant that marriage became only a matter of linking the throne to a "powerful prince" (Doran "Why Did Elizabeth Not Marry?" 30). However, Elizabeth's assumption of the title was based on several considerations strongly connected to the legitimacy of her rule. Basic consideration would have been the importance of her own, as well as England's, independence from the interference of a king consort, whether an Englishman or a foreigner. A king consort would have been closer to the Queen in stature than any other male in the kingdom while at the same time deserving her uxorial obedience. Misogynist objections to gynaecocracy would have been inflamed even further with the presence of such a person. However, and above all these practical considerations, Susan Doran points out a very important background to Elizabeth's assumption of the Virgin Queen status:

> Elizabeth was aware of the value of symbols, fictions and drama in the exercise of political power, and it is often said that she fashioned for herself a public persona as a virginal goddess, which would give her a special mystique as a female ruler and allow her to command the respect and awe reserved for kings. Similarly, through the image of the Virgin Queen she was able to present herself as no ordinary woman, but as an exceptional woman whose purity made her worthy of devotion, even adoration. (Doran *Monarchy* 9)

Elizabeth's virginity was a far more complex concept than a mere assumption of chastity and purity. The importance of this view is that it shows a more serious side to attacks on Elizabeth's moral conduct. In other words, if Elizabeth is shown as the opposite of the chaste and virgin queen she purports to be, it follows logically that her very position on the throne becomes moot. Dismantling Elizabeth from the robe of virginity can also be seen as a counterattack on the pseudo-Christian association she tried to gain by aligning herself with the Virgin Mary. As Carole Levin notes, Elizabeth and her government "deliberately took over the symbolism" of the cult of Virgin Mary in order to promote "a cult of the Virgin Queen" (Levin *The Heart and Stomach* 70). Therefore, Percy's allegory of Elizabeth through Epimenide must be studied carefully under this light: Epimenide's morality reflects the Queen's morality, and the Queen's morality is linked to her right to rule.

The other concept, which would help us appreciate the gravity of the attacks on the Queen's chastity, is the doctrine of the king's two bodies. Theorized by Ernst Kantorowicz in 1957, the concept originated from medieval political and religious thought but it was "codified and disseminated in a highly polemical form during Queen Elizabeth's reign" (Carroll 127). Kantorowicz also noted that it was the body of Elizabeth that revealed the whole concept of a dual body to him, though the theory is medieval in its origins (Kantorowicz vii). The doctrine proposed that kings had two bodies: a body natural and a body politic. In other words, a distinction is drawn between the human being and the position he or she occupies. Applied to Elizabeth's position as a "king" and a woman at the same time, Elizabethan jurists and courtiers found in it a proper explanation for some questions raised about Elizabeth's life and personal conduct.[24] Thus, the idea that Elizabeth had two bodies in her person, her mortal body and the immortal body of the "king-who-never-dies" was used to insure that "the ills to which all mortal flesh was subject (including femaleness) did not diminish the aura of divine authority attaching to her ruler's person" (Weil 166). This view was expressed early on in Elizabeth's reign as part of John Aylmer's defence of gynaecocracy. Aylmer used the theory of the king's two bodies to defend the Queen's weaknesses and female frailty which he considered as part of the body natural not the body politic (Jansen 38-9).

Moreover, Elizabeth's celibacy was central to the view she fostered of her two bodies. Her unmarried body became a symbol in its integrity (natural and politic) for the integrity of the realm (Loades 306-7). David Loades refers to the Tilbury speech, quoted above, as proof of the presence of this concept in Elizabeth's own understanding: "when in 1588 she rhetorically juxtaposed the body of a weak and feeble woman with her "foul scorn" that the prince of Parma should seek to invade her realm, the imagery was quite deliberate" (307).

However, this view of two bodies in one was not shared by everyone. Elizabeth's critics did not distinguish her personal actions from her position. For example, in 1563, an Edmund Baxter "openly expressed the not uncommon view that Elizabeth's reputed unchastity disqualified her as a monarch" (Levin *The Heart and Stomach* 76). Baxter had said that "Lord Robert [Dudley] kept her majesty and that she was a naughty woman and could not rule her realm" (Cressy 70). Levin further notes the grave importance of female chastity in relation to femaleness. To a queen, being unchaste was equivalent to a king being unable to keep his word or being shamed on the battlefield. Having sexual relationships meant Elizabeth was not fit to rule "something that had never been said of her father or any other heterosexual male ruler" (Levin *The Heart and Stomach* 76).

At home, some subjects talked of the Virgin Queen's immorality with apparent bile. The connection between chastity and right to rule is implicit in these "seditious words." For example, in 1589 one Parson Wylton was reported to have said "openly in church ... that the Queen's majesty was an arrant whore" since "the Queen is a dancer," and "all dancers are whores" (Levin "Gender, Monarchy" 89-90). Abroad, one of Elizabeth's severest critics on the Continent, Cardinal William Allen, wrote in 1588 an invective diatribe against Elizabeth entitled *Admonition to the Nobility and People of England*. In this work, apart from the routine accusations of

---

[24] On the different dimensions of the doctrine that the queen had a body politic and a body natural see Axton 11–25.

Elizabeth being "an incestuous bastard, begotten and born in sin," Allen used and created a great deal of rumours and libels against the Queen including accusations of insatiable sexual lust which she used Dudley to satisfy. Elizabeth's lust is only increased with time and "the older she gets, the more debased is her court" (Levin *The Heart and Stomach* 81). Allen hinted that the Queen abused her body natural and politic saying that "with divers others [other than Dudley], she hath abused her bodie against God's lawes, to the disgrace of princely majestie." He added that she hazarded the throne and country by refusing to get married "because she cannot confine herself to one man" (qtd. in Levin *The Heart and Stomach* 80). Cressy also noted that the doctors at Louvain insisted that Elizabeth was "not a righteous queen, and ought to be put out of her seat" (Cressy 75).

Attacks that linked Elizabeth's sexuality with her policy continued even posthumously. *Pruritanus* [sic], a Catholic book published in France in 1609 and smuggled to England, was highly critical of Henry VIII, Elizabeth and James. The "mock-catechism" accused Elizabeth of "immodesty, of having given birth to sons and daughters, of having prostituted her body to many different nationalities, of having slept with *blackamoors*"[25] (qtd. in Watkins 136-7, italics mine). England's sovereignty is thus compromised through the Queen compromising her body (see Schulte for more).

In Percy's *Mahomet and his Heaven*, Epimenide is presented as the centre of her male subjects' sexual fantasies. The action in the play shows that she is largely responsible for the fantasies cherished about her. She double deals lovers, gives false promises, derides them and avoids commitment to any of them. Compared to Lyly's Pandora, who at least gets married to one of her suitors, she is a playful woman who, although not involved in a sexual act during the action of the play, is understood to be immoral. The following discussion sheds light on this side of Epimenide and compares her further to Lyly's Pandora through studying scene I.iv in *Mahomet* in comparison to scene II.i, in *The Woman*. The two scenes were linked by Dodds in her study of the sources of *Mahomet and his Heaven*.

Both scenes present the heroine in a position where she is being approached by suitors and she rejects them. Pandora's suitors are the Utopian Shepherds (Stesias, Learchus, Iphicles and Melos) and Epimenide's suitors are Tubal and Caleb (both pastors of the desert).

---

[25] This libel can be seen as part of the Catholic outcry against Elizabeth's relationships with Al-Mansour of Morocco, which intensified after the battle of Alcazar and the Moroccan ambassadors' three visits to London in the last years of Elizabeth's reign (the last visit being in 1600).

Despite the thematic similarity, the two playwrights handle their topic differently. The presentation of the heroine is my primary interest here. Percy's Epimenide falls short of Pandora on the moral level.

The similarity between the two scenes stems from the theme of a beautiful woman whose love is being sought by a group of humble suitors. The heroine in both plays does not reject the pleas immediately but rather asks for a tangible proof for love. Under Jupiter's influence, Pandora expresses her hunger for "rule," "empery," "sovereignty," "princely sway" and "crown" (II.i.8–12). When the shepherds enter, they speak of their infatuation and their speeches take one form of a rhetorical question like "how long shall sorrow's winter… before my suit obtain thy…" and "how long shall death … abridge the course of my … life, / before Pandora love poor Iphicles." After giving them a task to prove their love, "slay the savage boar" (152), the shepherds leave and Pandora expresses her intention to keep them busy with "dangerous exploits" (159). In the corresponding scene in *Mahomet and his Heaven*, Tubal and Caleb present their cases to Epimenide who shows little interest in the pastors' words. Her responses to the suitors range from demanding actions, rather than words, to mocking their offers. Finally, like Pandora, she asks them to perform a task and makes them swear on the "Alcorans cover" (I.iv.128). In this case, the suitors are asked to steal Geber's signet and purse. Apart from the negative moral implications of stealing, the task itself is selfish and personal in nature if compared to Pandora's task for the latter will rid Utopia of a nuisance while this will only shift magic from the hands of one "Figure-Setter" (103) to another.

Percy's portrayal of love proposals is quite different from Lyly's. It is clear that the pastors in Percy are not seeking decent matrimony with Epimenide and that they seek her for both of them at the same time. There is little doubt about this as neither Islam nor Christianity allows such a relationship (polyandry) and, after all, the idea of marriage is never referred to by any of the characters. Neither of the two suitors shows jealousy or even objection to the other's attempts. In fact, as they leave to perform the task she gave them, *together* but in different directions, Tubal asks her "And love *us*?" (I.iv.123, italics mine) and Caleb confirms the question in the same line "Unfeynedly?" Here we see Epimenide apparently promising an amorous relationship to two of her subjects with no intention of marriage. The possibility that she is only being playful and not serious does not preclude criticism against a character that mingles in such a manner with commons and takes these matters lightly. Thus, as explained earlier, Elizabeth's detractors were focused on discrediting her chastity in order to discredit her rule, and Percy's presentation of Muslim women via Epimenide is heavily loaded with this highly dangerous issue.

5.3. Other women

The other female characters in *Mahomet and his Heaven* are Nabatha and Shebe, Epimenide's maids and Tib, the Chiause's[26] wife. Nabatha and Shebe are what may be termed "twin characters." Like Haroth and Maroth, and Tubal and Caleb, these two characters act and speak in identical manner. None of them has any distinguishing feature from the other. None of them even appears in a scene if the other does not. As Epimenide's maids, Nabatha and Shebe accompany her throughout the action. Their characters are promoted at the expense of Epimenide. More often than not, they take the role of an obedient follower and their comments usually echo Epimenide's words. At times, however, they play the role of an intercessor between Epimenide and Haroth and Maroth, which shows them in a more humane and favourable light in contrast to their mistress's arrogance. However, there is the incident, noted above, when in III.iv their relationship with Epimenide seems to change to become more like a common and informal interaction between equals. This incident has opposite reflections on the characters involved. Playing tricks with servants brings Epimenide down but lifts them up. It also gives us a different view of the maids where they are shown to have a sense of humour befitting to their position. Contrary to this, Epimenide's humour makes her clown-like and less respectable.

The important piece of action related to the two handmaids happens in the final scenes of the play. When Epimenide, Haroth and Maroth are sent to punishment, Nabatha and Shebe receive a different end. They are asked by Mahomet to marry Tubal and Caleb and they happily accept. This shows that the two maids are chaste in nature and attaining marriage is one of their dreams. The opposite to this throughout the play has been Epimenide whose typical inconsistency meant that she kept playing love games with five or six characters and ended up in punishment. What comes to play an important role in our understanding of these two characters is Leah Scragg's note that Lyly introduced the two handmaids who wait upon Pandora to make her even more like Elizabeth. Percy only followed suit in this regard. Thus, the logical extension of the idea of associating Epimenide with Elizabeth is associating Nabatha and Shebe

---

[26] From Turkish *çavus*, A Turkish messenger, sergeant, or lictor, *OED*. See also Dimmock p. 189 n.38.

with Elizabeth's ladies-in-waiting. The fact that Nabatha and Shebe get married while Epimenide is punished and never marries is another topical element closely connected to events in the Elizabeth court.

Elizabeth's avowed celibacy and adoption of the Virgin Queen status was not viewed positively by her detractors. Combined with alleged sexual promiscuity, celibacy becomes a state of prolonged life in sin. The views of Elizabeth's critics on her marriage were perhaps given more ground for conjecture by rumours and actual events about what many historians have termed Elizabeth's "notorious sexual jealousy" (Hammer "Sex and the Virgin Queen" 80-1). Examples cited in reference to this sexual covetousness are numerous. For example, when Elizabeth Throckmorton, lady-in-waiting to Elizabeth, married Sir Walter Raleigh in secret, Raleigh was arrested and imprisoned in the Tower of London and Throckmorton was expelled from court. On another occasion, Mary Shelton, a lady of the Privy Chamber, married widower John Scudamore. Upon hearing the news, Elizabeth "exploded" and "according to one witness: "The queen hathe usid Mary Shelton very yell for hir mariage. She hath telt liberall bothe with bloes and yevell wordes and hathe not yet graunted hir consent. I thinke in my conscience never woman bought hir hosbaunt more derare then she hath done." Elizabeth was so angry with her servant that she attacked her with a candlestick and broke the woman's finger" (Hammer "Sex and the Virgin Queen" 80-1; Doran "Why Did Elizabeth Not Marry?" 32-3).

It is difficult to judge whether the Queen's responses to the marriages and sexual misdemeanours of her courtiers were the result of an attempt to maintain strict court discipline centred around her, or from this assumed jealousy. But for the critics of Elizabeth, one interpretation was certainly favoured above the other. Thus, Percy's presentation of the two maids bears strong links to contemporary negative views on Elizabeth's conduct as a queen and her relationship with her women of her court. Her failure to attain the sacrament of matrimony is linked to sexual promiscuity and is also seen as a defect in her character. "Natural" women were not supposed to remain celibate but get married like Shebe and Nabatha.

In opposition to this presentation comes Tib, the Chiause's wife. She is a minor character who only appears in three consecutive scenes with few lines to speak. However, she plays the role of an unfaithful wife who has an extramarital relationship with the "Fryar" (or "Dervis" as he is sometimes called). Her husband is presented as a greedy officer who exploits the drought to accumulate a wealth especially from the Friar and his mosque. When the Friar visits them to arrange water supply for the mosque, she secretly talks to him and they agree to meet near the mosque after the "the Evensong," when Tib will be "at my Prayers and at my beades" (II.v.61). The fact that the mosque is being used as a place for amorous rendezvous gives the cuckoldry more negative connotations. What adds to Tib's unfaithfulness is the fact that during the conversation between the Chiause and the Friar, Pyr,[27] the angel in the comic subplot, kidnaps her husband and she is left alone with the Friar to arrange for their meeting. The fact that her husband is taken away in a mysterious way does not have any effect on her. As the Friar celebrates the disappearance of the Chiause, interpreting it that the devil took him in answer to the Friar's prayers, she only says one mysterious sentence "the Tyme requireth other wordes, other Fashions" (II.v.55) and then she agrees to meet the Friar. Percy's stage direction leaves no room to ponder about the nature of their relationship: "*Here they kiste each in the Mouth without smack or other Foolerye*" (II.v.72SD). Kissing on the mouth is obviously a sexual act and interestingly it was reported that Elizabeth "was seen to kiss Robert [Dudley] at a crossroads once, on the lips as spouses do" (Thomas 105). Tib is presented not only as an unfaithful wife, but also as a careless woman who shows no emotions or regret about her husband's strange disappearance.

Tib's name is worth some attention here. Despite the great deal of effort expended by Matthew Dimmock in his notes on character names in his edition of the play, he surprisingly does not comment on the name of Tib. Nonetheless, research into the background of the name gives important findings. One of the countless slanders against Queen Elizabeth collected by modern critics is one by a "Cornish recusant named John Trevelyan who declared in 1628 that 'Queen Tibb (meaning Queen Elizabeth) was as arrant a whore as ever breathed, and that she was [tupped?] by Essex and Leicester and others'" (Cressy 73). Thus, the name Tibb was used as a pet name for Elizabeth. The *OED* confirms this fact and adds an enlightening piece of information. The name is a shortened form of Isabel which is the Latin version of Elizabeth. More importantly, the dictionary notes that the name is:

> Formerly, a typical name for a woman of the lower classes, as in *Tib and Tom* (cf. Jack and Gill). Also, A girl or lass, a sweetheart, a mistress; dyslogistically, a young woman of low or loose character, a strumpet. Obs.

Apart from the actual slander in his words, in calling Elizabeth "Queen Tibb," John Trevelyan was insulting her with the use of a nickname whose

---

[27] The name Pyr may have been taken from the Greek word for fire πῦρ (*OED*), which would also indicate a devilish nature.

connotations included being a whore. Percy's use of the name Tib is not coincidental then. This view is supported by the characterization of Tibb in the play. The rare occurrence of the nickname Tib in reference to Elizabeth in early modern sources can be seen as a result of censorship against its use because of its negative connotations. Percy's use thus breaks this taboo and presents a Tib who plays out her name to the full by being a cheating wife and a mistress.

If we want to take the allegory a step further, we can link Tib's behaviour, not only her name, to Elizabeth as well. I am not referring to the already discussed allegations of promiscuity but rather to the mystical relationship fostered between Elizabeth and her England as husband and wife (See King "Queen Elizabeth" 30). Shortly after her coronation, in 1558, Elizabeth gave a famous speech to the Parliament in which she said:

> I have already joyned my self in Marriage to an husband, namely, the Kingdom of England. And behold (said she which I marvaile ye have forgotten,) the Pledge of this my wedlocke and marriage with my kingdom, (and therewith, she stretched forth her Finger and shewed the ring of gold). (qtd. in Levin *The Heart and Stomach* 41)

If admirers of Elizabeth saw in her a Virgin Queen who renounced marriage of the flesh to get married to her country, people on the other side of the spectrum saw in her relation to England an allegory of a cheating wife who cuckolds her husband. And Percy's Tib is an apt personification of such sentiment.

Stemming from the above-noted misogynistic views on a woman's inability to rule "properly," one major form of English Catholic tracts criticizing the state of the country is what Michael C. Questier refers to as the "evil counsellor" genre which attributed all the blame for any social or political failures to Elizabeth's advisors. In this literature:

> [The Queen's] alleged good parts are admitted but turned, or potentially turned, against her by reference to the political company she kept. For in such company, her good qualities became mere weakness. Her consequent failure to root out the corrupt influences around her threatened a colossal failure of leadership and the imminent collapse of good government, the law, national security, and godliness. (Questier 77)

Questier gave an example of this theme from the *Treatise of Treasons* 1572, perhaps by John Leslie. Apart from the main argument that Cecil and Bacon were the real traitors who deceived and pushed Elizabeth into injustice, the author likens her to Eve who was weak and was tempted by a serpent. In her case, Elizabeth was tempted "to intrude and entangle her self in the ecclesiastical ministry" (qtd. in Questier 80). Elizabeth was deceived by a serpent who told her that if she established a Protestant church in England, "all the princes her neighbours would follow her therein" (80). Thus, Questier comments, "Elizabeth had fallen into the sin of schism. The implication is that she must submit to Catholics' judgment as well as beg the pope's mercy in order to be saved, politically as well as spiritually" (80).

This connection between female weakness and schism provides an appropriate link for our study here. For in the same way that Percy views gynaecocracy as a flawed form of government, he also seems critical of the hard-line Protestant policy followed by the government as a schism and an innovation in religion.

6. Schism and unity

Percy used his knowledge of the existing schism between the two major Muslim sects in order to present his view on the way the Christian schism should ideally be solved. The play shows how while Percy called for reconciliation between the two sects, his view was essentially that Catholicism was the basic and true form of Christianity and that Protestantism was but a misled offshoot. Nonetheless, Percy's allegory calls for a reconciliation between the two Christian sects and adopts a peacemaking approach. But what happens in this part of the play exactly?

Right at the end of the play, Percy inserts an episode into the action which has no link to the main action of the play. After judging each of the trespassing characters, Mahomet is astonished by the sight of Haly (Ali) who arrives in Heaven with a retinue of "*all sortes and conditions of men, Preist, King, Clown, Soldier, Merchand, Saylour, Phisitian, Lawyer etcæt*" (V.xiii.opening SD). Mahomet first describes Haly as "our Enemye" (V.xii.108) but Haly immediately explains that he has come in repentance with the intention to "subscribe" to Mahomet's "Booke" (V.xiii.3) because what divides them is but a "silly quirk" (13). Haly then narrates that on his dying bed, he reviewed the little difference that divided his sect from the other one, and prayed to God to show him which is true through showing him whose book was "weightier" (53). Seeing that Mahomet's book is the heavier, he "instantly" subscribed to Mahomet's book and thus he was saved and "On a Camel my pleased soule flew hither, / And all these soules, with mee unite, in Trayne" (61–2). Mahomet then accepts Haly's repentance and asks him to sit on his "better hand" so that he judges with him. Percy converts the original Islamic preference and explains that the left hand is the one to which he is referring.

The episode highlights three important areas of concern for this study. It is essential to study the conciliatory approach adopted by Percy towards Christian schism and its pertinence to contemporary politics and Percy's religious and family background. In trying to understand this approach, we need to probe the significance of the use of Muslim Shiite-Sunni schism as an allegory for contemporary Christian schism. It is also necessary to note and discuss the use of the figure of Mahomet as an antichrist and the relationship between this presentation and the overall conciliatory call of the scene.

6.1. Muslim and Christian schism

Percy's depiction of the two sects of Islam shows little actual knowledge of the real division that existed amongst Muslims. For example, Mahomet calls Haly an enemy and the latter confirms by saying that their enmity resulted in "Theft's and Massakers" (V.xiii.11). In fact, the Prophet Muhammad was never involved in the schism that ensued only after his death (See Reid 140ff). Thus, generally speaking, the play is just another example of the scant knowledge about the nuances of the Islamic faith in the late sixteenth and early seventeenth centuries. As Dimmock notes, any knowledge of the distinction between the two sects of Islam was "often referenced in terms of territorial war rather than religious dispute" (Dimmock *Mahomet* 237).

Nor was Percy's presentation novel in linking the schisms on the two sides. In many examples of works that referred to the Muslim schism, parallels were drawn between Muslim and Christian two-sidedness. For example, in 1600 George Abott published his *A Briefe Description of the Whole Worlde* in which while describing Persia, Abott noted that:

> The Persians are all at this day Sarazens in religion, beleeuing on *Mahomet*: but as Papists and Protestants do differ in opinion concerning the same Christ: so do the Turkes and Persians about their *Mahomet*; the one pursuing the other as heretikes with most deadly hatred. Insomuch, that there be in this respect, almost continuall warres betweene the *Turkes*, and the *Persians*. (qtd. in Dimmock *Mahomet* 237)

This awareness of the current geopolitics of the Turco-Persian difference rather than the religious and ideological background of the schism was characteristic of early modern views towards this issue. Importantly, as Kenneth Parker notes, the symmetry between the two religious entities of Islam and Christianity was utilised by "Turkey and Persia, as well as England, Spain and the Holy Roman Empire" in order to build political and diplomatic alliances (Parker 4). Thus, no novelty exists neither in Percy's depiction of the Muslim schism, nor in the link between the Muslim and Christian sects. Nonetheless, Percy's reproduction of the Muslim schism is unique in the aims it pursues as well as in its topicality and politico-religious allegory. Percy uses the Muslim Other to promote a call to peace and unity unlike the theologians who used the symmetry for purposes of dissent as the following discussion shows.

Throughout the Reformation, the Turk was a figure that was used by both sides of the division as a sounding board against which the other side's distance from "true" Christianity was measured. Martin Luther himself started the debate by arguing that "a living creature consists of body and soul. The spirit of Antichrist is the pope, his flesh the Turk. One attacks the Church physically, the other spiritually" (qtd. in Setton 151) he also called the Catholic canonical texts "our Korans" (Quinn 43). Another example from the Protestant camp was John Foxe, author of *Actes and Monuments*. In the 1570 edition of the book, Foxe added a history of the Turks, *The Turkes Storye*, in this section he pondered "the relationship between the Turk and the papacy as persecutors of the Godly" (Highley 56).

The camp to which Percy belonged, the Catholic, was not economical with the trope of the Turk either. For example, Luther's arch-antagonist, the Catholic controversialist Johannes Cochlaeus, produced a pamphlet in German and Latin that featured a monstrous seven-headed Luther on its title page. "One of the heads attached to Luther's body wears a Turban, marking him as a Turkish infidel" (Highley 56). In one of his works, written while he was in the tower, Sir Thomas More used allegory to hint at the Henrician reformation that was being introduced to England (Chew 101 n.1). In *A Dialogue of Comfort Against Tribulation*, More discusses the case of Hungary under Ottoman occupation describing the "blasphemies of Mahomet," but in reality "he is referring to the coming into England of the doctrines of the Lutherans, Sacramentarians, and other heretics or schismatics" (Highley 59).

The Catholic point of view towards Turk and Protestants was that both represented the same process. Essential to this view was the Catholic allegation that Islam was originally a schism within the Eastern Church. That Muhammad was tutored by a certain Sergius, who features prominently as a cleric in our play, was a Christian "universal" belief according to Norman Daniel (105). Even before the Reformation, Catholic theologians as early as Peter the Venerable (c. 1094–1156), adopted the idea that a heretic Nestorian monk, distraught at not becoming Pope, taught Muhammad the new religion of Islam (Quinn 39-40). Thus,

Catholic contemporaries of the Reformation warned that the Lutheran heresy was but a new misled movement that would end in exactly the same situation as the Turk: a sworn enemy of the true church. In this context, it is not surprising to see how Luther was compared to Sergius as only "another lapsed monk and breeder of schism in the Church" (Highley 62).

Percy's use of the Muslim other in his allegory is different. He uses the Islamic schism for quite different reasons to the ones adopted by Catholics and Protestants noted above. No other writer would write, even fictionally, about the two sects of the Muslim enemy coming to terms with each other and reconciling in a heart-warming scene. If anything, Christian writers, on both sides of the Christian schism, would wish for the two versions of "Mahometism" to annihilate each other.[28] Percy's use of the metaphor was most likely an allegorical call for Christian reconciliation. This call for peace in itself has deep topical background in contemporary politics. Written by a Catholic gentleman living in Protestant England towards the end of Queen Elizabeth's reign, soon after the fall of Essex, and expecting the accession of James VI of Scotland to the throne, Percy's short but meaningful episode on religious unity and tolerance has a lot to offer for our current study.

6.2. Calls for peace and unity

Catholics did not have an easy life under Elizabeth who finalized England's transformation into a Protestant nation. Soon after Elizabeth assumed the throne, the parliament passed two acts, the Act of Supremacy, which confirmed Elizabeth as Supreme Governor of the Church of England, and the Act of Uniformity, which made it a legal obligation to go to church every Sunday. During her reign, Catholics were not treated on equal terms with their Protestant fellow citizens. Catholicism was also linked with incidents of civil unrest, like the Northern rebellion of 1569. It was the pretext behind external Catholic powers waging war against England, like the Spanish war and Armada of 1588. The papal bull excommunicating Elizabeth and urging her subjects to depose her was another landmark that meant little tolerance towards Catholicism in general and recusancy in particular (Dickens 311). Despite the assertions of some historians that Elizabeth was "naturally moderate" towards

---

[28] On a similar note, Walsingham instructed Harborne, English Envoy to the Porte, to encourage a military attack on Spain in the Mediterranean wishing to see the "two limbs of the devil" set against one another (Baumer 39).

Catholics (Questier 72), there were plenty of examples to the contrary and stories circulated among the Catholics that "commemorated Elizabeth's personal vindictiveness and brutality" (Questier 73). Her relationship with the Catholic nobility, to which our author belonged, was understandably more complex than with Catholic clergy and laity. The Percys professed loyalty to the Queen and, as shown above in Ch.2 section 2, Henry Percy did a lot to prove his allegiance. However, this was always doubted as mere politics and as Questier notes, Elizabeth's relationship to the Catholic gentry was marked with tension and mutual distrust (Questier 74).

As the sixteenth century drew to a close, and as the Queen grew older, calls for peace and reconciliation became strong, especially by Catholics. On the foreign front, the hostility against Spain had cost England dearly in both money and men (Redworth 7) and peace with the Catholic empire would have seemed advisable for the country's prosperity. At home, as James VI of Scotland, not the Spanish infanta, appeared as the most likely successor to Elizabeth, Catholics started to make calculations for their future under James. But things were not straightforward. Externally, peace with Spain was difficult to achieve especially in the presence of militant politicians and advisors like the Earl of Essex. Internally the situation was not very clear because although the Scottish King promised tolerance, he was ambiguous in his views on English Catholics (Houliston 137).[29]

In this light, the fall of Essex was an important factor that supported hopes for peace with Spain. As one of the strongest advisers in Elizabeth's government, Essex is often described as one of the "hawks" who "were deeply disappointed that [Elizabeth] did not continue to fight against Spain" (Doran *Foreign Policy* 59).[30] He was an enthusiastic patriot and Protestant who saw the relations with Spain in grand biblical terms: "as a holy war" as Shapiro describes it (47). Essex was convinced that any peace made with Spain "would be dishonorable and treacherous" (Shapiro 46). In other places, he wrote that the Spanish were "an insolent, cruell and usurping nation that disturbed the common peace, aspired to the conquest of my countrey, and was a generall enemie to the libertie of Christendome" (qtd. in Hammer *Polarisation* 246).

Essex's views were stopping the court from pursuing an end to the costly war with Spain and Catholicism. Elizabeth had explored the

---

[29] I am indebted to Kurosh Meshkat, PhD candidate at Queen Mary, University of London, for pointing out the fall of Essex and the succession of James as two important factors opening up room for negotiations with Spain (Meshkat).

[30] Cf. Muly Seth's hawkish call for pursuing military confrontation with the enemy and its links to the Armada, discussed in Ch. 1, section 4.3.

possibilities in 1595 but met with little Spanish enthusiasm. After Philip II's death in 1598, his son Philip III gave positive hints towards peace which resulted in a division in the English council. "Cecil favoured peace, but Essex and the hawks argued that the war had to be pursued until Spain was on its knees, since the word of Catholic rulers could never be trusted" (Doran *Foreign Policy* 61).

Therefore, Essex represented a big hurdle for Elizabeth and her pragmatic councillors, as well as Catholics who wanted to see an end to their country's enmity towards Spain. William Percy and his brother the Ninth Earl of Northumberland might well have been among these Catholics who disliked this undiplomatic attitude in Essex. But what was the relationship like between the two newly related families?[31] Devereux's relations with the Percys were not straightforwardly simple. The younger brothers, Charles and Josceline, were his admirers and took part in his fatal *coup d'état*. The older Percys, William and Henry, had relationships that fluctuated from good to strained. Towards the end of 1590 the Earl's relationship with Essex deteriorated and he was once "on the brink of a duel with Essex's friend, the earl of Southampton" (Hammer *Polarisation* 281). Moreover, Henry Percy's friendship with Raleigh "placed him in direct opposition to his brother-in-law" (Kincaid 10). Essex's stubbornness was proving a heavy load for the Catholic Earl who struggled to keep a friendly link with the likes of Walsingham and Burghley.

The play does make hints that could be understood as references to the Essex rebellion. Dodds noted that the lines in the Prologue: "Comædyes be not for sad dayes, you seye, / Tragædyes too will not this blissed day fit" (Prol.8–9), are a reference to the Essex rebellion as Percy was glad for his brothers' release while sad at Essex's fall (Dodds "A Dreame" 190). Early into the first scene, there is another hint at the rebellion. As Mahomet is giving a list of the sins of Arabia he mentions:

> One blown, with bellowes of Ambition,
> Does reare, ungratefully, rebellious armes,
> Against his sworne Lord, and anoynted Prince, (I.i.13–15)

In 1601, there is only one person who could be thought of as an ambitious rebel and that is Essex. William Percy's stance here is reflective of his brother's. The Earl made sure to distance himself from his brother-in-law and strived to save his brothers from punishment for their part in the revolt.

---

[31] Henry Percy married Essex's sister in 1594.

When Percy wrote the play, and after Essex's execution, the winds of change in the political arena of Anglo-Spanish relations were already blowing hard. On the theological side, certain members of the clergy were also starting to adopt the ecumenical idea of a general Christian council that united Europe's princes and the papacy without one side excluding the other. The most prominent example is Richard Hooker (1554–1600), one of the most notable apologists for the Elizabethan religious settlement. In his *Of the Laws of Ecclesiastical Polity* (published between 1593 and 1597), Hooker defined the Anglican Church and laid down the basics upon which it is still known today (Pollard 177). Hooker's adoption of the *via media* (middle way) policy was translated into the stance taken by the Anglican Church which simultaneously distanced itself and took certain features from both extreme ends of the Christian Spectrum at the time: Reformed Protestantism and Roman Catholicism. Prominent within Hooker's theories was his conviction in the importance of general Christian councils that brought everybody together in order to "resolve theological issues, settle conflicts over matters indifferent in themselves, heal rifts and schisms and deal with matters of politie, order and regiment" (qtd. in Patterson 64).

Hooker's teachings were carried further and put to the test by two of his former students: George Cranmer and Edwin Sandys. They toured the Continent in 1593 to get in touch with other Christian churches and probe the possibility of unity. Later, Sandys wrote a report on their findings entitled *A Relation of the State of Religion* (1599). Despite the many differences that separated Christians, Sandys proposed that unity was possible on certain bases he set forth in detail. One of his important suggestions was that unity could be defined "by some generall councell assembled and composed indifferently out of both sides" (qtd. in Patterson 65). His views concur with King James's views, discussed below, in that Sandys gave Christian princes supremacy in their council over papal authority. As Patterson notes, although Sandys praised pope Clement VIII's enthusiasm for "the quiet of Christendom," he did not object to his authority being overruled by the princes should he stand in the way of the project (65). Thus, apart from the political and diplomatic interests in peace and unity, certain members of the Protestant clergy were keenly seeking a form of unity that did not discuss differences about minor details and at the same time emphasised shared areas and common interests.

6.3. James and Catholic Hopes

The greatest prospect of the change towards tolerance at home and peace with Roman Catholicism abroad was coming from the north. King James VI of Scotland was the closest to the English throne and he had a background and proven attempts in seeking unity and concord among different branches of Christianity. James was the son of Mary Stuart (1542–1587) the Catholic Queen who was associated with many plots to overthrow Elizabeth and bring back Catholicism to England. Although he was a Protestant himself, it was generally believed, as Glyn Redworth notes, that the new king would be "more accommodating to his mother's co-religionists" (Redworth 7). James's position was quite unique and the question of his accession was associated with a heated polemical debate which saw each of the two Christian sides claim James their own. While Protestants claimed him the heir of Elizabeth, Catholics argued that he was essentially heir to Mary Stuart, the "martyr" of Catholicism (Questier 87).

James Stuart's position as heir apparent prompted feelings of optimism and anxiety among English Catholics. They had hoped "that Elizabeth would be succeeded by a Catholic monarch," or that James "would extend more or less full toleration to Catholics" (Houliston 135). Some Catholics even entertained a hope that James would restore Catholicism to England (Redworth 7). However, as it became clear that none of these unrealistic hopes was going to be fulfilled and with the rise in James's stakes at inheriting the English throne, many overtures by Catholic personages started to be made to him with the aim of securing as good a future for their co-religionists as was politically possible. William Percy was very close to the Catholic circles that discussed the issue of James's accession and his plans for the country, as his brother Henry was involved in direct correspondence with the Scottish king.

The correspondence between the Earl and the King concentrated on tolerance of the Catholics in James's England. Percy made it clear that he was no Catholic himself but many of his "retinue and dependants" were, and thus he felt responsible for them. He offered the King his unconditional support if "toleration for the Catholics" was part of the King's policy. James "promised abundant favour to all, Catholic or Protestant" (Brenan 79). As the discussion below shows, James was not merely distributing promises in order to secure support but he was genuinely interested in this policy.

James's coming to London radically changed English Catholicism. Even the most ardent of its supporters had to review their stances. In another line of correspondence, James was approached by Robert Parsons

(1546–1610), the famous Jesuit priest. Trying to probe the prospective king's faith, Parsons wrote to James in 1602 that he was "willing to support James to the death if only he would change his religion" (Houliston 137). It seems that Parsons, otherwise a staunch Catholic with a history of many attempts to restore England to the old religion, was sure that the Scottish King was never going to fulfil any of his Catholic fantasies, so he sought a *via media* settlement with him. Thus, when James was crowned, Parsons wrote a letter to him in October 1603 in which he made mention of his own role in the succession and expressed his hope that he would not be like Elizabeth who persecuted the Catholics and as a result ruined "her soul" (Houliston 135). Interestingly, in the preface to his *A Treatise of Three Conversions*, published later in 1603, Parsons expressed a very similar opinion to the one expressed by Haly in our play: that the two sects are only different in very minor issues. Thus, he wrote, he was sure the King would be of the opinion that "no one reason at all can be found, why a man should rather be of one sect, than another" (qtd. in Houliston 136).

Henry Percy seeking conciliation with James would not be a surprise then. After all, he denied being Catholic himself. Even if he were Catholic, he would never have been as devoted to Catholicism as the diehard Robert Parsons, who himself sought conciliation. Moreover, the Percys were justified in any optimism they might have had about the new monarch's pluralist view on religion for during his Scottish reign James did make actual attempts at uniting the Catholic and Protestant churches together.

In the winter of 1589–1590, as he was celebrating his wedding to Princess Anne in Denmark, James proposed to the Danish king a project for European peace. According to Patterson, behind this attempt by James there was his concern for the inter-European conflicts in which England, Spain and France were involved. His wish, as expressed to his ambassadors was "a nombre of Princes weill affected to Christian peax and trew religioun, wolde be commoun resolutioun direct a joinct legatioun of a few persones authorized and instructed from thame all to the said Princes of Englande France and Spayne" in order to make peace (qtd. in Patterson 29). Patterson further notes that this attempt did not go through because of lack of support (29). Interestingly, as Baumer notes, this was the same year that James wrote a poem commemorating the victory at Lepanto (Baumer 44). Although Protestant, James found no problem in celebrating a Christian victory even if the winning party was Catholic.

A decade later, James proposed another plan for a Christian union which also had opposing the Turk as its aim. Basically, he intended to bring together moderates from all sides with the aim of working against the Turk. He worked on his plan with Pope Clement VIII, moderate Catholic princes of Italy and the King of Denmark. His aim from all this was to unite Catholic and Protestant Europe "to withstand the common enemy of the Christian name" (qtd. in Baumer 45-6). Although he had ulterior motives, securing support for his accession to the English throne, James's sincere concern for Christian unity cannot be doubted, Baumer concludes (46).

James adhered to his peacemaking policy and ecumenical projects after his English coronation. In 1603, over a period of time which included his coronation date, James corresponded with the Pope to effect a Christian form of unity. The idea was again rather vague as Baumer notes (45) but it included a council sponsored and monitored by European princes with the Pope as *primus inter pares* (first among equals) but without supreme authority. The result, it was hoped, would be "a re-unified church, founded on the Roman Catholic communion but mildly reformed" (Houliston 139). Foreign powers certainly saw in James a reconciler. For example, in 1603, upon his crowning, James received a congratulatory letter from Jacques-Auguste de Thou, president of the Parlement of Paris. Among other formal issues, the letter asked James "to promote "the concord of the church with common consent" rather than "[limit] himself to establishing peace within his own borders" (Patterson 1). James replied positively assuring de Thou of his total dedication to the enterprise saying that he had never been "of a sectarian spirit nor resistant the well-being of Christendom" (Patterson 2). Houliston notes that it is important to study James's ecumenical view for Europe as it served as the blueprint for his religious policy at home. On the home front, James's view was that "under royal guidance and patronage Catholics would be brought into the ecumenical fold, shedding their corruptions, still affording the Pope his due as spiritual leader without supreme authority" (Houliston 139).

6.3.1. James I and Islam

Another facet of James's view on Christian unity manifested itself in a clear definition of friends and foes. For James, Christians of different denominations cannot be enemies while the Turk, the real enemy, is threatening their very existence. English Catholics expecting the coming of James were very likely to be in favour of his anti-Ottoman stance especially because it shifted enmity from amongst Catholic and Protestant European states to a united effort to curb Ottoman endeavours to subdue Christendom.

In his poem, *The Lepanto*, in addition to celebrating a Catholic victory, King James displayed his hearty dislike towards the Turk. The poem celebrates:

> A bloodie battell bolde,
> . . . .
> Which fought was in LEPANTOES gulfe
> Betwixt the baptiz'd race,
> And circumsised Turband Turkes (6, 9–11)

The poem uses the general epithet Christian to refer to the European Catholic league, which was actually a coalition of several powers including Spain, Venice, the Vatican, Genoa, and others. In the poem, God, called Jehova, expresses his view on Christian differences in a rather all-inclusive way: "All Christians serves my Son though not / Aright in every thing" (79–80). Then, he orders Archangel Gabriel to inspire the Christians that:

> No more shall now these Christians be
> With infidels opprest,
> . . . .
> Go quicklie hence to Venice Towne,
> And put into their minds
> To take revenge of wrongs the Turks
> Have done in sundrie kinds. (81–82, 89–92)

Nabil Matar rightly recognizes in this poem a clear tendency towards defining the main conflict as one between Christendom and the Turk. This "religious polarization" of the conflict is further highlighted by the fact that references to the turban and circumcision, the cultural signifiers of the Turk, were only introduced in the English translation of the poem which was republished at James's coronation in 1603 (Matar *Turks, Moors* 143). The poem was studied by Emrys Jones in 1968 as a possible influence of Shakespeare's *Othello* (1604) especially in its antagonising of the Turk and the use of certain expressions. Interestingly, Jones notes that the poem had an immense influence on contemporary writers who welcomed the new King and his policies. For example, Richard Knolles dedicated his *Generall Historie of the Turkes* (1603) to King James and praised him because "he hath not disdained" to praise the victory of the "Christian confederate princes obtained against these the *Othoman* Kings or Emperors" (qtd. in Emrys Jones 48).

Another incident indicative of James's, perhaps anachronistic, views on the relations with the Turk is narrated by Franklin Baumer. In 1594, at his son Prince Henry's baptism, the King of Scotland participated in a masque that included three Knights of Malta opposed by three Turks. The King predictably played one of the Christian knights fighting against the Turks (Baumer 37 n.59). James displayed awareness of the enmity between the two empires representing the Shiite and Sunni sects, as Baumer also notes the fact that in 1601, the year our play was written, James sent a letter to the Safavid Shah of Persia congratulating him on a recent victory against the Ottomans and hinting at cooperation against the Turk (Baumer 37 n.59).

James took his anti-Turkish views with him to London. After his accession, he categorically denied to sign commercial letters to the Turk. His argument was that as a "Christian Prince" he ought not to do things that did not fit with this title "for Merchants causes." Even when he later accepted to do similar things, he made it clear that the purpose was trade and trade only (Baumer 37 n.58). His views were not restricted to Turks only as evidence seems to suggest he had similar views on Moors as well. Nabil Matar stresses that James's anti-Muslim position was "so widely known" that soon after his coronation, the English representative in Morocco Henry Roberts urged the king to wage war against the Moors describing such an act as "godly and christianlike" for it would "subdue [Morocco] from Mahomet to the knowledge of Christ" (qtd. in Matar *Turks, Moors* 143).

James was to take an even tougher and more militant approach later in his reign for, in 1622, James ordered his ambassador in Constantinople to object to the imminent Turkish attack to be launched against Poland. Sir Thomas Roe was to inform the Sultan of the "jealousy that we and all other Christian princes had of such an attempt." This course of action against Poland "would engage us necessarily, though unwillingly, to take arms against him . . . [because] there are no respects of friendship so dear unto us, as the obligation we have to defend those princes and states that be fellow-professors with us of *the same Christian faith*" (qtd. in Baumer 37, italics mine). Thus, not only was James ecumenical in his views, but he was also ready to go to war to defend a fellow Christian prince, even if he was Catholic.

6.4. Percy's allegory for peace and reconciliation

The cultural backdrop to the themes of Muslim schism, Christian schism and calls for Christian peace as well as the political atmosphere in England at the turn of the century, are all factors that we need to consider if we want to fully appreciate the depths of Percy's writing of the Haly episode. However, the episode itself still needs closer analysis and study.

As far as allegory is concerned, the episode can be divided into two parts. First, there is the proposal for unity and second there is the part where Mahomet becomes a visual representation of the antichrist. The second part is not separate in its implications from the first as it is used as a supporting point in the argument for Christian unity.

It has to be established here that although the religion of Percy's Arabia is supposed to be Islam, it still bears strong links to Roman Catholicism, which can be seen as an attempt by Percy to make his allegory more apprehensible to his audience. This is achieved through many Catholic-related references throughout the play. To start with, in "The Names of the Persons" the Dervis is introduced as a "Mahometaine Fryar" (32). As Matthew Dimmock notes, throughout the play the name of this character keeps shifting between "Dervis" and "Fryar" (Dimmock *Mahomet* 29). Dimmock sees this and similar references as part of an "amalgam" of Christianity and Islam which Percy is trying to establish. However, Dimmock does not recognize the vital detail that this and other "Christian" hints are more specifically "Catholic" references, a fact that gives us a better understanding to the play's allegorical dimension as a whole. In post-reformation England, friars were one of the emblems of Catholicism. Not only did Protestant England link them with the old religion, but she also associated them with "fraudulent theatricality" seeing their "humblest habits" as "a false disguise" (Huston 395). This is especially true of *Mahomet and his Heaven* where the friar is the one exploiting the drought and monopolizing water supplies in his Meschit. Percy's friar might not be a wise choice on his part as it confirms Protestant negative views on Catholic religious orders as corrupt and materialistic. However, it may be the case that a religiously "relaxed" Percy had no problem denouncing malpractices by clergy as a gambit to get his message of reconciliation through. Admitting the existence of individual misconduct can be a good strategy to defend a theory or doctrine against petty accusations and shifts focus to bigger and more theoretical issues.

In another instance, the adulterous Tib tells the Fryar that she will meet him for an amorous rendezvous behind his "Meschit" when she will be at her "Prayers" and her "beades" (II.v.61). Again, the string of beads or rosary was a Catholic symbol and as Holt notes, most Protestants would not use it to repeat or say prayers (Holt 383; see also Doran and Durston 90). Upon Epimenide's arrival in the heavenly scene, Gabriel, trying to discover who this creature could be, says: "Doubtles some witch she is

who, by chaunce having / Seene our feynd formes paint on some boarde"
(IV.v.10–1). As Dimmock notes, iconography was used by "Protestant
propagandists" to attack Catholic idolatry which was seen as worse than
the Turks who did not approve iconography as well (*Mahomet* 222–3).[32]
Moreover, the use of shrines and the prevalence of saint worship was
another Catholic trademark attacked by Protestants. As Doreen Rosman
notes, pilgrimages to shrines were banned and later shrines were
demolished as part of Henry's reformation of the Church of England
(Rosman 74; see also Bowker 76). In *Mahomet*, a good number of the
scenes take place in a shrine and Epimenide and her retinue clearly pay a
special religious visit to Mahomet's tomb in order to pray for mercy (e.g.
scenes I.iii and I.iv). Other subtle references that confirm the identification
of Mahomet's followers with Catholic Christian are recurrent oaths uttered
by the characters as well as references to saints like St. Anne (IV.ix.61), St
Mary (IV.ix.68), "Sancto Domingo" (III.i.37), and Mary Mieu (V.xiii.110)
(Dimmock *Mahomet* 29, 239).

Having established parallels between Mahomet's followers on Earth
and Catholics, the scene becomes set for the reconciliation episode. What
remains in this scene is to link Haly's sect, the Shia, with Protestantism.
The first and most basic form of linkage between the two sects, at least
from Percy's point of view, is the fact that both are deviations from the
norm. As the excerpt quoted above from George Abbott indicates, there
was a certain amount of information available for English literati which
was enough to know the basics of the Muslim schism. How much of this
awareness Percy possessed is beyond our ability to know but at least we
can confirm that Percy knew that the Ottomans' sect antedated the
Persians'. Thus, the chronological link could be established.

Haly's speech gives more hints about the intended symmetry.
Narrating his death-bed story, Haly tells Mahomet that as he was in agony,
ghosts of dead people from both sects came to him. Each group were
carrying their Quran: "Yours brought their Alcoran, by you confirmed, /
The other it of late by mee reformed" (V.xiii.30–1). The specific use of the
word "reformed" in reference to a different version of the Quran is a clear
allusion to the Protestant reformation of the sixteenth century. Describing
Mahomet's book as "confirmed" is another stress on the legitimacy of the
original as opposed to the offshoot. Moreover, when visions of the two
sects speak to Haly, the "former Order and Institution" or Catholicism is
praised as follows:

---

[32] For more on Protestants and icons see Hart 273–4.

Maintaine, by all the Art thou may, thy former
Order and Institution, which ever
Hath beene, by most wisards of the world,
Accounted best. (40–43)

Percy also gives a more immediate reference to contemporary Catholic-Protestant debate relating to the different versions of the Bible adopted by the two parties. Seeking guidance from God on which path to follow, Haly requests that "The weightier may weigh down th'one hand of myne, / Th'other, as lighter, may mount with the other" (53–4). Upon holding both books, he discovered that "by one graine, ours to be more light" (57). This small difference between the two versions with the "newer" or "reformed" book being lighter in weight clearly refers to the Lutheran calls to purge the Vulgate Bible from the "erroneous" books (Dimmock *Mahomet* 238).[33] Finally, the two Muslim patriarchs reconcile and "strike a lasting league" (68) and Mahomet invites Haly to sit on his "better hand" (67).

Having made his call for peace, Percy starts the second phase of this allegory with the following stage direction:

> *The left syde is the worthier among the Turks, According which be the Goates on the right hand of them, the sheepe on the left, so now Haly on the better or left syde of Mahomet* .(72 SD)

In a clear reversal of the conventional Christian view of judgement day, Mahomet becomes the opposite image of Jesus Christ and, as a result, the Islamic final abode becomes the opposite of Christian Heaven. The Christian view is set out in Matthew 25:

> 31 When the Son of man shall come in his glory, and all the holy angels with him, then shall he sit upon the throne of his glory:
> 32 And before him shall be gathered all nations: and he shall separate them one from another, as a shepherd divideth his sheep from the goats:
> 33 And he shall set the sheep on his right hand, but the goats on the left.
> 34 Then shall the King say unto them on his right hand, Come, ye blessed of my Father, inherit the kingdom prepared for you from the foundation of the world.
> 41 Then shall he say also unto them on the left hand, Depart from me, ye cursed, into everlasting fire, prepared for the devil and his angels: (Matthew 25.31–4, 41 *The Bible*)[34]

---

[33] For more on the issue of purging see Greenslade 169.

[34] See note no. 6 in the Bibliographical note above.

Significantly, the better hand as Percy presents it is the left hand. Later, when Mahomet stands to give judgment he is portrayed thus

> *He gave sentence with either hand on either syde*
> *of him, with hand down and hand up, contrary to*
> *christs in judgement, Left hand up, and Right hand down.* (V.xiii.128SD)

An image recurrent throughout medieval and Renaissance iconography is that of Christ on judgment day. Inspired by the verses quoted above, these paintings focus on the idea of right and left with many of them depicting Jesus in a pose quite opposite to Mahomet's pose in the play. This is the case in *Last Judgment* by Michelangelo (1475–1564) and *Day of Judgement* by Fra Angelico (1395–1455). Thus, Percy's stage direction enacts an image which clearly presents Mahomet as the opposite to Jesus Christ and associates him with the Antichrist both literally and physically.

Some confusion may be traced here. Percy has presented Mahomet in a fairly positive light so far. Apart from the humiliation he receives at the hands of Epimenide, he has been described as a heaven dweller, a just judge and a favourer of learning and knowledge. Moreover, in the reconciliation scene, his sect is identified as the true version of religion to which heretics must return. So why would Percy choose to make this abrupt change in characterization and change Mahomet from the supreme arbiter for heavenly residents to the Antichrist? There is little doubt that such a change represents a shock to the audience. It is like a wake-up call at the end of this Oriental tale which absorbed them for some time. The effect would be to remind them that the real enemy is the Turk. They are the followers of the Antichrist and they are threatening the existence of Christendom. Thus, the visual demonization of Mahomet at the end of the play is used as another ploy by Percy to support his call for peace and unity by showing who he thinks the real enemy is in order to unite Christianity.

It is of paramount importance that Percy's demonization of Mahomet and pointing out of the Turks as the real enemies runs along the lines of King James's views on the issue. Not only did James once and again call for unity but he, as explained above, associated Christian unity with war against the Turk whom he saw as the real enemy. James's refusal to continue Elizabeth's policies with the Ottomans and the Moors was a manifestation of the King's anti-Muslim sentiments expressed earlier in his life as King of Scotland. These sentiments of aversion towards the Turk and interest in unity must have been well known to Henry Percy who was approaching the King at the time and thus William Percy was very likely to have come across them himself.

Percy's call for reconciliation springs from heated contemporary debates and concerns regarding Christian unity. He uses allegory to call Protestants to revert back to Catholicism and employs mime to show the real enemy of Antichrist. Thus, Percy's take on Islamic schism and his final demonizing of Muhammad stem from topical concerns which were behind this episode's conception as well as composition.

7. Conclusion

The argument of this chapter has been to show that although Percy's play is set in Arabia and populated by Muslim characters, the messages it carries and the characterization of many of its characters do not depart from the England of Percy's times. The playwright's ideological agenda, stemming from family and sectarian concerns, makes its presence strongly felt throughout the play. Three main areas support this argument and special sections were dedicated to them.

By way of setting the argument into the context of the playwright's ideological agenda, the biographical section has shown the delicate situation the Percy family was going through in the year 1601. Their uneasy relationship with Queen Elizabeth, culminating in the death of William Percy's father in prison, preoccupied a great deal of their political and literary careers. The Percy family were seen as members of the Catholic Nobility. Regardless of whether they liked this association or not, and regardless of whether they were really pro-government as they claimed or not, Elizabeth's privy councillors viewed them with suspicion. The Earl of Northumberland was trying hard to clean up his family's image and saw the coming reign of James VI of Scotland an appropriate opportunity to start afresh with a new government. Thus, William Percy's *Mahomet and his Heaven* is best seen as the product of this vital historical moment in the life of the Percys and England in general.

One negative aspect that stuck itself to the Earl and might have damaged his political chances is rumours of his eccentricity and his links to the new sciences often mistaken for magic. Northumberland was a polymathic gentleman with an interest in science and the supernatural. The Earl himself and members of his circle ventured to show the importance of the hermetic tradition and positive magic (*magia*) to the development of humanity. William Percy took his share in polishing his brother's image through presenting a magician who saves his country from the fallible and fickle woman who runs it. The image of the magus in the play is William Percy's attempt to defend his brother against accusations of witchcraft and black magic.

Women's rule was a topic for intense debate throughout the second half of the sixteenth century. The Percys did not prosper under Elizabeth and, given the general zeitgeist of misogyny, would have seen in gynaecocracy a cause for their troubles. England's weariness with female rulers led to a warm welcome for James as a king with a proper family and a secure heir. William Percy expressed negative contemporary views on Elizabeth's reign through the character of Epimenide by describing her as fickle, sinful and immoral. In a hint that shows preference for androcracy, Percy also insinuated the inferiority of women, especially as rulers, to men by having a male figure punish Epimenide for her behaviour. Thus, the image of the Muslim woman in the play interacts with these contemporary local debates on women and their fitness to rule. Very little, if anything, of the Muslim woman is present in the play.

On the religious front, distancing themselves from Catholicism was not a successful policy for the Eighth and Ninth Earls of Northumberland. Thus, coming to terms with this fact meant that the Earl wanted to secure the best deal with the coming monarch. The reconciliation of the two branches of Christianity was thus allegorized by Percy through the use of the Muslim schism. Mahomet and Haly's peace-making episode at the end of the play represents a genuine need by the Percys to find themselves able to live peacefully within a Protestant nation without being persecuted or marginalized.

These three motifs in the play show the extent of Percy's involvement in current day ideological and political debates through his art. This involvement works at two levels: conscious and unconscious. Certain parts of the play are clearly written with a purpose in mind, like the reconciliation scene, while others are part of contemporary debates on vital issues like the characterization of women in the play and its relationship with the gynaecocracy debate. Regardless of the level of the playwright's intentionality, the product is highly topical in its presentation of Islam and it is constructed from various contemporary issues that are not in any way Islamic. Similar to *Alcazar*, *Mahomet and his Heaven* sees the Muslim Other through a topical lens and portrays it using ideological colours and shades.

GENERAL CONCLUSION

The field of Islam in English Renaissance culture is a fascinating area of research that has introduced so much to our understanding of that period. Critics and historians have explored many interesting areas and brought into attention plenty of new ideas. In the area of Elizabethan theatre in particular, studies have covered major and minor plays and explored them from different angles. This work tries to make its contribution to the field first through studying two important and relatively ignored plays in great depth, and second through drawing attention to the important factor of topical agency in the formation of Muslim image in these plays, with the hope that subsequent critics will extend the results of this approach to other works and authors.

This work has shown how several factors play an important role in the creation and formation of the image of Muslims in George Peele's *The Battle of Alcazar* and William Percy's *Mahomet and his Heaven*. Personal ideology, political and religious commitment, as well as the wish to pass certain messages were all part of the web of mutual influences surrounding the plays and their production. The resulting image is constructed from these elements as much as, if not more than, it is representative of original sources about Islam and Muslims.

The conclusions reached in both plays confirm this proposition. Peele's *Alcazar* presents Moors in a mostly positive light with some exceptions. It has been found that Peele's political agenda governs his views on Moors. Thus, because the Queen's alliance with Ahmad Al-Mansur necessitated some justification, Peele portrays him and his predecessor in the most appealing of colours and so are Moors in general. As a result, Al-Mansur's enemy, another Moor, is both portrayed as a pariah not representative of his people and as an evil schemer. The Moors' war is also adjudged as a just cause in the face of the less favourable papal crusades. The Moroccan Embassy of 1589 is seen as both the instigator and the political framework of Peele's construction of Islam. The Spanish Armada is also strongly present and makes the presentation of Spain less than approving. These are all topical elements that feature significantly in the presentation of Muslims in the play and render it a construction from topical elements rather than a representation from original sources.

Percy's *Mahomet* is more an allegorical parable than just an Islamic story from the Quran. The interests of Percy's family and sect feature heavily in this work. His positive depiction of the Muslim magus lives in the late Elizabethan world and tries to challenge contemporary views on new science and magic as well as defend the playwright's polymathic brother against accusations of wizardry. The image of Muslim women in the play shares very little, if anything, with available sources on Islam. Epimenide, an allegory for Queen Elizabeth, is portrayed in a misogynistic manner and is given a chastising treatment. The tumultuous history of the Percy family with Queen Elizabeth, including the suspected murder of Percy's father, had its mark on his views on the Queen in particular and gynaecocracy in general. The play's final call for peace and reconciliation between religious sects resonates strongly with King James's imminent succession and his promises of toleration, which were expressed in correspondence with Percy's brother. Thus, Percy's play constructs these motifs and characters from personal interests and topical concerns to the extent that Islamic elements derived from sources can hardly be detected.

Moreover, in line with the argument of this work, the two plays work in similar ways despite their seeming difference. In both plays, original information is passed through a topically-informed filter of and presented in a topically-relevant manner. The result is a construction that merges whatever is left from the original sources with contemporary concerns to give us a final result that may claim to represent Muslims and Islam, but is in fact more of a reflection, or rather a refraction, of very local issues.

The two plays complement each other in their relationship to government policies. Taking into consideration that politics and religion are the two inseparable factors informing the composition of the plays, the two plays accommodate themselves in relation to contemporary politico-religious ideology in ways that serve their purposes. Thus, *Alcazar*'s message is clear and open for all to see. Its characters are the real historical figures to whom reference is being made. Its ideological agenda runs smoothly with the dominant ideological agenda of the government and censorship is not a concern. On the other hand, *Mahomet and his Heaven*'s messages are hidden inside an Islamic story and setting. Allegory is used to camouflage dangerous messages against the Queen and against Protestantism. Its ideological agenda is oppositional and it conflicts with the dominant government ideology.

Both plays use the Muslim element to promote their respective ideologies: Peele to justify alliance with the Moors and Percy to denounce Elizabeth and support his brother's views on science and religious tolerance. Thus, the Muslim Other falls victim to these topical factors and is reduced to a mere construction made from little original knowledge and much more from topical issues and interests.

These two plays, significant yet relatively marginalized, have been given an in-depth study in this work to an extent never attempted before. What this book shows is that although the two plays seem to show certain knowledge of Islam, this knowledge is subordinate in importance to the playwright's ideological agendas and topical interests. In other words, the plays do not display an encyclopaedic, tourist-like interest towards the Muslims, but rather they use Islamic themes and motifs to perform completely different cultural work. Peele's cultural work is to confirm and promote the government position, while Percy's is more covert and relates to an undeclared dislike of Elizabeth and her policies.

The question that deserves an answer at this stage is how important are these findings and this approach to research in the field of Renaissance drama and Islam. The answer, I argue, relates to two levels. On the level of the two plays themselves, the study has linked close textual reading with the author's general output and politico-religious texts and events that informed the writing of the plays. The result showed consistency between these three elements in both cases, especially in relation to ideological commitment. Had this approach been taken by Matar in his study of *Alcazar*, for example, he would possibly have changed his views on the play. Although Matar finds the correct topical elements informing the plays, as we saw earlier, he does not read the text correctly nor does he appreciate the playwright's literary output.

On the level of the field itself, this work has hopefully enlarged an alternative and extremely promising perspective on studies of Islam in Renaissance drama. Topical historical readings are firmly entrenched in general critical studies, but somehow their impact on this particular field has not been as strong as it should be. The application of this approach to other works of import would definitely lead to new findings and a re-evaluation of the image of Muslims in works like *Othello* with its naturalized Moor, or *The Fair Maid of the West* with its two parts written more than twenty-five years apart.

The field of Islam in Renaissance drama is in bloom and I think that it would benefit from the approach and the findings of this study. It is to the scrutinous eye of this field that I present my work, and at its disposal do I leave this book.

APPENDIX I:
SEBASTIAN'S LITERARY AFTERLIFE

Don Sebastian's death on the battlefield of Alcazar was so shocking that it was easier to disbelieve than believe. Eventually, a legend grew claiming that the young prince escaped miraculously from slaughter in Africa and was preparing a return to reclaim his throne. The myth was mainly propagated by proponents of Portuguese independence (W. H. Roberts 308–9). However, the "advent" of King Sebastian was metaphorically achieved through his literary afterlife. As early as January 1579 (less than six months after Alcazar), literary works about the lost king appeared in England. Hundreds of years after Sebastian's death, works in English appeared that either featured the young prince or alluded to his tragedy.

In Thomas Churchyard's verse work, *The miserie of Flaunders. The Calamities of Fraunce, misfortune of Portugall, unquietness of Ireland, troubles of Scotland and the blessed state of England,* a special section is dedicated to describe the fall of Sebastian. Churchyard praises the Portuguese King thus:

> There was a kyng, who had greate gifts of grace,
> A Princely sparke, of goodly porte and state:
> And as his shape, was semely to the sight (Churchyard 10).

Churchyard further narrates Portugal's "misfortune" through describing the king's "noble mynde" that always urged him "to doe some mightie deede, / Against the Turkes" (11). Sebastian's bravery is lamented as he lost the battle against "the Mores" only because their "strength and force, were stronger treble fold" (11). The story is used to support the writer's overall message of the importance of peace and stability, which are abundant in England. The loss of the monarch is portrayed as an omen for more ill fated events.

> For since thy kyng, is taken from thee thus,
> That was before, sent thee to thy greate ioye:
> There is behinde, a sorer plague yewus [certainly], (11–2)

After Churchyard, the story of Sebastian's ambiguous death or escape fascinated many writers. Maria Leonor Machado de Sousa has listed as many as twenty-two literary works where Sebastian features either as an actual character or through a telling of his story. These literary works start with Churchyard's poetical work and reach to the second half of the twentieth century (see Table I-1). Prominent among these are, of course, Peele's *Alcazar* and John Dryden's *Don Sebastian* (1689). In Dryden's work, we see a Sebastian who has survived Alcazar but who has been captured by Muley-Moluch (Peele's Muly Seth). In Moroccan captivity, Sebastian shows patience and strength that serve to highlight the ruthlessness of his barbarous captors. The only noble Moor is a woman, Almeyda who turns out to be his illegitimate sister (Barthelemy 193).

One reference to the story in *The Conspiracie, And Tragedie of Charles Duke of Byron* by George Chapman mentions Sebastian very briefly but it encapsulates contemporary sentiments about Sebastian.

> Truth is a golden Ball, cast in our way,
> To make vs stript by falsehood: and as Spain
> When the hot scuffles of Barbarian arms
> Smothered the life of Don Sebastian,
> To guild the leaden rumour of his death
> Gave for a slaughtered body, held for his,
> A hundred thousand crowns, caused all the state
> Of superstitious Portugal to mourn
> And celebrate his solemn funerals; (II.i.156–164)

In brief, Sebastian is presented as a victim of "Barbarian arms" whose death is capitalized on by a pragmatic Spain. Peele in *Alcazar* negates the former assumption and reinforces the latter.

Table 1-1: Literary Treatment of Sebastian. * refers to works that are lost; ** refers to the day and month of publication (Sousa 17–8)

No.	Literary Work
1.	1579. *(A book in meter compiled by Thomas Churchyard) The miserie of Flaunders. The Calamities of Fraunce, misfortune of Portugall, unquietness of Ireland, troubles of Scotland and the blessed state of England.* Stationers' Register, 2.1.**
2.	1579.* *A briefe Rehersall of the bloodie Battell fought in Barbary.* Ballad. Stationers' Register, 19.2. **
3.	1594. *Tke Battell of Alcazar. Fought in Barbarie, betweene Sebastian King of Portugall, and Abdelmelec King of Marocio. With the death of Captaine Stukaley.* Tragedy by George Peele,
4.	c. 1600. *The Life and Death of the Famous Stukely. An English Gallant in the time of Queen Elizabeth, who ended his Life in a Battel of three Kings of Barbary.* Ballad.
5.	1600.* *Ye history of the Life and Deathe of Captaine Thomas Stucley, with his Mariage to Alexander Curtis his daughter, and his valiant endinge of his life at the battell of Alcazar.* Ballad. Stationers' Register, 11.8.
6.	1601.* *A ballad Intituled the Wonder of the world of Don Sebastian I. King of Portugall that lost him self in the battell of Affrick Anno 1578 & C.* Stationers' Register, 12.4.
7.	1601.* *Sebastian King of Portugal.* Tragedy by Chettle and Dekker.
8.	1605. *The Famous Historye of the life and death of captaine Thomas Stukely. With his rnariage to Alderman Curteis Daughter, and valiant ending of his life at the Battaile of Alcazar.* Tragedy.
9.	1631. *Believe as you list.* Tragedy by Philip Massinger
10.	1683. *Don Sebastian King of Portugal. An Historical Novel* Translated from French (1679) by Ferrand Spence. London.
11.	1690. *Don Sebastian* Tragedy by Dryden.

12.	1769. *The captive*. comic opera by Isaac Bickerstaff, adapted from Dryden.
13.	1809. *Don Sebastian; or, The House of Braganza*. An historical romance by Anna Maria Porter. London
14.	1812. *Portugal*. A poem in two parts (part II). By Lord George Grenville
15.	1812. *The Renegade: a Grand Historical Drama, in three acts*. By Frederick Reynolds.
16.	1831 *Ode on the Defeat of King Sebastian of Portugal, and his Army, in Africa*. Translation from the Spanish poem of Fernando de Herrera by Felicia Hemans
17.	1822, *Sebastian of Portugal*. Dramatic poem by Felicia Hemans.
18.	1823. Lockhart, *The Departure of King Sebastian*. Translation of an original anonymous Spanish ballad.
19.	1831. *Sebastian of Portugal*. Dramatic piece by Felicia Hemans (and a new version of the 1822 text)
20.	1845. *Don Sebastian*, ballad by Terence Hughes
21.	1944. *King Sebastian*. Verse-Drama by Ernest Randolph Reynolds. Lisbon.
22.	1955 *The Hidden King*. Verse-Drama by Jonathan Griffin.

WORKS CITED

1. Manuscripts

Percy, William. *Plays and Other Material*. DNP MS509. The Archives of the Duke of Northumberland at Alnwick Castle, Alnwick.

2. Primary sources

Abbot, George. *A Briefe Description of the Whole World*. Fifth ed. London: Printed for Margaret Sheares ... and John Playfere, 1664.

Allen, William. *An Admonition to the Nobility and People of England and Ireland*. Antwerp, 1588.

Bedwell, William. *Mohammedis imposturae: that is, A discouery of the manifold forgeries, falshoods, and horrible impieties of the blasphemous seducer Mohammed*. London: Imprinted by Richard Field dwelling in great Wood-streete, 1615.

Biddulph, William. *The Travels of certaine Englishmen into Africa, Asia, Troy, Bithnia, Thracia, and to the Blacke Sea*. London: T. Haveland for W. Apsly, 1609.

Boorde, Andrew. *The fyrst boke of the introduction of knowledge The whych dothe teache a man to speake parte of all maner of languages...* London: William Copland, 1555.

Bullein, William. *A Dialogue bothe Pleasaunte and Pietifull wherein is a Goodly Regimente against the Feuer Pestilence...* London: Imprinted By Ihon Kingston, 1564.

Calendar of State Papers, Domestic Series, of the Reign Elizabeth, 1598–1601. Ed. Mary Anne Everett Green. London: Longman, Green, and co., 1869.

Churchyard, Thomas. *The miserie of Flaunders, calamitie of Fraunce, misfortune of Portugall, vnquietnes of Irelande, troubles of Scotlande: and the blessed state of Englande*. London: [By Felix Kingston] for Andrewe Maunsell, 1579.

Dolorous Discourse of a Most Terrible and Bloudy Battle, Fought in Barbarie (A). Imprinted at London: By John Charlewood, and Thomas Man, 1579.

Geuffroy, Antoine. *The Order of the Greate Turckes Courte, of hys Menne of Warre, and of all hys Conquestes, with the Summe of Mahumetes Doctryne. Translated out of Frenche.* London: Ricardus Grafton, 1542.

Here begynneth a lytell treatyse of the turkes lawe called Alcaron. And also it speketh of Machamet the nygromancer. London: Wynkyn de worde, 1519?

Holy Qur'an (The): Text, Translation and Commentary. Trans. Abdullah Yusuf Ali. Elmhurst, N.Y. : Tahrike Tarsile Qur'an, 2002.

James I, King of England. *Daemonologie in forme of a dialogue, diuided into three bookes.* Edinburgh: Printed by Robert Walde-graue printer to the Kings Majestie, 1597.

—. *Selected Writings.* Eds. Neil Rhodes, Jennifer Richards and Joseph Marshall. Aldershot: Ashgate, 2003.

Jonson, Ben. *The Works of Ben Jonson with Notes, Critical and Explanatory and a Biographical Memoir.* Eds. William Gifford and Francis Cunningham. Vol. 3. 3 vols. Whitefish, Mont.: Kessinger, 2004.

Knolles, Richard. *The generall historie of the Turkes from the first beginning of that nation to the rising of the Othoman familie: with all the notable expeditions of the Christian princes against them...* London: Printed by Adam Islip, 1603.

Knox, John. *The First Blast of the Trumpet against the Monstruous Regiment of Women.* Geneva: J. Poullain and A. Rebul, 1558.

Kyd, Thomas. *The Spanish tragedy.* Revels Student Editions. Ed. David M. Bevington. Manchester: Manchester UP, 1996.

Lyly, John. *The Woman in the Moon.* Ed. Leah Scragg. Manchester: Manchester UP, 2006.

Mandeville, John Sir. *The Voyages & Travels of Sir John Mandevile.* c. 1366. London: Printed for R. Scott, T. Basset, J. Wright, and R. Chiswel, 1677.

Marlowe, Christopher. *Dr Faustus.* The New Mermaids. Ed. Roma Gill. London: A & C Black, 2002.

—. *Tamburlaine the Great.* The Revels Plays. Ed. J. S. Cunningham. Manchester: Manchester UP, 1999.

Montecroce, Riccoldo de. *Ricoldi ex ordine fratru praedictatoru confutatio legis a maledicto Mahomete [translated by B. Pincernus from Demetrius' Greek version of the original Latin text]* Location unknown, 1520.

Newton, Thomas. *A Notable Historie of the Saracens* London: by William How, for Abraham Veale, 1575.

Peele, George. *The Battle of Alcazar*. Ed. Charles Edelman. Manchester: Manchester UP, 2005.

—. *The Life and Works of George Peele*. Ed. Charles Tyler Prouty. 3 vols. New Haven: Yale UP, 1952.

Percy, Herny. *Advice to his Son*. Ed. G. B. Harrison. London: Ernest Benn, 1930.

Percy, William. *Mahomet and his Heaven*. Ed. Matthew Dimmock. Aldershot: Ashgate, 2006.

Polemon, John. *The Second Part of the Booke of Battailes, fought in our age: taken from the best authors and writers in sundry languages*. London: Gabriell Cavvood, 1587.

Raleigh, Sir Walter. *The History of the World*. London: Printed by William Stansby for Walter Burre, 1617.

Read, Alexander. *The Chirurgicall Lectures of Tumors and Vlcers*. London: Printed by I[ohn] H[aviland] for Francis Constable and E[dwin] B[ush], 1635.

Selden, John. *Table-talk, being discourses of John Seldon*. London: Printed for *Jacob Tonson*, at the Judge's Head near the *Inner-Temple Gate in Fleetstreet*... 1696.

Shakespeare, William. *The Norton Shakespeare: Based on the Oxford Edition*. Eds. Stephen Greenblatt, et al. New York: Norton, 1997.

Teonge, Henry. *The Diary of Henry Teonge, Naval Chaplain on Board His Majesty's Ships Assistance, Bristol and Royal Oak, anno 1675 to 1679*. London: Charles Knight, 1825.

3. Secondary sources

adh-Dhahabi, Muhammad bin Uthman. *The Major Sins Or al-Kaba'ir*. Trans. Siddiqui Mohammed Moinuddin. Beirut: Dar al Fikr, 1993.

Al-Ghunaimi, Abdulfattah. *Mawsuat Tareekh Al-Maghrib Al-Arabi (Encyclopaedia of Moroccan History)*. Cairo: Madbouli Press, 1999.

Alcock, Antony Evelyn. *A History of the Protection of Regional Cultural Minorities in Europe : from the Edict of Nantes to the Present Day*. Basingstoke: Macmillan press, 2000.

Andrea, Bernadette. "Islam, Women, and Western Responses: The Contemporary Relevance of Early Modern Investigations." *Women's Studies* 38.3 (2009): 273–92.

Andrews, Kenneth R. *Trade, Plunder, and Settlement: Maritime Enterprise and the Genesis of the British Empire, 1480–1630*. Cambridge: Cambridge University Press, 1984.

Ardolino, Frank. *Apocalypse & Armada in Kyd's Spanish Tragedy.* Kirksville, MO: Sixteenth Century Journal Publishers, 1995.

—. "The Protestant Context of George Peele's 'Pleasant Conceited' *Old Wives Tale.*" *Medieval and Renaissance Drama in England* 18 (2005): 146–65.

Axton, Marie. *The Queen's Two Bodies: Drama and the Elizabethan Succession.* London: Royal Historical Society, 1977.

Bailey, Alfred. *The Succession to the English Crown: A Historical Sketch.* London: Macmillan, 1879.

Baker, H. Kendra. "Queen Elizabeth's Reputed Children." *Notes and Queries* 158.5 (1930): 84–85.

Baldick, Chris. *The Concise Oxford Dictionary of Literary Terms.* 2nd ed. Oxford: Oxford University Press, 2001.

Barbour, Reid. "Peele, George (bap. 1556, d. 1596)." *ODNB.* Eds. H. C. G. Matthew and Brian Harrison. Online ed. Oxford: OUP, 2004.

Barbour, Richmond. *Before Orientalism: London's Theatre of the East, 1576–1626.* Cambridge: Cambridge UP, 2003.

Bartels, Emily C. "Making More of the Moor: Aaron, Othello, and Renaissance Refashionings of Race." *Shakespeare Quarterly* 41.4 (1990): 433–54.

—. *Speaking of the Moor.* Philadelphia: University of Pennsylvania Press, 2008.

—. *Spectacles of Strangeness: Imperialism, Alienation, and Marlowe.* Philadelphia: University of Pennsylvania Press, 1993.

Barthelemy, Anthony Gerard. *Black Face, Maligned Race:The Representation of Blacks in English Drama from Shakespeare to Southerne.* London: Louisiana State UP, 1987.

Bate, Jonathan. "Othello and the Other—Turning Turk: The subtleties of Shakespeare's treatment of Islam." *Times Literary Supplement* 19 October 2001.

Batho, G. R. "The Library of the 'Wizard' Earl: Henry Percy, Ninth Earl of Northumberland (1564–1632)." *Library* 25 (1960): 246–61.

Baumer, Franklin L. "England, the Turk, and the Common Corps of Christendom." *The American Historical Review* 50.1 (1944): 26–48.

Bekkaoui, Khalid, ed. *The Battle of Alcazar.* Casablanca: Moroccan Cultural Studies Centre, 2001.

Benbow, R. Mark. "The Araygnment of Paris by George Peele." *The Life and Works of George Peele.* Ed. Charles Tyler Prouty. Vol. 3. New Haven: Yale UP, 1970. 1–131.

Berek, Peter. "Tamburlaine's Weak Sons: Imitation as Interpretation before 1593." *Renaissance Drama* 13 (1982): 55–82.

Bernard, G. W. "Seymour, Thomas, Baron Seymour of Sudeley (b. in or before 1509, d. 1549)." *ODNB*. Eds. H. C. G. Matthew and Brian Harrison. Online ed. Oxford: OUP, 2004.

Berry, Philippa. *Of Chastity and Power: Elizabethan Literature and the Unmarried Queen*. London: Routledge, 1994.

Bertens, Johannes Willem. *Literary Theory: The Basics*. 2nd ed. Oxford: Routledge, 2008.

Birmingham, David. *A Concise History of Portugal*. 2nd ed. Cambridge: Cambridge UP, 2003.

Blanks, David R., and Michael Frassetto, eds. *Western Views of Islam in Medieval and Early Modern Europe: Perception of Other*. London: Macmillan 1999.

Bond, Richard Warwick. *The Complete Works of John Lyly*. 3 vols. Oxford: Claredon, 1902.

Bovill, E. W. *The Battle of Alcazar: an account of the defeat of Don Sebastian of Portugal at El-Ksar el-Kebir*. London: Batchworth Press, 1952.

Bowker, Margaret. "The Henrician Reformation and the Parish Clergy." *The English Reformation Revised*. Ed. Christopher Haigh. Cambridge: Cambridge UP, 1987.

Bradley, David. *From Text to Performance in the Elizabethan Theatre: Preparing the Play for the Stage*. Cambridge: Cambridge University Press, 1992.

Braunmuller, A. R. *George Peele*. Boston: Twayne, 1983.

Brenan, Gerald. *A History of The House of Percy: from the Earliest Times down to the Present Century*. Ed. William Alexander Lindsay. 2 vols. London: Fremantle, 1902.

Breuer, Heidi. *Crafting the Witch: Gendering Magic in Medieval and Early Modern England*. New York: Routledge, 2009.

Brotton, Jerry. *Trading Territories: Mapping the Early Modern World*. London: Reaktion Books, 1997.

Burns, Clayton Joseph. "William Percy's *Arabia Sitiens*." unpublished doctoral thesis. University of New Brunswick, 1984.

Burton, Jonathan. *Traffic and Turning: Islam and English Drama, 1579–1624*. Newark: University of Delaware Press, 2005.

Caldwell, Robert G. "The Anglo-Portuguese Alliance Today." *Foreign Affairs* 21.1 (1942): 149–57.

Campbell, Lily Bess. *Shakespeare's "Histories": Mirrors of Elizabethan Policy*. London: Routledge, 2005.

Carroll, Robert, and Stephen Prickett, eds. *The Bible: Authorized King James Version*. Oxford: Oxford UP, 1998.

Carroll, William C. "Theories of Kingship in Shakespeare's England." *A Companion to Shakespeare's Works: The Histories*. Ed. Richard Dutton. Oxford: Blackwell, 2006. 125–45.

Cavanagh, Sheila. "The Bad Seed: Princess Elizabeth and the Seymour Incident." *Dissing Elizabeth: Negative Representations of Gloriana*. Ed. Julia M. Walker. Durham, NC: Duke UP, 1998. 9–29.

Chambers, Robert. *The Book of Days: a miscellany of popular antiquities in connection with the calendar, including anecdote, biography & history, curiosities of literature, and oddities of human life and character*. Vol. II. 2 vols. London: W. & R. Chambers, 1869.

Chapman, Annie Beatrice Wallis. *Commercial Relations of England and Portugal*. 1907. Eds. Violet Mary Shillington and Annie Beatrice Wallis Chapman. New York: Burt Franklin, 1970.

Cheffaud, P. H. *George Peele: 1558–1596?* Paris: Alcan, 1913.

Chew, Samuel Claggett. *The Crescent and the Rose: Islam and England during the Renaissance*. 1937. Oxford: Oxford University Press, 1965.

Christian, Margaret. "Elizabeth's Preachers and the Government of Women: Defining and Correcting a Queen." *The Sixteenth Century Journal* 24.3 (1993): 561–76.

Clay, William Keatinge. *Liturgical Services: Liturgies and Occasional Forms of Prayer Set forth in the Reign of Queen Elizabeth*. Cambridge: Cambridge UP, 1847.

Clegg, Cyndia Susan. "Censorship and the Problems with History in Shakespeare's England." *A Companion to Shakespeare's Works, Volume II: The Histories*. Eds. Richard Dutton and Jean E. Howard. Oxford: Blackwell Publishing Ltd, 2003. 48–69.

Cohen, I. Bernhard, ed. *The Cambridge Companion to Newton*. Cambridge: Cambridge University Press, 2004.

Cohen, Stephen. "New Historicism and Genre: Towards a Historical Formalism." *The Historical and Political Turn in Literary Studies*. Ed. Winfried Fluck. Tübingen: Gunter Narr Verlag, 1995. 405–24.

Colebrook, Claire. *New Literary Histories: New Historicism and Contemporary Criticism*. Manchester: Manchester UP, 1997.

Coyle, Martin. *Encyclopedia of Literature and Criticism*. London: Routledge, 1990.

Cressy, David. *Dangerous Talk: Scandalous, Seditious, and Treasonable Speech in Pre-Modern England*. Oxford: Oxford UP, 2010.

Croft, Pauline. *King James*. Basingstoke: Palgrave, 2003.

Cruz, Jo Ann Hoeppner Moran. "Popular Attitudes Towards Islam in Medieval Europe." *Western Views of Islam in Medieval and Early*

Modern Europe: Perception of Other. Eds. David R. Blanks and Michael Frassetto. London: Macmillan 1999. 55–81.

Cunliffe, John W. "Gascoigne and Shakspere." *The Modern Language Review* 4.2 (1909): 231–33.

D'Amico, Jack. *The Moor in English Renaissance drama*. Tampa: University of South Florida Press, 1991.

Daniel, Norman. *Islam and the West: the Making of an Image*. Oxford: Oneworld Publications, 1993.

Davies, Norman. *Europe: A History*. Oxford: Oxford University Press, 1996.

Davies, Tony. *Humanism*. 2nd ed. London: Routledge, 2008.

De Fonblanque, Edward Barrington. *Annals of the House of Percy: from the Conquest to the Opening of the Nineteenth Century*. Vol. II. London: Printed by R. Clay & Sons for private circulation only, 1887.

Dickens, A. G. *The English Reformation*. London: B.T. Batsford, 1964.

Dijkhuizen, Jan Frans van. *Devil Theatre: Demonic Possession and Exorcism in English Drama, 1558–1642*. Cambridge: Brewer, 2007.

Dimmock, Matthew. *New Turkes: Dramatizing Islam and the Ottomans in Early Modern England*. Aldershot: Ashgate, 2005.

—. *William Percy's Mahomet and his Heaven: a Critical Edition* Aldershot Ashgate, 2006.

Disney, A. R. *A History of Portugal and the Portuguese Empire: from Beginnings to 1807*. 2 vols. Cambridge: Cambridge UP, 2009.

Dixon-Kennedy, Mike. *Encyclopedia of Greco-Roman Mythology*. Santa Barbara: ABC-CLIO Ltd, 1998.

Dodds, Madeline Hope. "*A Dreame of a Drye Yeare*." *Journal of English and Germanic Philology* 32 (1933): 172–95.

—. "The Financial Affairs of a Jacobean Gentleman." *Archaeologia aeliana, or, Miscellaneous tracts relating to antiquity* New Series 4.xxii (1944): 91–109.

—. "*A Forrest Tragaedye in Vacunium*." *The Modern Language Review* 40.4 (1945): 246–58.

—. "William Percy and Charles Fitzjeffrey." *Notes and Queries* CLX (1931): 420–22.

—. "William Percy and James I." *Notes and Queries* CLXI (1931): 13–14.

—. "William Percy's '*Aphrodysial*'." *Notes and Queries* CLXI (1931): 257–61.

—. "William Percy's '*Aphrodysial*'." *Notes and Queries* CLXI (1931): 237–40.

Dollimore, Jonathan, and Alan Sinfield. *Political Shakespeare: Essays in Cultural Materialism*. 2nd ed. Manchester: Manchester UP, 1994.

Doran, Susan. *Elizabeth I and Foreign Policy, 1558–1603*. London: Routledge, 2000.

—. *Monarchy and Matrimony: the Courtships of Elizabeth I*. London: Routledge, 1996.

—. "Why Did Elizabeth Not Marry?" *Dissing Elizabeth: Negative Representations of Gloriana*. Ed. Julia M. Walker. Durham, NC: Duke UP, 1998. 30–59.

Doran, Susan, and Christopher Durston. *Princes, Pastors, and People: the Church and Religion in England, 1500–1700*. 2nd ed. London: Routledge, 2003.

Drabble, Margaret, ed. *The Oxford Companion to English Literature*. 6th ed. Oxford: Oxford University Press, 2000.

Drake, George A. "Percy, Algernon, tenth earl of Northumberland (1602–1668)." *ODNB*. Eds. H. C. G. Matthew and Brian Harrison. Online ed. Oxford: OUP, 2004.

Eales, Jacqueline. *Women in Early Modern England, 1500–1700*. London: UCL Press, 1998.

Edelman, Charles. *The Stukeley plays*. Manchester: Manchester UP, 2005.

Edgeworth, R. J. "The Death of Dido." *The Classical Journal* 72.2 (1976): 129–33.

Eggert, Katherine. *Showing Like a Queen: Female Authority and Literary Experiment in Spenser, Shakespeare, and Milton*. Philadelphia: University of Pennsylvania Press, 2000.

Fairholt, Frederick William. *Lord Mayors' Pageants*. London: Percy Society, 1843.

Feingold, Mordechai. "The Occult Tradition in the English Universities of the Renaissance: A Reassessment." *Occult and Scientific Mentalities in the Renaissance*. Ed. Brian Vickers. Cambridge: Cambridge University Press, 1984. 73–94.

Fenn, Robert Denzel. "William Percy's *Faery Pastorall*: An Old Spelling Edition." unpublished doctoral thesis. University of British Columbia, 1997.

Fletcher, Anthony, and Diarmaid MacCulloch. *Tudor Rebellions*. Seminar Studies in History. London: Longman, 1997.

Flynn, Dennis. *John Donne and the Ancient Catholic Nobility*. Bloomington: Indiana University Press, 1995.

Forker, Charles R. *Richard II*. Shakespeare: the Critical Tradition. London: The Athlone Press, 1997.

Forshaw, Peter. "Two Occult Philosophers in the Elizabethan Age." *History Workshop Journal* 64.1 (2007): 401–10.

Fox, Adam. *Oral and Literate Culture in England, 1500–1700*. Oxford: Oxford UP, 2000.

Freadman, Anne. "Representation." *New Keywords: A Revised Vocabulary of Culture and Society*. Eds. Tony Bennett, Lawrence Grossberg and Meaghan Morris. Oxford: Blackwell, 2005. 306–9.

Freeman, Thomas S., and Elizabeth Evenden. *Religion and the Book in Early Modern England: the Making of John Foxe's 'Book of Martyrs'*. Cambridge: Cambridge UP, 2011.

French, Peter J. *John Dee: the World of an Elizabethan Magus*. London: Routledge and Kegan Paul, 1972.

Frye, Susan. *Elizabeth I: The Competition for Representation*. Oxford: Oxford University Press, 1993.

Gair, Reavley. "Percy, William (1574–1648)." *ODNB*. Ed. Lawrence Goldman. Online ed. Oxford: OUP, 2004.

Games, Alison. *The Web of Empire: English Cosmopolitans in an Age of Expansion, 1560–1660*. Oxford: Oxford UP, 2008.

García-Arenal, Mercedes. *Ahmad al-Mansur: the Beginnings of Modern Morocco*. Oxford: OneWorld, 2009.

Gatti, Hilary. "Giordano Bruno: The Texts in the Library of the Ninth Earl of Northumberland." *Journal of the Warburg and Courtauld Institutes* 46 (1983): 63–77.

Gazzard, Hugh. "'Many a Herdsman more disposde to morne': Peele, Campion, and the Portugal expedition of 1589." *Review of English Studies* 57.228 (2006): 16–42.

Gill, Roma. *Christopher Marlowe's Dr Faustus Based on the A Text*. New Mermaids. London: A & C Black, 2002.

Glick, Thomas F., Steven John Livesey, and Faith Wallis. *Medieval Science, Technology, and Medicine: an Encyclopedia*. New York: Routledge, 2005.

Greenblatt, Miriam. *Elizabeth I and Tudor England*. New York: Marshall Cavendish, 2001.

Greenblatt, Stephen. "Invisible Bullets." *The Greenblatt Reader*. Ed. Michael Payne. Oxford: Blackwell, 2005. 121–60.

—. "Towards a Poetics of Culture." *The New Historicism*. Ed. H. Aram Veeser. New York: Routledge, 1989. 1–14.

Greenblatt, Stephen, et al., eds. *The Norton Shakespeare: Based on the Oxford Edition*. New York: Norton, 1997.

Greenslade, Stanley Lawrence, ed. *The Cambridge History of the Bible 3: The West from the Reformation to the Present Day*. Cambridge: Cambridge UP, 1963.

Griffin, Eric. "'Spain is Portugal/And Portugal is Spain': Transnational Attraction in The Stukeley Plays and *The Spanish Tragedy*." *Journal for Early Modern Cultural Studies* 10.1 (2010): 95–116.

Guinle, Francis. "Barbarous/Barbarian: The Ambiguity of b/Barbary in Peele's *Battle of Alcazar*." *Writing the Other: Humanism versus Barbarism in Tudor England*. Eds. Zsolt Almási and Michael Pincombe. Newcastle: Cambridge Scholars, 2008. 20–37.

Hackett, Helen. *Virgin Mother, Maiden Queen: Elizabeth I and the cult of the Virgin Mary*. Basingstoke: Macmillan, 1995.

Hakluyt, Richard. *The Principall Navigations, Voiages, and Discoveries of the English Nation*. Vol. VI. Glasgow: James MacLehose and Sons, 1904.

Hammer, Paul E. J. "Devereux, Robert, second earl of Essex (1565–1601)." *ODNB*. Eds. H. C. G. Matthew and Brian Harrison. Online ed. Oxford: OUP, 2004.

—. *The Polarisation of Elizabethan Politics: the Political Career of Robert Devereux, 2nd Earl of Essex, 1585–1597*. Cambridge studies in early modern British history. Cambridge: Cambridge UP, 2005.

—. "Sex and the Virgin Queen: Aristocratic Concupiscence and the Court of Elizabeth I." *The Sixteenth Century Journal* 31.1 (2000): 77–97.

Harris, Jonathan Gil. *Shakespeare and Literary Theory*. Oxford: Oxford UP, 2010.

Hart, Trevor. "Protestantism and the Arts." *The Blackwell Companion to Protestantism*. Eds. Alister E. McGrath and Darren C. Marks. Malden, MA: Blackwell, 2004. 268–86.

Highley, Christopher. *Catholics Writing the Nation in Early Modern Britain and Ireland*. Oxford: Oxford UP, 2008.

Hillebrand, Harold N. "William Percy: An Elizabethan Amateur." *Huntington Library Quarterly* 1 (1938): 391–416.

Hilliard, Stephen S. "Lyly's Midas as an Allegory of Tyranny." *Studies in English Literature, 1500–1900* 12.2 (1972): 243–58.

Hoenselaars, A. J. *Images of Englishmen and Foreigners in the Drama of Shakespeare and his Contemporaries*. London: Associated University Presses, 1992.

Holmes, Frederic Lawrence, and Trevor Harvey Levere. *Instruments and Experimentation in the History of Chemistry*. Cambridge, Mass.: MIT, 2000.

Holmes, Peter. "Paget, Charles (c.1546–1612)." *Oxford Dictionary of National Biography*. Eds. H. C. G. Matthew and Brian Harrison. Oxford: OUP, 2004.

—. "Stucley, Thomas (c.1520–1578)." *Oxford Dictionary of National Biography*. Ed. H. C. G. Matthew and Brian Harrison. Oxford: OUP, 2004.

Holmyard, Eric John."Jābir ibn Hayyān."*Proceedings of the Royal Society of Medicine, Section History of Medicine*. 1923. Vol. 16. 46–57.

—. *Makers Of Chemistry*. Oxford: Clarendon Press, 1931.

Holt, Bradley P. "Protestantism and Spirituality." *The Blackwell Companion to Protestantism*. Eds. Alister E. McGrath and Darren C. Marks. Malden, MA: Blackwell, 2004. 382–91.

Horne, David H. *The Life and Minor Works of George Peele*. Vol. 1. New Haven: Yale UP, 1952.

Houliston, Victor. *Catholic Resistance in Elizabethan England: Robert Person's Jesuit polemic, 1580–1610*. Aldershot: Ashgate, 2007.

Housley, Norman. *The Later Crusades, 1274–1580: From Lyons to Alcazar*. Oxford: Oxford UP, 1992.

--- RE: *The Battle of Alcazar*. E-mail to the author. 16 Jul. 2009.

Hughes, Alan, ed. *William Shakespeare's Titus Andronicus*. Cambridge: Cambridge UP, 2006.

Hume, Martin Andrew Sharp. *The Courtships of Queen Elizabeth: A History of the Various Negotiations for her Marriage*. Whitefish, Mont.: Kessinger, 2003.

Hunt, Jocelyn. *The Renaissance*. London: Routledge, 1999.

Huston, Diehl. "'Infinite Space': Representation and Reformation in *Measure for Measure*." *Shakespeare Quarterly* 49.4 (1998): 393–410.

Hyland, Peter. "Moors, Villainy and *The Battle of Alcazar*." *Parergon* 16.2 (1999): 85–99.

Ichikawa, Mariko. "What to do with a corpse?: Physical reality and the fictional world in the Shakespearean Theatre." *Theatre Research International* 29.3 (2004): 201–15.

James, Susan E. "Katherine [Katherine Parr] (1512–1548)." *Oxford Dictionary of National Biography*. Eds. H. C. G. Matthew and Brian Harrison. Oxford: OUP, 2004.

Jansen, Sharon L. *Debating Women, Politics, and Power in Early Modern Europe*. Basingstoke: Palgrave Macmillan, 2008.

Jawad, Haifaa A. *The Rights of Women in Islam: An Authentic Approach*. Basingstoke: Palgrave Macmillan, 1998.

Jones, Eldred. *Othello's Countrymen: The African in English Renaissance Drama*. London: Oxford UP, 1965.

Jones, Emrys. "Othello, 'Lepanto' and the Cyprus Wars." *Shakespeare Survey* 21 (1968): 47–52.

Jump, John Davies. *Doctor Faustus by Christopher Marlowe*. London: Routledge, 1965.

Kantorowicz, Ernst H. *The King's Two Bodies: A Study in Mediaeval Political Theology*. Princeton: Princeton UP, 1957.

Keßler, Eckhard. "Renaissance Humanism: the Rhetorical Turn." *Interpretations of Renaissance Humanism*. Ed. Angelo Mazzocco. Brill's Studies in Intellectual History. Leiden: Brill, 2006.

Kincaid, Patrick Clayton. "A Critical Edition of William Percy's *The Cuckqueans and Cuckolds Errants*." Unpublished doctoral thesis. The University of Birmingham, 1999.

King, John N. "Queen Elizabeth I: Representations of the Virgin Queen." *Renaissance Quarterly* 43.1 (1990): 30–74.

Kuhl, Ernest. "'The Wanton Wife of Bath' and Queen Elizabeth." *Studies in Philology* 26.2 (1929): 177–83.

Lee, Patricia-Ann. "A Bodye Politique to Governe: Aylmer, Knox and the Debate on Queenship." *Historian* 52.2 (1990): 242–61.

Levin, Carole. *The Heart and Stomach of a King: Elizabeth I and the Politics of Sex and Power*. Philadelphia: University of Pennsylvania Press, 1996.

—. "Percy, Henry, eighth earl of Northumberland (c.1532–1585)." *ODNB*. Eds. H. C. G. Matthew and Brian Harrison. Online ed. Oxford: OUP, 2004.

—. "'We Shall Never Have a Merry World while the Queene Lyveth': Gender, Monarchy, and the Power of Seditious Words." *Dissing Elizabeth: Negative Representations of Gloriana*. Ed. Julia M. Walker. Durham, NC: Duke UP, 1998. 77–95.

Levine, Mortimer. *The Early Elizabethan Succession Question, 1558–1568*. Stanford CA: Stanford UP, 1966.

Lewalski, Barbara Kiefer. *The Life of John Milton: A Critical Biography*. Oxford: Blackwell, 2003.

Lewis, Bernard. *Islam and the West*. New York: Oxford University Press, 1993.

Loades, David. *Elizabeth I: the Golden Reign of Gloriana*. London: Palgrave, 2003.

Lockyer, Roger. *Tudor and Stuart Britain, 1485–1714*. 3rd ed. Harlow: Pearson Longman, 2005.

Logan, Terence P., and Denzell Stewart Smith. *The Predecessors of Shakespeare: a Survey and Bibliography of Recent Studies in English Renaissance Drama*. Lincoln: University of Nebraska Press, 1973.

Loomba, Ania. *Shakespeare, Race, and Colonialism*. Oxford: Oxford UP, 2002.

Loomba, Ania, and Jonathan Burton. *Race in Early Modern England: a Documentary Companion*. Basingstoke: Palgrave Macmillan, 2007.

MacLean, Gerald M. *The Rise of Oriental Travel, English Visitors to the Ottoman Empire 1580–1720*. Basingstoke: Palgrave Macmillan, 2004.

Marcus, Leah S. "Dramatic Experiments: Tudor Drama, 1490–1567." *The Cambridge Companion to English Literature, 1500–1600*. Ed. Arthur F. Kinney. Cambridge: Cambridge University Press, 2000.

—. *Puzzling Shakespeare: Local Reading and its Discontents*. Berkeley: University of California Press, 1988.

Matar, Nabil. *Britain and Barbary 1589–1689*. Gainesville: UP of Florida, 2005.

—. "The Representation of Muslim Women in Renaissance England." *The Muslim World* 86.1 (1996): 50–64.

—. *Turks, Moors, and Englishmen in the Age of Discovery*. New York: Columbia UP, 1999.

Matthews, Michelle M. "Magician or Witch?: Christopher Marlowe's *Doctor Faustus*." Unpublished Master's dissertation. Bowling Green State University, 2006.

May, Steven W. *The Elizabethan Courtier Poets: the poems and their contexts*. Columbia: University of Missouri Press, 1991.

McAdam, Ian. *Magic and Masculinity in Early Modern English Drama*. Pittsburgh, Pa.: Duquesne University Press, 2009.

McJannet, Linda. *The Sultan Speaks: Dialogue in English Plays and Histories about the Ottoman Turks*. New York: Palgrave Macmillan, 2006.

McLaren, Anne. "Gender, Religion, and Early Modern Nationalism: Elizabeth I, Mary Queen of Scots, and the Genesis of English Anti-Catholicism." *The American Historical Review* 107.3 (2002): 739–67.

Mebane, John S. *Renaissance Magic and the Return of the Golden Age: the Occult Tradition and Marlowe, Jonson and Shakespeare*. London: University of Nebraska Press, 1989.

Meshkat, Kurosh Re: Schism E-mail to the author. 21/07/2010.

Metlitzki, Dorothee. *The matter of Araby in medieval England*. New Haven: Yale UP, 1977.

Meyer, Arnold Oskar. *England and the Catholic Church under Queen Elizabeth*. London: K. Paul, Trench, Trübner & Co., 1916.

Montrose, Louis Adrian. "Gifts and Reasons: The Contexts of Peele's *Araygnement of Paris*." *ELH* 47.3 (1980): 433–61.

—. "Professing the Renaissance: The Poetics and Politics of Culture." *The New Historicism*. Ed. H. Aram Veeser. New York: Routledge, 1989. 15–36.

—. "'Shaping Fantasies': Figurations of Gender and Power in Elizabethan Culture." *Representations* 2 (1983): 61–94.

Mitchell, W. J. T. "Representation." *Critical Terms for Literary Study.* Eds. Frank Lentricchia and Thomas McLaughlin. Chicago: University of Chicago Press, 1990. 11–22.

Moryson, Fynes. *Shakespeare's Europe: Unpublished Chapters of Fynes Moryson's Itinerary, Being a Survey of the Condition of Europe at the End of the 16th Century.* Ed. Charles Hughes. London: Sherratt & Hughes, 1903.

Mullaney, Steven. "After the new historicism." *Alternative Shakespeares.* Ed. Terence Hawkes. Vol. 2. London: Routledge, 1985. 17–37.

—. "Mourning and Misogyny: *Hamlet, The Revenger' sTragedy*, and the Final Progress of Elizabeth I, 1600–1607." *Shakespeare Quarterly* 45.2 (1994): 139–62.

Neale, John Ernest. *Queen Elizabeth I.* New York,: Harcourt Brace and Company, 1934.

Newitt, Malyn. *Portugal in European and World History.* London: Reaktion Books, 2009.

Nicholls, Mark. "'As Happy a Fortune as I Desire': the Pursuit of Financial Security by the Younger Brothers of Henry Percy, 9th Earl of Northumberland." *Historical Research* (1992): 296–314.

—. "The Enigmatic William Percy." *Huntington Library Quarterly* 70.3 (2007): 469–77.

—. "Percy, Henry, ninth earl of Northumberland (1564–1632)." *ODNB.* Eds. H. C. G. Matthew and Brian Harrison. Online ed. Oxford: OUP, 2004.

Nicholls, Mark, and Penry Williams. "Ralegh, Sir Walter (1554–1618)." *Oxford Dictionary of National Biography.* Eds. H. C. G. Matthew and Brian Harrison. Oxford: OUP, 2004.

Nicholson, Brinsley. "Sebastian of Portugal and Peele's *Battle of Alcazar.*" *Notes and Queries* s5–III.58 (1875): 107.

O'Malley, Gregory. "Pilgrimage, Crusades, Trade and Embassy: pre-Elizabethan English Contacts with the Ottoman Turks." *Crusades* 3 (2004): 153–70.

Obaid, Hammood. "Christians and Barbarians in Peele's *Battle of Alcazar.*" *Humanity and Barbarism in Tudor Literature.* Pázmány Péter Catholic University, Piliscaba, 2006.

Obaid, Thoraya Ahmed. "The Moor Figure in English Renaissance Drama." Unpublished doctoral thesis. Wayne State University, 1974.

Palazzolo, Grace V. "Misogyny, Gylany, Witchery: Intellectual Discourse on Women and Power in Early Modern England." *The Maxwell Review* Spring (2007): 103–16.

Palmer, D J. "'We Shall Know by This Fellow': Prologue and Chorus in Shakespeare." *Bulletin of the John Rylands University Library of Manchester* 64.2 (Spring 1982): 501–21.

Parker, Kenneth. *Early Modern Tales of the Orient: A critical anthology.* London: Routledge, 1999.

Partridge, Eric. *The Routledge Dictionary of Historical Slang.* 1937. Ed. Jacqueline Simpson. London: Routledge, 2006.

Paster, Gail Kern. *Humoring the Body: Emotions and the Shakespearean Stage.* Chicago: University of Chicago Press, 2004.

Patterson, William Brown. *King James VI and I and the Reunion of Christendom.* Cambridge: Cambridge UP, 1997.

Percy, Thomas. *Reliques of Ancient English Poetry.* Ed. Henry B. Wheatley. 3 vols. London: Bickers and Son, 1877.

Phillips, James Emerson. *Images of a Queen: Mary Stuart in Sixteenth-Century Literature.* London: Cambridge UP, 1964.

Pieterse, Jan Nederveen. *White on Black: Images of Africa and Blacks in Western Popular Culture.* New Haven: Yale UP, 1995.

Pincombe, Michael. *Elizabethan Humanism: Literature and Learning in the Later Sixteenth Century.* London: Longman, 2001.

—. *The Plays of John Lyly: Eros and Eliza.* The Revels Plays Companion Library. Manchester: Manchester UP, 1996.

Pollard, Arthur. "Richard Hooker (ca. 1554–1600)." *British Writers. Volume I, William Langland to the English Bible.* Ed. Ian Scott-Kilvert. New York: Charles Scribner's Sons, 1979. 176–90.

Potter, David. *A History of France, 1460–1560: the Emergence of a Nation State.* London: Palgrave Macmillan, 1995.

Prestage, Edgar. "The Anglo-Portuguese Alliance." *Transactions of the Royal Historical Society* 17.1 (1934): 69–100.

Pryor, Felix. *Elizabeth I: Her Life in Letters.* Berkeley: University of California Press, 2003.

Questier, Michael C. "Elizabeth and the Catholics." *Catholics and the 'Protestant nation': Religious Politics and Identity in Early Modern England.* Ed. Ethan Shagan. Manchester: Manchester UP, 2005.

Quinn, Frederick. *The Sum of All Heresies: the Image of Islam in Western Thought.* Oxford: Oxford UP, 2008.

Redworth, Glyn. *The Prince and the Infanta: The Cultural Politics of the Spanish Match.* London: Cambridge UP, 2003.

Reid, Patrick. *Readings in Western Religious Thought: the Middle Ages Through the Reformation*. New York: Paulist Press, 1995.

Rhodes, Neil, Jennifer Richards, and Joseph Marshall, eds. *King James VI and I: Selected Writings*. Aldershot: Ashgate, 2003.

Rice, Warner G. "A Principal Source of *The Battle of Alcazar* " *Modern Language Notes* 58.6 (1943): 428–31.

Roberts, Gareth. "Marlowe and the Metaphysics of Magicians." *Constructing Christopher Marlowe*. Eds. J. A. Downie and J. T. Parnell. Cambridge: Cambridge UP, 2000. 55–73.

—. "Necromantic Books: Christopher Marlowe, *Doctor Faustus* and Agrippa of Nettesheim." *Christopher Marlowe and English Renaissance Culture*. Eds. Darryll Grantley and Peter Roberts. Aldershot: Ashgate, 1999. 148–71.

Roberts, William H. "The Figure of King Sebastian in Fernando Pessoa." *Hispanic Review* 34.4 (1966): 307-16.

Rosman, Doreen. *From Catholic to Protestant: Religion and the People in Tudor England*. Introductions to History. Ed. David Birmingham. London: UCL Press, 1996.

Royan, Nicola. "Writing the Nation." *A Companion to English Renaissance Literature and Culture*. Ed. Michael Hattaway. Oxford: Blackwell, 2003. 699–708.

Rutter, Tom. "Marlovian Echoes in the Admiral's Men Repertory: *Alcazar, Stukeley, Patient Grissil*." *Shakespeare Bulletin* 27.1 (2009): 27–38.

Said, Edward W. *Orientalism*. 1978. London: Penguin, 2003.

Schmuck, Stephan. "England's Experiences of Islam." *A New Companion to English Renaissance Literature and Culture*. Ed. Michael Hattaway. Vol. I. Malden: Wiley-Blackwell, 2010. 543–56.

—. "From Sermon to Play: Literary Representations of 'Turks' in Renaissance England 1550–1625." *Literature Compass* 2.1 (2005): 1–29.

Schulte, Regina. "Conceptual Approaches to the Queen's Body." *The Body of the Queen: Gender and Rule in the Courtly World, 1500–2000*. Ed. Regina Schulte. New York: Berghahn Books, 2006.

Schwoebel, Robert. *The Shadow of the Crescent; the Renaissance Image of the Turk, 1453–1517*. New York: St. Martin's Press, 1967.

Scragg, Leah, ed. *The Woman in the Moon by John Lyly*. Manchester: Manchester University Press, 2006.

Setton, Kenneth. "Lutheranism and the Turkish peril." *Balkan Studies* 3 (1962): 133–68.

Sha'ban, Mohammed Fuad. "The Mohammedan World in English Literature, 1580–1642." Unpublished doctoral thesis. University of Duke, 1965.

Shapiro, James S. *A Year in the Life of William Shakespeare, 1599.* London: Faber, 2005.

Shepherd, Simon. *Marlowe and the politics of Elizabethan theatre.* Brighton: Harvester Press, 1986.

Shirley, John Williams. "The Scientific Experiments of Sir Walter Ralegh, the Wizard Earl, and the Three Magi in the Tower 1603–1617." *Ambix* IV.1 and 2 (1949): 52–66.

Simonds, Peggy Muñoz. *Myth, Emblem, and Music in Shakespeare's Cymbeline: an Iconographic Reconstruction.* Newark: University of Delaware Press, 1992.

Simpson, Richard. *The School of Shakspere: Including "The Life and Death of Captain Thomas Stukeley".* Vol. I. 2 vols. London: Chatto and Windus, 1878.

Sinfield, Alan. *Faultlines: Cultural Materialism and the Politics of Dissident Reading.* Berkeley: University of California Press, 1992.

—. *Shakespeare, Authority, Sexuality: Unfinished Business in Cultural Materialism.* London: Routledge, 2006.

Smith, Anthony D. *Myths and Memories of the Nation.* Oxford: Oxford University Press 1999.

Sousa, Maria Leonor Machado de. *D. Sebastão na Literatura Inglesa.* Lisboa: Instituto de Cultura e Língua Portuguesa, 1985.

Strong, Roy C. *The Tudor and Stuart Monarchy: Pageantry, Painting, Iconography, Vol. II Elizabethan.* Woodbridge: The Boydell Press, 1995.

Szőnyi, György Endre. *John Dee's Occultism: Magical Exaltation through Powerful Signs.* SUNY series in Western esoteric traditions. Albany: State University of New York, 2004.

Tazón, Juan E. *The Life and Times of Thomas Stukeley (c.1525–78).* Aldershot, Hants, England: Ashgate, 2003.

Tennenhouse, Leonard. *Power on Display: the Politics of Shakespeare's Genres.* London: Routledge, 2005.

Thomas, Jane Resh. *Behind the Mask: the Life of Queen Elizabeth I.* New York: Clarion Books, 1998.

Thoreau, Henry David. *Walden, Civil Disobedience and Other Writings.* 3rd ed. New York: W. W. Norton, 2007.

Tolan, John Victor. *Saracens : Islam in the medieval European imagination.* New York: Columbia UP, 2002.

Trim, David. "Early-Modern Colonial Warfare and the Battle of Alcazarquivir, 1578." *Small Wars and Insurgencies* 8.1 (1997): 1–34.

Ungerer, Gustav. "Portia and the Prince of Morocco." *Shakespeare Studies* 31 (2003): 89–126.

Veeser, H. Aram, ed. *The New Historicism Reader*. London: Routledge, 1994.

Vickers, Brian. *Shakespeare, Co-Author: a Historical Study of Five Collaborative Plays*. Oxford: Oxford UP, 2004.

Viguers, Susan T. "Peele's *The Battle of Alcazar* " *Explicator* 43.2 (1985): 9–12.

Vitkus, Daniel J. "Early Modern Orientalism: Representations of Islam in Sixteenth- and Seventeenth-Century Europe." *Western Views of Islam in Medieval and Early Modern Europe: Perception of Other*. Eds. David R. Blanks and Michael Frassetto. New York: St. Martin's, 1999. 207–30.

—. *Three Turk Plays from Early Modern England: Selimus, A Christian turned Turk, and The Renegado*. New York: Columbia UP, 2000.

—. "Turning Turk in *Othello*: The Conversion and Damnation of the Moor." *Shakespeare Quarterly* 48.2 (1997): 145–76.

Wann, Louis. "The Oriental in Elizabethan Drama." *Modern Philology* 12.7 (1915): 423–47.

Watkins, John. *Representing Elizabeth in Stuart England*. Cambridge: Cambridge UP, 2002.

Weil, Rachel Judith. *Political Passions: Gender, the Family and Political Argument in England, 1680–1714*. Manchester: Manchester UP, 1999.

Weimann, Douglas Bruster and Robert. *Prologues to Shakespeare's Theatre: Performance and Liminality in Early Modern Drama*. New York: Routledge, 2004.

Weiner, Andrew D. "Expelling the Beast: Bruno's Adventures in England." *Modern Philology* 78.1 (1980): 1–13.

Wernham, R. B. *The Making of Elizabethan Foreign Policy, 1558–1603*. Una's Lectures. London: University of California Press, 1980.

—. "Queen Elizabeth and the Portugal Expedition of 1589." *The English Historical Review* 66.258 (1951): 1–26.

Whigham, Frank, and Wayne A. Rebhorn, eds. *The Art of English Poesy by George Puttenham, A Critical Edition*. Ithaca: Cornell University Press, 2007.

White, Paul Whitfield. "Patronage, Protestantism, and Stage Propaganda in Early Elizabethan England." *The Yearbook of English Studies* 21 (1991): 39–52.

Wilson, Richard, and Richard Dutton, eds. *New Historicism and Renaissance Drama*. London: Longman, 1992.

Wood, Anthony à. *Athenae Oxonienses: an Exact History of all the Writers and Bishops who have had their Education in the University of Oxford*. 1691–2. Ed. Philip Bliss. London: Rivington, 1813–20.

Wright, Louis B. *Middle-Class Culture in Elizabethan England*. Ithaca: Cornell University Press, 1958.

Yates, Frances A. *Astraea: The Imperial Theme in the Sixteenth Century*. London: Routledge & Kegan Paul, 1975.

—. *Giordano Bruno and the Hermetic tradition*. London: Routledge and Kegan Paul, 1964.

—. *The Occult Philosophy in the Elizabethan Age*. London: Routledge, 2001.

—. "Queen Elizabeth as Astraea." *Journal of the Warburg and Courtauld Institutes* 10 (1947): 27–82.

Yoklavich, John, ed. *The Dramatic Works of George Peele*. Vol. 2. New Haven: Yale University Press, 1961.

Zetterberg, J. Peter. "The Mistaking of 'the Mathematicks' for Magic in Tudor and Stuart England." *The Sixteenth Century Journal* 11.1 (1980): 83–97.